BEHAVIOR SCIENCE MONOGRAPHS

The Eastern Carolines

John L. Fischer
with the assistance of
Ann M. Fischer

HUMAN RELATIONS AREA FILES PRESS

New Haven, Connecticut

1970

ACKNOWLEDGMENTS

This monograph, compiled under sponsorship of the Pacific Science
Board, National Academy of Sciences—National Research Council,
was originally published by the Human Relations Area Files in 1957,
with financial assistance from the Trust Territory of the Pacific Islands.

Grateful acknowledgment is also made to Yale University Publications in Anthropology and to Frank M. LeBar for the use in the present edition of illustrations from THE MATERIAL CULTURE OF TRUK.

TABLE OF CONTENTS

TABLE OF CONTENTS

TABLE OF CONTENTS

TABLE OF CONTENTS

LIST OF TABLES

INTRODUCTION

The purpose of this handbook is to provide for officials and others interested a non-technical summary of the contemporary scientific information of administrative relevance concerning Truk and Ponape Districts.

The bulk of the information reviewed here has been taken from anthropologists, geographers, linguists, and biologists. More material is included from anthropology than other fields. This is partly because the greatest volume of scientific work in Micronesia in recent years has been in the field of anthropology, partly because more of the anthropological material is of general administrative relevance, and partly because I am best qualified by training to deal with anthropological material. An understanding of the customs, beliefs, traditional rights and responsibilities, family life, and other aspects of the life of the islanders is of use to the general administrator, the doctor, the teacher, the agriculturist, and to anyone employing islander labor or trying to change and improve local life. Familiarity with the findings of anthropologists and other scientists in Micronesia can go far toward producing such an understanding.

The greatest contribution to the study of the people of Micronesia before the last World War was the series of volumes coming from the German anthropologists participating in the South Seas Expedition of 1908-10. The volumes on Truk, Ponape, Kusaie, and surrounding low islands summed up the previous writings and reported new findings. This material was translated into English and analyzed exhaustively during World War II and summarized in the military Civil Affairs Handbooks.

Following the war the United States Navy took over the administration of the islands of Micronesia from the Japanese authorities. A series of anthropological and other scientific investigations followed designed to provide information of both practical and pure scientific interest. The first of these was the United States Commercial Company economic survey of Micronesia in 1946. Both Ponape and Truk were included in this. This was followed by the extensive Coordinated Investigation of Micronesian

INTRODUCTION

Anthropology (CIMA) under which expeditions were sent to Ponape, Kapingamarangi, Mokil, and Kusaie in Ponape District and to Truk Lagoon
(Romonum) and Lukunor in Truk District, in addition to a number of expeditions to other parts of Micronesia. This program was under the joint
sponsorship of the Office of Naval Research and the Pacific Science Board
of the National Research Council. On completion of this program these
same agencies sponsored a further program of wider scientific scope although
with somewhat fewer participants. This program was termed Scientific
Investigations in Micronesia (SIM) and included biologists and other scientists as well as anthropologists.

"Applied" anthropologists were introduced into the district administrations as a consequence of the usefulness of the CIMA program to
American officials of the Trust Territory. Some of these anthropologists
have also made important contributions to the basic information on the
peoples of their districts, although the prime purpose in introducing the
position of anthropologist and probably the greatest value of it to date has
been to make available professionally competent advice, from some one
partly outside the power hierarchy and trusted by the islanders, on their
day to day reactions to specific administrative programs, both proposed
and already accomplished.

Most of the information in this handbook has been derived from the
works listed in the bibliography. The notes in the bibliography indicate
the principal works on which I have relied. On the other hand I have
included some information accumulated by myself in the course of residence
in the Eastern Carolines.

I lived in the area for four years, 1949-53, where I was employed
as District Anthropologist for two years by the Naval Administration and
then as District Island Affairs Officer for two years under the Interior
Department Administration. These jobs made it possible to become acquainted with all the separate low island communities in the area as well
as with the communities near the district administrative centers. I was in
Truk a little over a year and on Ponape three years.

As noted above, this handbook has been prepared for officials and
non-scientific laymen interested in the administration of Microneisa. Although it is trusted that some of the information will also be of interest to

specialists, anyone interested in pursuing specific subjects in more detail should consult the sources in the annotated bibliography at the end of the handbook. Some of the references listed there also contain bibliographies as noted.

An attempt has been made to use as few anthropological and other special terms as possible, in order to avoid burdening the average reader with the need for memorizing a long list of definitions. In a few cases technical terms such as "clan" have been introduced to avoid cumbersome circumlocutions but only after definition.

For similar reasons an attempt has been made to use as few terms from the native languages as possible. The use of native terms is easy for the anthropologist who has become familiar with them and also is a way of avoiding the unintended connotations of many English words. On the other hand, in works for the non-specialist an abundance of native terms sometimes gives the undesirable impression that the author is trying to show off his knowledge rather than transmit it; or conversely that he uses the native words because he is really not quite sure what they mean. If he should desire, the person in the field can easily learn the local terms for different native concepts discussed from the people themselves. Others can consult the bibliography, as most of the anthropological works listed contain some native vocabulary.

While every attempt has been made to convey the most information simply and concisely certain inherent limitations of this handbook must be noted. The first is the limitation of length. Most of the others may be summed up by saying that the handbook is not intended as and cannot be a substitute for the local applied anthropologist attached to the district administrations. It would be closer to the truth to say that this handbook, among other things, provides a basis for understanding how local anthropologists, properly utilized, can be of great assistance to a just and efficient administration of the Trust Territory, and what type of information they can provide.

The facts and trends reported herein are general and long term. No attempt has been made to spell out the exact character, influence, and shifting alliances of each island leader, for instance, which is the sort of thing the local anthropologist is especially suited to learning. To give an example of the difference between the kind of information which this handbook and the local investigator can provide, the handbook can inform the reader that many people on island X believe in sorcery. But only a local contemporary investigator trusted by the public is able to find that individual A believes that individual B recently killed A's brother C by sorcery. Thus the administrator would have to procede with care, to put it mildly, in attempting to arrange for A and B to work together in a project of economic benefit to their community.

While this handbook has been organized to provide a summary of the long term trends and persistent facts of the islander societies, no attempt has been made to include everything in this category reported in the literature. The aim has been rather to select basic information which will be relevant to the most common and important administrative problems. Obviously problems not foreseen by the authors of this handbook will arise which will require general information on the local cultures not reported herein. In some cases the desired information may be found in works listed in the bibliography. In many, further research of an anthropological or other nature will be required.

We would note that in spite of the great amount of basic information gathered by scientists to date and reported in the works listed in the bibliography there are still critical gaps in the basic data on all the local cultures in Truk and Ponape Districts. Detailed anthropological reports are entirely lacking for a number of culturally distinct communities. Especially critical are Pingelap, Ngatik, Nukuoro, Losap, the Halls, Namonuito, and Puluwat and nearby islands. Even where considerable work has been done by a number of scientists, as on Ponape, there are still many basic questions left unanswered, such as, whether on the average farmstead much copra is cut by others than the owner of each piece of coconut land and his sons? Just what do these and more distant relatives or outsiders get beside a share of the cash proceeds? Why really do they do this work? These questions have important bearing on both scientific and practical problems yet the answers are only very roughly known, and cannot be given reliably without considerable further research. The absence of certain facts from this handbook does not therefore always mean that they were considered to be of insufficient importance. It may simply mean that there is as yet no reliable information on them.

Cambridge, Mass. June, 1955

CHAPTER I

GEOGRAPHY AND CULTURAL CLASSIFICATION

LOCATION

Truk and Ponape Districts are two of the six administrative districts of the Trust Territory of the Pacific Islands, the others being the Marshalls, Yap, Palau and Saipan Districts. Truk and Ponape Districts together constitute roughly the eastern half of the Caroline Islands, Yap and Palu Districts constituting the western half. Accordingly the term "Eastern Carolines" has sometimes been used in this handbook as a convenient way of referring to the islands included in Truk and Ponape Districts as a group. The Eastern Carolines by this definition include about one-third of the land area of the Trust Territory and nearly one-half of its population.

The U. S. administered Trust Territory of the Pacific Islands includes most of the cultural and geographic area known as Micronesia—the "small islands". Micronesia includes from southeast to northeast the Gilberts (British-administered), Marshalls, Carolines, and Marianas. Ocean (Banaba) and Nauru, also British-administered, two isolated islands west of the Gilberts, are also included. The Ellice Islands, south of the Gilberts, are sometimes included in Micronesia by virtue of their proximity to the Gilberts but culturally they are Polynesian. Aside from the British-administered islands the only part of Micronesia outside the Trust Territory is Guam, the largest island of the Marianas and in fact in the whole of Micronesia. Guam is an American possession not under trusteeship. although closely tied to parts of the Trust Territory by geography and culture.

The Eastern Carolines as defined above, lie roughly between 1° and 9° north latitude, Kapingamarangi being the farthest south, and Namonuito the farthest north. East to west the Eastern Carolines lie from about 163° to 149° east longitude, a distance of roughly 850 miles. The three most important groups, Truk, Ponape, and Kusaie, are located respectively about

1

600, 900, and 1200 miles to the south and east of Guam. Ponape and Kusaie both lie about 300 miles away from the atomic testing area of Eniwetok in the northwestern Marshalls, to the southwest and south respectively. The main islands of the Western Carolines, Yap and the Palaus, lie about 800 and 1100 miles to the west of the Truk respectively, although there is a series of lesser islands intervening. Rabaul, New Britain, lies about 700 miles south of Truk but is separated from the Mortlocks, the southernmost islands in Truk District by a considerable stretch of sea with few island way stations.

The three largest groups, Kusaie, Ponape and Truk, lie in a roughly east-west line bending a little to the southeast. Pingelap and Mokil lie along this line between Kusaie and Ponape. The uninhabited atoll of Oroluk lies along it between Ponape and Truk. A westward continuation of the line bisects the Puluwat area. The other islands in Truk District can be regarded as on two more or less north-south lines which cross cut this main axis. The most important cross-axis runs from the Halls south past Truk through Nama, Losap, Namoluk, the Mortlocks and extends to Nukuoro in Ponape District. A second cross-axis runs south from Namonuito through the three groups of the Puluwat area. This mnemonic scheme omits only Ngatik, on a line between Ponape and Nukuoro, and Kapingamarangi, to the south of Nukuoro.

TOPOGRAPHY

The islands of Micronesia and other parts of the Pacific are often divided into high and low islands by geographers and by the islanders themselves. Low islands are composed of sand bars washed up on coral reefs by the waves. High islands may be formed in a variety of ways but volcanic action is the most common for the islands more remote from continental shores. The high islands of the Eastern Carolines are all composed mostly of basalt and considered to be of volcanic origin.

In the Trust Territory the Marianas District is composed almost entirely of high islands, while the Marshalls District is composed entirely of low islands. Each of the districts in the Caroline Islands (Ponape, Truk, Yap, Palau, from east to west) contains both high and low islands. Truk and Yap Districts contain most of the low islands in the Carolines however.

There are many fewer high islands (ignoring the uninhabited raised coral islets of southern Palau) in the Carolines than low islands but the total area of the high islands is much greater than that of the low islands.

Approximate figures for the total high and low island areas of Truk and Ponape Districts are as follows:

TABLE 1

AREA OF TRUK AND PONAPE DISTRICTS
(sq. mi.)

District	Total Area of High Islands	Total Area of Low Islands
Truk	37	10
Ponape	172	4
Total	209	14

(Various estimates of the high island areas are given depending largely on how much mangrove swamp one counts as land. These are conservative.)

Most of the low islands in Truk and Ponape Districts are atolls: a ring of coral reef with a number of sand islands on top, the whole enclosing a lagoon. Two of the inhabited low islands in Truk District, Nama and Pulusuk, are single islands without any lagoon, although Pulusuk does have a small brackish lake in its center. Pulap and Tamatam together form a sort of half atoll. The two islands are connected by a single linear reef which makes an incomplete circuit. There is one uninhabited isolated low island in the Truk District, East Fayu, between Namonuito and the Halls. There is also an uninhabited atoll, Oroluk, about halfway between Truk and Ponape.

Atolls in Truk and Ponape District vary considerably in size. In the smallest atolls — Puluwat, Namoluk, Etal, Pingelap, and Mokil— the lagoon area is small relative to the land and reef area. The latter three lack any deep channel from the sea into the lagoon. In the largest atolls— Namonuito, Satawan, and Ngatik— the reef and land areas are but a small fraction of the lagoon area and islands on the other side of the lagoon are below the horizon.

All the atolls except the five smallest have ship channels of a sort so that foreign sea-going vessels can use the lagoons as harbors. Of the

3

five smallest Puluwat has quite a respectable sized boat channel but the other four lack any marked natural channel. The ship channels of the other atolls are of varying quality.

The water over the reef of Namonuito on the lee sides (west and south) is deep enough for good sized ships to sail over in many places, although not with too much comfort. The reefs of the other atolls are shallow enough to be exposed at low tide and only small boats and canoes can pass over them in most places, and this only at high tide.

In general the channels are good in Truk District and not so good in Ponape District. However, the channels of Kapingamarangi and Ngatik and possibly Nukuoro could be greatly improved by reliable markers and the blasting of a few coral heads. The lagoons are generally deep enough for ships although scattered coral heads necessitate careful navigation.

It is generally believed by geologists that coral atolls are formed by the gradual sinking of a high island accompanied by a continuous upward growth of coral around it. Several stages in this process can be demonstrated in the Eastern Carolines. Kusaie is the closest to the initial stage. It is a high island with only a narrow reef around it and no large deep lagoons between the reef and the shore. Ponape is further along in the process. As the island has subsided the sea has drowned the lower parts of the river valleys. Around most of the island the reef is separated from the mainland by a deep lagoon, although the lagoon is lacking on parts of the southeast coast. Truk, which is sometimes described as a complex atoll, is a still further stage. The land has sunk so much that the land mass has been broken up and only the tops of the highest mountains show above the water. The encircling reef is five to twenty miles distant from the main islands. The numerous atolls among the low islands illustrate the completion of the development. Isolated coral islands such as Nama and Pulusuk may illustrate a further stage of shrinking or fragmentation of the atoll. Shoals south of Kusaie and Pulusuk may illustrate a final stage where for some reason the atoll itself disappears beneath the waves.

The soil of the low islands consists of coral sand and vegetable matter and can support only a limited variety of wild and domestic plants. On the other hand on the high islands much land is not usable because it is too rocky or steep or is overgrown with coarse grass or is at too high an elevation. On the low islands nearly the entire land surface is usable agriculturally and is in fact under intensive use on nearly all the atolls.

Most of the land area of the inhabited low islands can be divided into three zones. Around the shore is a zone where the ground water is mixed with sea water and where heavy salt spray blows in at times with high winds. In this zone the main cultivated plants are coconut and pandanus. Further inland is a zone where the ground water is fresher and which is more protected from sea spray. In this zone the main cultivated plant is breadfruit, although other plants, wild and cultivated, are also found. In the center of most of the inhabited islands is a third zone of taro swamp. These swamps are probably in part natural but have been extended by excavation. The soil is a muck formed largely of decaying vegetation. The islanders have added to this by bringing dead leaves from the other two zones.

The agricultural productivity of all three zones depends on the presence of reasonably fresh ground water. The coral rock and sand composing the low islands is porous and the land is so low that with prolonged absence of rain or with excessive consumption of ground water sea water would eventually underlie the whole area. As it is the fresh water in the ground is kept reasonably pure by its lesser density which enables it to float on deeper layers of denser sea water. Mixture occurs all along the edges of the islands and even the water in the central swamps is somewhat brackish most of the time. At places cracks in the underlying coral rock may let the sea water penetrate far inland with the rise and fall of the tides. The islanders sometimes come across such spots in extending their taro swamps and then must fill the place up again.

On the high islands supplies of fresh water are generally better than on the low. All have fresh springs and Ponape and Kusaie have a number of sizable streams.

CLIMATE

Throughout the Eastern Carolines humidity is normally very high and rainfall is generally adequate and even abundant. Rainfall is greater on the high islands than on the low. The mountains of Ponape, Kusaie, and to a lesser extent Truk cause the moisture laden winds to rise on hitting them, expand, and cool which produces more rain. The mountain tops of Ponape are in fact hidden in clouds most of the time for this reason.

Rainfall on the high islands appears to decrease from east to west: Kusaie being the most rainy and Truk the least. Some old figures for

5

average annual rainfall at two sites in Kusaie were 187 and 255 inches per year; for three places in Ponape from 168 to 186 inches; for two places in Truk 90 and 129 inches. Rainfall on Kusaie and Ponape varies considerably from place to place due to the conformation of the mountains and detailed observations representative of the different parts of the islands are not available for comparison. Rainfall evidently varies considerably on Truk as well due to the conformity of the mountains, but the Truk mountains are lower and the differences in rainfall caused by them are not as noticeable to the casual observer.

Even on the low islands rainfall is usually adequate to support extensive productive plantations of breadfruit, a tree which grows poorly or not at all on drier coral islands in other parts of the Pacific (for instance, the Northern Marshalls within the Trust Territory). Within the Eastern Carolines Kapingamarangi is the island most disturbed by occasional prolonged drought but even on this island the breadfruit tree grows, although it does not always bear well.

Temperature generally ranges from about 75° in the middle of the night to 85° in the middle of the afternoon. It rarely falls more than a degree or two below 70° or rises above 90° Truk appears to be about a degree or two warmer than Ponape and Kusaie due to less cloud cover. The greater protection of buildings and pedestrians from the sun's rays afforded by the cloud cover on the latter two islands gives people the impression of a greater difference in temperature with Truk than actually appears to exist.

The northeast trades blow most of the year in the Eastern Carolines but die down in the summer months, when the wind is variable. The trades are important to sailing and "upwind" and "downwind" are commonly used to refer to direction in everyday speech. On the high islands the force of the winds varies considerably depending on what side of a mountain one is on.

Typhoons occur occasionally but with less frequency and intensity than farther west in the Carolines. When they occur they move west and slightly north. The most severe typhoons within the lifetime of people now alive were those of 1905, striking Kusaie, Pingelap, Mokil, Ponape, Ngatik, the Halls, and Namonuito, and of 1907, striking the Mortlocks. Typhoons are especially disastrous to the low islands. Waves may completely sweep across the land drowning people and destroying all the standard vegetable food so that many who escaped drowning later died of famine.

6

Kapingamarangi alone appears to be far enough south so that it escapes typhoons, but it has the compensating disadvantage of severe droughts.

CULTURAL CLASSIFICATION OF THE ISLANDS
OF TRUK AND PONAPE DISTRICTS

The most basic cultural division of the islands of Truk and Ponape
District is into Micronesian and Polynesian. There are only two Polynesian
islands, Kapingamarangi and Nukuoro. The main historic cultural ties of
the people of these two islands are with islands farther east outside of Micronesia such as Samoa, Tahiti, and Hawaii.

A threefold basic division of the Micronesian islands is also apparent:
Kusaie, Greater Ponape area, Greater Truk area. There is no other island
very closely related to Kusaie culturally. Ponape and Truk appear to be
more closely related to each other than Kusaie although this statement
could bear further study. The islands of the Truk area are also closely related in culture to the low islands east of Yap in Yap District and south of
Palau in Palau District. Cultural relations of the Eastern Carolines with
Yap and Palau proper, the Marianas are more distant. The Marshalls and
the Gilberts to the east may be more closely related. The greater Truk
area includes the islands within the Truk Lagoon (thirteen permanently inhabited high islands and the single inhabited reef island of Pis), eleven low
island communities to the south, and thirteen low island communities to the
north and west. Truk and Ponape share many features of culture and language which can only be explained by a common historical origin at some
time in the past. They have nevertheless diverged in many of their customs, and the languages, while related, are now mutually unintelligible.
The difference may be about on the order of that between English and
German.

Within each area there are also considerable cultural differences
among some of the low islands and between low and high islands. Six main
sub-areas may be distinguished in the Truk area and four in the Ponape
area, as follows:

Truk Area	Ponape Area
Truk Lagoon	Ponape and satellite
Mortlocks and Nama	islands
(seven communities)	Ngatik

7

Truk Area	Ponape Area
Losap (two communities)	Mokil
Halls (four communities)	Pingelap
Namonuito (five com- munities)	
Puluwat and nearby islands (four communities)	

Within the greater Truk and Ponape areas the high islands have
served as centers of trade and cultural influence since prehistoric times. In
spite of the important differences of custom and language among the low
islanders and between low and high islanders many adults on the low islands,
including probably all of the older men, understand the dialect of their high
island trade center, and can speak it when necessary, if with an accent.
Low island children and women, who have less contact with high island
people, find the high island dialects largely unintelligible at first, although
they can learn them quickly and easily if need arises. High islanders usually
do not bother to learn the low island dialects and find it hard or impossible
to understand two low islanders talking among themselves.

The high island sub-areas and the more populous of the low island
sub-areas are further divisible by lesser differences of custom and dialect.
Each of the larger high islands of Truk constitutes from one to several communities with its own special accent and vocabulary and unique variations
of custom. The island of Ponape is divided into five traditionally independent districts each with its own variations of customs and dialect, and these
districts also have noticeable though small internal variations.

Ponape also has a number of immigrant colonies most of which were
established in the German period. These include colonies from all of the
low islands in Ponape District (Mokil, and Pingelap, Ngatik, Nukuoro and
Kapingamarangi) from some of the Mortlock islands (especially Ta, Satawan,
and Lukunor), from Yap, Truk Lagoon, and Losap. Most of these immigrants or their ancestors were settled in the petty state of Jokaj by the German regime on lands confiscated from the original Ponapean population
after the rebellion of 1911 in which the district administrator was killed.
The Germans exiled the original population of Jokaj to Yap and Palau but
later the Japanese allowed them to return. Only some were able to resettle
in Jokaj and the rest scattered throughout the island.

A list of the main sub-areas of the Greater Truk and Ponape areas according to similarity of custom and language coincides with an east-west list according to geographic proximity: Pingelap, Mokil, Ponape, Ngatik, Mortlocks, Losap, Truk, Halls, Namonuito, Puluwat group. The biggest jump in this list is between Ngatik in the Ponape area and the Mortlocks in the Truk area, but it is still clear linguistically at least that these two sub-areas are the most closely related of any sub-areas separated by the boundary between the two major areas. These similarities are no doubt the result of continuing contact in prehistoric times in trade, visiting, and war as well as of a common origin in the remote past.

A list of the main communities and inhabited islands of the Eastern Carolines follows. The first name is the most commonly used one in the English literature. The second name represents the one used in speech by the islanders themselves. The official Ponapean spelling is used for islands in the Greater Ponape area. Elbert's spelling is used for names in Truk District (with indication of prolonged vowel sounds by repeating the letter).

Polynesian Islands
    Kapingamarangi, Greenwich (Kapingamarangi)
    Nukuoro (Nukuoro)
Kusaie (Kosrae)
    Lele (Lelu, offshore island, capital of Kusaie)
Greater Ponape Area
    Pingelap (Pinglap)
    Mokil (Mwekil)
    Ngatik (Ngetik)
    Ponape (Pohnpei)
        Matolenim, Metalanim (Moadolenimw)
            Tamon (Temwen, island in Matolenim)
        U (Uh)
            Tabak (Dehpehk, island in U)
            Takaiu (Takaieu, island in U)
            Mant Paitak (Mwand Peidak, island in U)
            Mant Paiti (Mwand Peidi, island in U)
        Kitti (Kiti)
            Ant (And, atoll attached to Kiti)
        Not (Net)
            Parem (Parem, island in Net)
            Langar (Lenger, island in Net)
        Jokaj (Sokehs)

Palikir (Palikir, mainland part of Jokaj)
Pakin (Pakein, atoll attached to Jokaj)
Greater Truk Area
    Mortlocks, Ku or Nomoi Islands (Nömwun Kküwu)
        Etal (Ettal)
        Satawan Atoll (no native name)
          Satawan (Sätawan)
          Ta (Töö)
          More (Mwóóch)
          Kutu (Kütü)
        Lukunor Atoll (no native name)
          Lukunor (Lükünoch)
          Oneop (Oneop)
        Namoluk (Nómwoluuk, often considered separate from Mort-
          locks but culturally close)
      Losap Atoll (Loosòpw)
        Losap (Loosópw)
        Pis (Piis)
      Nama (Nömö, culturally related to Mortlocks)
    Truk Lagoon (Chuuk)
      Moen (Wööna)
        Falo (Fönó, subsidiary to Moen)
      Dublon, Toloas (Tonowas)
      Uman (Uumaan)
      Tsis (Siis)
      Fefan (Feefen)
      Parem (Pärem)
      Udot (Útööt)
      Eot (Ööt)
      Falabeguets (Fanapenges)
      Tol (Toon)
        Pata (Paata)
        Polle (Pwene)
        Wone (Wone)
      Ulalu (Romonum)
      Pis (Piis, also known as Fanöw)
    Hall Islands (Nomwun Paaföng)
      Murilo Atoll (no native name)
        Murilo (Mwirilö)
        Ruo (Ruò)
      Nomwin Atoll (no native name)
        Nomwin (Nómwin)

Fananu (Fanaanü)
Namonuito Atoll (Nómwun Weitö)
Ulul (Onoun)
Magur (Möktïr)
Onari (Ünaanü)
Ono (Ono)
Pisaras (Pisarach)
Puluwat Area (no native name)
Puluwat (Pwolowót)
Pulap Atoll (no native name)
Pulap (Pwollap)
Tamatam (Tamatam)
Pulusuk (Houk; Trukese Suuk)

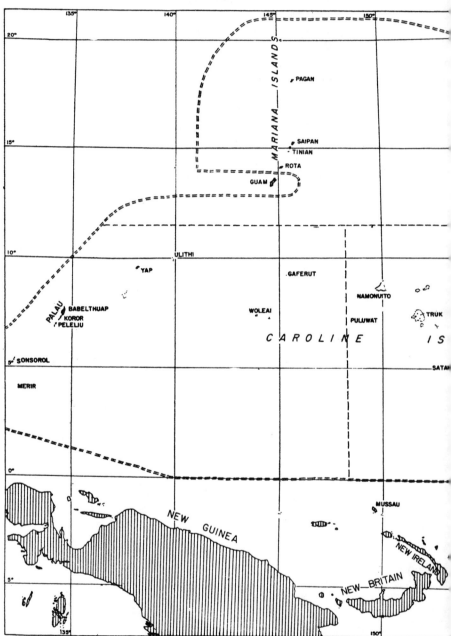

Courtesy of Herold J. Wiens

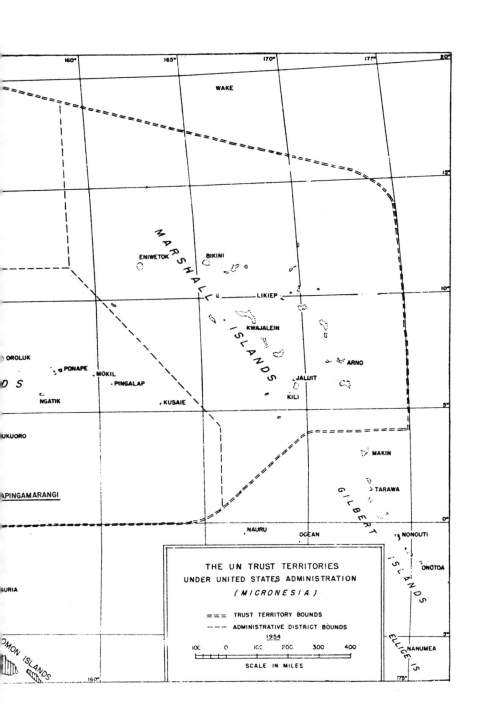

THE UN TRUST TERRITORIES
UNDER UNITED STATES ADMINISTRATION
(MICRONESIA)

=== TRUST TERRITORY BOUNDS
--- ADMINISTRATIVE DISTRICT BOUNDS
1954

100   0   100   200   300   400

SCALE IN MILES

CHAPTER II

THE PAST

This chapter gives a brief survey of the prehistory and recorded history of the Eastern Caroline Islands. The intention is in part simply to satisfy the curiosity of administrators and other interested persons about some common questions on the history of the area. However the record of the contact between European and islander, which forms the greater part of this chapter is intended to serve a more important purpose as well. This record gives an idea of the sorts of events which have helped form the islanders' conceptions of "civilized" people. It also contains some object lessons in descriptions of actions of foreigners which have worked and some which have not.

PREHISTORY

Written records of any sort involving the Eastern Caroline Islands are lacking before the sixteenth century while written records giving signif icant information about the islands do not start until the nineteenth century. Events and conditions before this must be inferred by anthropologists and archaeologists from studies of the physical traces of the life and dwellings of people of former times and by studies of customs and traditions found at time of discovery from which inferences can be drawn about earlier times. Such evidence is necessarily less precise than full written records but when the various types of unwritten evidence are combined and compared surprisingly consistent chronologies of the movements of peoples may be inferred.

The techniques of archaeology are usually the most effective in de termining prehistory where there are sufficient material remains to apply them. The recently developed technique of measuring amounts of radio active carbon in plant and animal remains is capable of giving rough dates back into the glacial age. No carbon dates are available as yet for the

12

Truk and Ponape areas but a date of about 1500 B.C. has been determined for a site on Saipan which was investigated by Dr. Alexander Spoehr (now director of the Bishop Museum in Honolulu). It seems plausible that the Carolines also were settled by this time.

Archaeological investigation in the Eastern Carolines so far has been mostly limited to the great ruins of Ponape (the artificial islands of Nan Matol in the petty state of Matolenim) and Kusaie (the enclosures etc. at the capital at Lele). These are unlikely to provide much information on the early periods of prehistory since they appear to have been constructed well after the islands had been settled, the population increased, and integrated governments developed. Whatever the original dates of construction the Ponape and Kusaie ruins were still in use at the time of first foreign contact. It is not true, as one sometimes reads in speculative articles, that modern Ponapeans have no traditions of the construction and purpose of the islands of Nan Matol. These traditions are further mentioned below.

Other archaeological sites, ranging from house sites to forts, tombs and ceremonial places are found on the three high island groups. Ponape appears to be especially rich in such sites. The site of Sahpw Takai (literally "Rocky Land") in Kiti deserves special mention. According to tradition, it was built in imitation of parts of Nan Matol and was the capital of Kiti District.

Archaeological investigation of many of these sites at present would be somewhat hampered by Ponapean sentiment. Many Ponapeans still feel strongly that the remains of the people of olden times should not be disturbed and will refuse to approach these sites. Many others however have considered that these taboos are pagan superstitions and have demonstrated their Christian zeal by building pigpens or other structures out of ancient rock tombs and sacred enclosures. This destruction of sites valuable to science and as monuments to the achievements of the past will continue unless counteracted by both adult education and enforcement of conservation laws.

The most encouraging places for early remains are the high islands, since there are better chances for preserving sites there. It is likely that the first settlers would make at least occasional use of caves and overhanging cliffs near the shore which afford about as good conditions for preservation of small archaeological remains as can be hoped for. The scientific importance of such sites is equal to the larger, more spectacular sites and they deserve full protection from disturbance by any one except properly authorized scientists.

On the other hand in the low islands the whole surface is liable to occasional inundation by storms and old islets are sometimes eaten away by changing currents or new ones built up. Also it is easier for the inhabitants to avoid rubbish heaps (the archaeologist's delight) by throwing their unwanted things into the sea.

Local tradition in many parts of the world has been compared with the results of archaeological digging and the tradition vindicated or disproved. In Truk and Ponape Districts Ponape Island offers an especially rich body of semi-historical legends. Many of the local traditions concerning Nan Matol were recorded by the German anthropologist Paul Hambruch in 1910. Most of these could still be recorded in fuller form on Ponape today, as well as others which he missed.

According to Ponapean tradition construction of the islands began under the direction of two immigrant magicians, Sihpa and Sohpa. They became the site of the capital of the petty state of Deleur, which eventually conquered all of Ponape, and whose chiefs bore the title of Sau Deleur or Lord of Deleur. Whatever the origin of the original legendary immigrants their successors were evidently absorbed into Ponapean society for the later rulers bear clearly Ponapean names whose meaning is apparent today (e. g. "Foremost Reign", "Straight Reign"). This line of rulers was allegedly terminated by an invading force from Kusaie, which Kusaiean tradition also recalls.

Other traditions relate the legendary history of the immigration of various clans to Ponape and other islands, the direction or islands from which they came, and the first place of settlement. Archaeological investigations might find useful hints in some of these legends. If any are vindicated by the findings this would increase the significance of both the traditions and archaeological material in question.

Allegedly historical traditions may be considered along with other stories told for amusement and studied not for their truth but in terms of their distribution, that is, what other tribes or communities tell them. Historical contact direct or indirect can be assumed at some time in the past where two communities share what is recognizably the same tale. The degree of similarity of the two versions and the numbers of distinct tales shared allow inferences on directness and age of historical contact. A thorough up-to-date comparative study of Micronesian tales has yet to be made. Studies made to date indicate strong connections of most of Truk and Ponape Districts with the rest of Micronesia, and outside the area to both the islands of Melanesia to the south (New Guinea, Solomons, etc.) and Polynesia to the east (Samoa, Hawaii, Tahiti, etc.)

Linguistics offers another means of learning something of tribal and racial history. Even with unwritten languages it is possible to establish common historic origins by present similarity. For this purpose similarity of grammar, word endings, and the words for the most common everyday objects and concepts is more important than a mere count of the proportion of shared words in dictionaries of the two languages. In general the more alike the more closely connected historically.

Recently rather precise statistical methods have been proposed for dating the point of divergence of related languages by counting the number of related basic words used for common everyday concepts. The assumption is that the basic vocabulary of any language is highly resistant to change and that it will change in any language at about the same rate. Results of the application of this technique of linguistic dating to Micronesian languages are not yet available, but may be forthcoming as an outcome of the CIMA and SIM studies of Micronesian languages, including Trukese and Ponapean. The main thing that can be said now is that all languages in the two districts fit into the great Malayo-Polynesian family, whose speakers are found principally in Indonesia and the Philippines, parts of Southeast Asia, parts of Melanesia, and all of Micronesia and Polynesia (that is all the islands in the Pacific from New Guinea north to Hawaii, and from New Guinea and New Zealand to east of Tahiti).

It also appears likely from the geographic distribution of languages that the ancestors of the present speakers of Nuclear Micronesian languages (the people of all islands in the two districts except Kapingamarangi and Nukuoro and possibly Kusaie) came into the area first and that the ancestors of the speakers of the other languages arrived later. If this is true other relative latecomers in Micronesia would be the ancestors of the present Palauans, Yapese, and Chamorros. There is no suggestion however that any of these invasions were very recent.

The distributional studies of folk tales and language are single examples of a general technique which may be applied to any aspect of cus tom, although folk tales and vocabulary are especially suited because of their arbitrariness and immense variety. Archaeologists apply the same principle of similarity in working out connections between different sites. Stone and shell adze heads and stone food pounders are examples of material objects whose form is determined by custom. Because of their durability they are especially suited for tracing historical connections in the distant past. Much remains to be done along these lines in Micronesia.

The study of physical types can provide evidence about the prehistoric contacts of people. If the people of two areas have sufficiently similar physical types it can be inferred that they have a common ancestry.

There are a couple of precautions to be observed here, concerning the effect of environment on physical type and the magnification of random genetic variations in small populations.

For instance, in Truk District German measurements show that the low islanders on the average are a little taller than the people of Truk Lagoon. It is plausible that this difference might have been caused by a wave of immigration of some taller race into the area, such as the Polynesians who also settled Kapingamarangi and Nukuoro. A fleet of immigrants which was absorbed into the population would be liable to have a bigger effect on the low islands with their relatively small populations than on the larger populations of the high islands.

On the other hand it is clear that the low islanders and high islanders have different diets. The low islanders in general depend more on taro and coconut while the high islanders get more breadfruit. The low islanders may also get more fish. With this much information one might argue that the difference in stature is due to diet. A full assessment of the strength of heredity and environment here requires further study.

Because of the influence of environment on many of the bodily measurements used by early physical anthropologists, many modern workers are attaching increasing importance to blood types, which are strictly hereditary and do not change with environment. A number of series of blood types are now known besides the original A, B, and O and populations may be described in terms of the frequencies of the various types in each series. Similarity of frequencies implies common ancestry.

A large-scale study of blood types in Truk and Ponape Districts is yet to be made. The frequency of A and B blood types on Kapingamarangi is similar to other Polynesian populations, if known descendants of Micronesian immigrants are excluded. The general physical type of the Kapingamarangi people is similar to other Polynesians so the evidence from physical anthropology confirms the evidence of culture and language about these people.

On most Micronesian islands except for the two Polynesian atolls in Ponape District some investigators distinguish several racial types. The proportions of the mixture vary somewhat. Most notably within the Carolines, Kusaie shows more mongoloid admixture than average, while the high islands of Yap and Palau show both more mongoloid and negritoid (Pacific pygmy, as found on Bataan, Luzon).

Persons familiar with the appearance of the various islanders within Truk and Ponape Districts can often recognize certain physical traits as being especially common on certain islands. Thus on Losap Atoll there is an unusually large proportion of fat people, although still a minority of the population. The hair of the Kusaieans tends to be straighter than most other islands, while the hair of the people of Pingelap tends to be wiry and high-bridged noses are fairly common. The men of Puluwat and nearby islands have especially well-developed musculature. Many of the men of Truk Lagoon and the low islands north and west of Truk have unusually broad lower jaws.

It is hard to judge the import of these variations. The population of most of these islands is not large and the number of original settlers may have been quite small. Also before foreign contact there may have been times when most of the population of one or more of the low islands has been wiped out in a typhoon or the ensuing famine. It is likely that the physical peculiarities of a single individual or family surviving a typhoon or initially settling an island have been inherited by a large proportion of the current population. Many of the noticeable differences among the islanders therefore may not imply separate immigration from different parts of the world.

Nevertheless physical anthropologists partly account for this variation by postulating multiple origins. Besides the mongoloid and negritoid strains noted above a "generalized" strain is said to be important. This is especially prominent around Ponape but evident throughout most of the Carolines and Marshalls. It lacks most of the specialized characteristics of the other races in the area, such as the straight hair and broad faces of

17

the mongoloids, or the frizzly hair, thick lips, and black skin of the negritoid, or the heavy build of the Polynesian. Besides this, a slight Polynesian admixture is also postulated for the low islands throughout most of the Carolines, but is less evident on the high islands. A study of modern physical types alone, however, does not indicate clearly when, where, or in what order these mixtures took place.

Since Western contact there has been another series of mixtures taking place: with whites of European origin until World War I, then with Japanese through World War II and again with whites after World War II. The islands of Ngatik, Mokil, Kusaie, and Ponape show considerable white admixture. Truk Lagoon and Ponape both show considerable Japanese admixture. With the present limited travel facilities and restrictions on immigration into the Territory the rate of new admixture has decreased considerably, and there is the prospect that in the next few generations existing intrusive racial strains will be thoroughly mixed with the rest of the population, as they already are socially.

INITIAL DISCOVERY AND EXPLORATION PERIOD: 1529-1800

The first European discovery of islands in the Eastern Carolines was more than four centuries ago, only a few decades after the discovery of the New World. Due to the relatively small size of the islands and the lack of products for trade little interest was manifested in them for another two and a half centuries. Even reports of the existence of the islands are often fragmentary and inconclusive, and they were certainly sighted and contacted following discovery by more Western ships than are known to historians. None of these contacts appear to have been of crucial significance in the life of the islanders although they were sometimes considered to be portentous events to judge from a legendary account reported from Ponape by the German anthropologist Hambruch. Here is one report:

> A strange ship came to Nalap at the entrance to
> the harbor of Rohn Kiti. The natives thought they
> were gods and brought kava to sacrifice. As some of
> the men landed, however, their human nature be-
> came evident. The sacrificial greeting was soon
> followed by hostility. Immediately at the mouth of
> the Kiti River behind the bar the strangers climbed
> on land. The landing place was at Sakaren Iap.
> They were clad in iron and a man in black with a

crucifix was with them. As a result of a misunderstanding, a battle followed with many Ponape people
killed. The strangers were unwoundable because of
their "strong skin" yet they were finally overpowered
and one was speared in the eyes through the visor
opening.

The first recorded sighting of islands in the Eastern Carolines was by
Alvaro Saavedra, a Spaniard, who passed through the area on his way from
Mexico to the Moluccas in 1529. He may have sighted all three of the high
island groups, Kusaie, Ponape, and Truk, but did not land or leave clear
enough reports to make clear just what he did see. Magellan on his circum-
navigation of the globe a few years earlier sailed near or through East Carolines but saw no land until he reached the Marianas.

Following Saavedra another Spaniard, Grijalvares, is believed to
have sighted Kapingamarangi on a trip from Peru to the Moluccas in 1536.
He recorded little beyond the fact that he sighted an island at the approximate position of Kapingamarangi.

Truk was clearly visited by Arellano, another Spaniard, on the ship
"San Lucas" in 1565. In a hostile encounter with the Trukese twelve canoes
full of armed men came out to meet the ship and the Spaniards felt compelled to fire on these with cannon, inflicting great damage. Arellano also
discovered Pulap Atoll and in a hostile encounter with the inhabitants of
Tamatam islet the islanders killed three Spaniards so he gave this group the
name of "Los Martires" or "The Martyrs". In a second trip by Arellano,
his pilot, Lope Martin, with thirteen soldiers and as many sailors, was put
off on Namonuito because he had murdered the captain of one of the ships.
Two years later Mendana found material evidences of whites having been on
the island, but no people were found. Nothing more was ever heard of
them.

Ponape was clearly visited by the Spaniard Quiros in 1595 on the one
remaining ship of Mendana's expedition. Quiros also sighted Ngatik. Alvaro de Mendana died on October 18, 1595 in the Santa Cruz islands. Pedro
Fernandez de Quiros, the first pilot, took command in his place. At this
time, one of the four ships with which they had started the voyage had disappeared and only one of the remaining ships was seaworthy. Quiros set out
on a direct course for Guam and then Manila. Men died daily during this
trip and the remainder of the crew was more or less sick. In December the

two ships which had been in bad condition disappeared. The remaining ship, the "San Jeronimo" held to its course, but currents carried it far to the east, and on December 23, 1595 Quiros sighted an unknown high island which from the description is clearly Ponape. Quiros could not find a safe way into the lagoon. Natives came out in canoes, but only one dared to come outside the reef. To Quiros he appeared to be naked, had long hair, signaled the direction from which he had come, broke something white which he ate, and raised coconuts to his lips to drink. They called to the man to come on board, but he would not.

During most of the seventeenth and eighteenth centuries the islands of Truk and Ponape Districts were mostly ignored by ships and there are few reports although sporadic contact probably continued. Toward the end of the eighteenth century some other discoveries are reported.

A Spaniard, Don Felipe Tompson, saw Ngatik in 1773 and believed himself the discoverer, although Quiros probably also saw it.

A Captain Musgrave of the ship "Sugar-Cane" sighted Ngatik and Pingelap in 1793. Pingelap has at times carried his name.

The eighteenth century closes with the Spaniard Ibargoitia sighting Puluwat and Pulusuk in 1799. These islands had been recorded on maps before then but it is not known if this was done because of information received from inhabitants of other islands or because of the now lost report of some ship which actually sighted them before this. Ibargoitia also visited Tamatam and Pulap in 1801.

INTENSIFIED FOREIGN CONTACT: 1800-1887

After the beginning of the nineteenth century whalers were active in the islands of the Eastern Carolines but the exact details of their contact with the islanders are largely lacking. Further recorded contacts early in the century were Crozier's sighting of Kusaie in 1805, the discovery of Nukuoro by the Spanish frigate "Monteverde" in 1806, and the sighting of Pingelap in 1809 by a Captain MacAskill of the "Lady Barlow". Pingelap was formerly sometimes called MacAskill's Island. MacAskill may also have visited Truk in the same year.

In 1814 the Spaniard Dublon visited Truk and has been considered by some to be the discoverer of the group. The island of Tolowas, the site of the administrative center of Truk District under the Germans and Japanese is still often called by his name.

In the years 1817 to 1820 the Frenchman Freycinet made a voyage around the world on the corvette "L'Uranie". In 1819 he sighted a number of islands in the Eastern Carolines including Kapingamarangi (possibly), Truk, Puluwat, and Pulusuk. He did not go ashore at Truk but he did get wooden bowls from there.

Freycinet gives accounts of Trukese voyaging to other islands. In 1807, he says, about fifteen Trukese with a king, went to Guam, were fired upon and returned to their boats in the night, although they were hungry. In 1816 there are reported to have been about 120 boats put out from Truk and about 110 of these were lost in storms. In 1815 many are said to have gone to Saipan and in 1818 a colony was formed there by six leaders, five children and eighty adults. Other reports indicate that these individuals may have been low islanders from the culturally related atolls north and west of the Truk Lagoon.

In 1824 Captain John Hall passed along the east side of Truk Lagoon and sighted Nomwin and Murilo Atolls to the north of Truk which are still often called the Hall Islands after him.

Three months later in the same year the French Captain Louis Isidore Duperrey, commanding the corvette "La Coquille", visited Truk and made the place known. Duperrey also visited some of the other islands including Kusaie where the ship stayed for ten days. Mokil was sometimes called Duperrey's Island in honor of his visit there. The naturalist A. P. Lesson accompanied the ship and made notes on the islands visited. A map maker was also aboard.

In 1825 it is reported that Kapingamarangi was sighted and named Greenwich, a name still used for it on occasion. The "discoverer" is unknown however. In 1827 a Captain Macy discovered Namoluk and named it Harvest.

In 1827 the Catholic priest Bachelot came to Ponape. He worked for several years on the island of Na in Matolenim. He was unsuccessful in making converts but in Hambruch's time the Matolenim people, Catholic and Protestant alike, had heard tales of his kindness from their grandparents. In Hambruch's time his house location was still shown on Na although his

21

grave had disappeared. Father Bachelot had no successor and the beginning of continuous mission work on Ponape was with the Protestants in 1852.

In 1828 the Russian explorer Lütke, captain of the "Senyavin", visited Kusaie, Pingelap, Ponape, Ngatik, Lukunor, Namoluk, passed by Truk Lagoon and went on to the Halls, Namonuito and many of the low islands in Yap District. This trip was the fourth Russian voyage around the world. Ponape with nearby islands are still sometimes referred to as the Senyavin Islands in memory of this visit.

Lütke stayed at Kusaie for three weeks and like other early visitors reported that the Kusaieans were very friendly. They liked Europeans and the affection was reciprocated. In spite of this, they kept their women out of reach of the white sailors, when they learned that the sailors were looking for them.

Relations with the nobility of Kusaie were never so good as they were with the common people. In Duperrey's and Lütke's time there was a chief named Sesa who tried to provoke trouble with the Europeans who managed to avoid it only with difficulty. This caused Lesson, who reported for Duperrey, to take a dislike to chiefs. Lütke liked them better than Lesson had, but still he did not like them as well as he did the common people. The ships "Coquille" (Duperrey's) and "Senyavin" introduced metal to Kusaie, and it quickly became prized above all gifts.

Lütke was surprised to find Ponape. In the night he came very near the reef and he felt that it was just by chance that he had not missed Ponape or been wrecked on the reef. At daybreak he was outside Matolenim Harbor. He thought himself to be the discoverer and mentions that it was strange that the largest and highest of the Carolines was the last to be discovered. Large canoes, which carried fourteen men and small ones which carried only two came out. The people in the canoes sang, danced, and gesticulated with heads and hands. With difficulty he got one on board, and says "Their wild visages are full of mistrust, the great blood-filled eyes, the savagery and the wildness of these island dwellers made on us a right unpleasant impression because we had not yet forgotten the pleasant stay with our friends on Kusaie from whom they are distinguished by speech as well as by appearance." One man tried to get Lütke's sextant but finally swam to his canoe. Later at Mutok Harbor they were again surrounded by canoes and in one there was a woman. They noticed the natives had spears and slings in their canoes which they tried to keep concealed under mats.

The next day they found people on the reef who barked like dogs at them which indicated to Lütke that they had the dog. On this day some leaders came aboard the most distinguished of which was the iros lapalap who had a scar of a bad wound on his leg. This caused Lütke to conjecture that they had wars. When the ship went into the lagoon the natives shrieked a great deal and the ship had to push its way through the canoes. Finally one threw a spear at Lütke who fired over his head. At this the natives scattered and the ship went out of the lagoon, cruised about and found Ant and Pakin.

Next day they saw Sokas and set a boat to investigate Langar Harbor. Again the natives crowded so about them that they feared evil intentions. Shots fired above the heads of the crowd only increased the furor. The boat returned to the ship. Lütke expressed a desire to set foot on the "newly discovered" shore, but not at the expense of the blood of his own men or that of the natives. The night before when the natives had gone away Lütke mentions the sound of the triton "which in these waters is the call to battle". They were becalmed on Ant and almost went on the reef there. Both Ant and Pakin appeared to them to have been visited but uninhabited. Six men who were on Pakin shoved canoes into the water and came toward the boat singing and making signs with a bit of red material. These were answered with a red handkerchief. They brought gifts of fruit but would not accept the invitation to come on board. Lütke went to them in a skiff but complains of their speaking so loudly and quickly that communication was not much possible. He recorded the name of the big island as Pouynipeti or Painipete. One man had elephantiasis and another a skin disease which Lütke says is common in these islands. The next day they went back to the big island and found some natives whom Lütke considered to be more intelligent. He discovered from them that the name of the big island was indeed Pouynipete and that the southerly of the atolls was called Andema (there is Ant) and the northerly Paghenema (there is Pakin). They got some other names from the natives, most of them just misunderstandings but the name of Pingelap is recorded correctly.

Lütke reported that on the coast there were very few dwellings yet smoke rose in many places and the great coconut stands showed the great population of the island, especially in the north. The southwest appeared to be less populated as it is today. He estimated that they saw about five hundred men and with women and children he felt the island would have a population of about two thousand.

Lütke's expedition was accompanied by Kittlitz, a geologist and botanist, and Mertens, a mineralogist and draftsman. Kittlitz's reports give details on the islands.

Lütke's expedition took an English sailor, one William Floyd, off Murilo where he had been stranded for one and a half years. During his stay Floyd visited Truk by island sailing canoe. This incident serves as a reminder of the early presence of commercial ships without interest in making scientific reports of their voyages.

The French explorer Dumont d'Urville passed by Truk and visited Pulap in 1828. He returned to Truk in 1838 for a more notable visit described below.

In 1830 the American Captain Benjamin Morrell visited Truk, Pulap, and Nukuoro. Morrell believed himself to be the discoverer of Truk and named the islands after his friend Edwin Bergh, Bergh's Group. Bergh was a shipbuilder in New York. Morrell found the reef full of mother of pearl and bêche de mer and sandalwood on the mountains. The natives he said were shy but friendly. Two to three hundred boats were often around the ship. Morrell presented the natives with many seeds— apple, pear, peach, plum, melon, pumpkin, yam, potatoe, onion, cabbage, turnip, carrot, pea, parsnip, and bean. Outside of the pumpkins or cucumbers, which may stem from him, nothing has grown from them.

On Morrell's visit to Nukuoro the islanders first brought food and exhibited shyness. The crew responded with old knives, hardware, and trinkets and the islanders gave back their clothing and fishing gear and signified their desire to go ashore and get more things for trade. When the ship went closer in however the island men suddenly began preparations for fighting evidently intending to capture the ship. Morrell sailed away before any casualties occurred. On a second visit he could not sail away as easily and was forced to open fire in self defense.

The Irish sailor James O'Connell was stranded on Ponape for the years 1826-1833. He was on the island during and after Lütke's visit, although he made no contact with him. O'Connell says that there were six foreign vessels stranded on the island shortly before the arrival of Lütke. His book, "A Residence of Eleven Years in New Holland and the Caroline Islands; being the Adventures of James O'Connell" was edited from his verbal narrative by B.B. Mussey of Boston in 1836. O'Connell served on the bark "John Bull" in 1826. Missionaries were going to Kusaie on the same ship which was stranded on a reef. The men left the ship. O'Connell, five of the men, and the wife and daughter of the missionary escaped in a boat. Their comrades disappeared from view. In the heat and cold the women died.

After three days land was sighted. Natives saw the boat and attacked but O'Connell and his vessel offered no opposition. They were brought to a canoe house and accepted as guests. They feared they would be eaten. O'Connell danced to the delight of the natives. His acceptance of his plight and what appears to be determination to enjoy it was no doubt in large part responsible for his safety while on Ponape. Dogs were roasted and kava drunk at this first welcome feast. Leaders from other parts appeared and the strangers were divided among them. O'Connell and his comrade Keenan were put in a canoe and taken to an uninhabited hut where women began to tatoo them. Keenan complained and they stopped work on him, but insisted on tatooing O'Connell. The wounds from this job took a month to heal. Then O'Connell was taken back to his native home where there was a last bit of tatooing which he reported did not hurt much. There was music and dancing. Keenan made a flute and entertained the natives with it. O'Connell was given the woman who did the last bit of tatooing on him as a wife. They lived with his father-in-law and his wife went everywhere he did. O'Connell says they got along as well as most civilized couples.

There were many eels on Ponape at this time; they had probably multiplied as a result of a taboo on eating them or killing them. O'Connell, who knew of the taboo, found the forbidden fruit difficult to resist and finally he and Keenan killed and ate eels in secret. The bones of the eels were found by the natives and there were three days of wailing. O'Connell says this was more of a deterrent for the future than all the laws of Massachusetts. If the sinners had been discovered it is difficult to say what might had happened to them.

O'Connell was but one of a considerable number of Western sailors who through accident or choice resided for a time or for the rest of their lives on Ponape, Kusaie, and other islands of the Eastern Carolines beginning in the early decades of the nineteenth century. Island chiefs often found it profitable to keep such foreigners attached to them to handle trade with foreign ships and to give advice on the use of foreign goods.

A gruesome incident of the 1830's was the wreck of the "Falcon", an

English ship. When the ship was wrecked the captain and crew settled themselves on the island of Nahpali in Matolenim with as much of their gear as they could salvage. An argument developed with the people of Matolenim, according to one story because the Nanmarki (senior chief) wanted to confiscate the ship's goods, while according to another, members of the ship's company made advances towards Ponapean women. The captain of the "Falcon" and many of the crew were killed and the remnants of the ship burned at the Nanmarki's order.

In 1836 two warships, the "Lambton" and the "Unity", arrived and learned of the fate of the "Falcon" and its crew. Obtaining the details was not difficult as there were about forty Europeans living on the island at the time including some survivors of the "Falcon". In league with certain other Ponapeans, who were apparently of a political faction opposed to the incumbents, a punitive expedition was organized. The offending Nanmarki was shot by people of Wene, Kiti, while his brother, who held the title of Nahnawa, was captured and shot and then hanged to the mast of the "Lambton" as an example. Other supporters were likewise killed and their property destroyed. Following this incident a junior sub-clan of the chiefly clan of Matolenim assumed power and has kept the title of Nanmarki to the present.

Whaling ships made Kusaie and Ponape favorite stopovers. It is not known when the first whaling ships visited the two islands. They had begun to visit the islands before Lütke's time and their number increased as the islands became better known. A report in 1840 says that forty-seven ships had visited Ponape in six years, mostly whalers. A later report for 1852 estimated that fifty to sixty American whalers put into Ponape each year between November and April for water, wood, and provisions. Whaling ships likewise were visiting Kusaie in great numbers at this time. Truk however was largely spared because of its reputation of being hostile to foreigners. Its harbors were also less satisfactory. The low islands in general also received fewer visits because they had less to offer in the way of supplies. Whaling in this part of the Pacific declined during the 1860's and was practically extinct by 1870 as the whales were killed off.

The French explorer d'Urville returned to Truk in 1838 with two corvettes, "L'Astrolabe" and "La Zelée". After visiting Losap he entered Truk Lagoon in the southeast part and went on the west side of Sis (Tsis) south of Fefen to anchor. Thirty to forty boats came alongside, each with seven to eight men. They came as the anchor fell and boarded immediately.

Evidently up to this time the natives had a friendly attitude to whites on ships coming into the lagoon. The captain was received on land in a friendly manner in a boathouse. The chief was there but the women fled. It was said that if a woman gave herself without permission of her spouse or parents she was killed.

D'Urville explored the islands fairly well but eventually a misunderstanding arose which led to fighting. D'Urville fired on the Trukese and fled with his two ships. This episode may have been the beginning of the Trukese reputation for hostility to strangers.

The island of Ngatik is one of the few low islands which had significant contact with foreign ships during this period. The whole island was taken over by a group of white sailors who killed all the adult men and settled with the women. Men from other islands in Micronesia, including especially Ponape, came in after this to settle the island.

Captain Godby, an Englishman, reported that one of these men accosted his ship off Ngatik in 1841. The man said that he and his companions had killed the men of Ngatik in retribution for the previous killing of two European captains. Other reports and tradition now current on the island itself say that the foreign sailors were in search of a rumored treasure of tortoise shell and that they killed the local men for refusing to disclose its whereabouts. Actually there was only a small amount of tortoise shell on the island it is said.

Godby without knowing this suspected that the foreigners had piratical intentions and were trying to lure his ship closer to shore in order to seize it. Later visitors around this time expressed similar suspicions.

The island of Mokil appears to have had the next most intense contact with foreigners of all the low islands in the two districts during this period. Several white deserters from whaling ships were on the island from about 1830 on. The history of Westerners on Mokil is not as tragic as that of Westerners on Ngatik but some of these men met violent deaths themselves and outraged the islanders by their behavior. Others introduced Christianity, taught useful arts, and assisted at visits of foreign ships and were on the whole well regarded by the Mokilese.

The influence of these early whites was probably especially great because the population of Mokil had been nearly wiped out by a severe typhoon a few decades before the arrival of the foreigners. The population may have been no greater than sixty or so on the foreigners' arrival and the customs and patterns of living were apparently rather fluid as a result of the catastrophe.

In 1844 another hostile contact with the Trukese occurred with two English ships under the command of Andrew Cheyne. According to Cheyne two thousand men surrounded the boat with spears and stones. The figure two thousand for the attackers sounds exaggerated. They quickly emptied the water casks, which showed they knew what they were doing. This meant that a landing had to be made. During the day spears and sling-stones prevented the landing. At night the beach was clear and the long boat landed, destroyed houses and boats. Many knives were found. It is unclear where the Trukese obtained their iron knives at this date and earlier. Some may have come from Guam by trade via island sailing canoes and others may have been brought by unrecorded Western trading ships.

In the same year Cheyne visited Ponape and stayed for almost two months gathering trepang. He reported that the coming of Europeans and guns had caused war to be almost absent. In Ponape Awak and Matolenim were at war, yet the terror of the deadly effect of the guns made them usually stay out of shooting range and they soon concluded a peace.

The prices for local produce quoted by Cheyne are of interest: For a dozen chickens, twenty-four sticks of nigger-head tobacco or four ells (one ell may be anywhere from twenty-seven to forty-five inches) of cheap cotton; for one hundred yams, ten sticks of tobacco; for one hundred bread-fruit or one hundred coconuts, ten sticks of tobacco; for one stalk of ba-nanas, two sticks of tobacco.

Cheyne said that the natives were not cannibals and as far as he could ascertain they abhorred cannibalism as much as we do.

As a result of a reconnaissance trip of the Eastern Carolines in 1849 American Protestant missionaries were established on Ponape and Kusaie in 1852. The Reverend B. G. Snow settled on Kusaie in 1852 and in early September the missionaries Gulick and Sturges arrived and later established themselves at Matolenim and Kiti respectively. The Hawaiian pastor Kaaikaula accompanied Sturges at Kiti. All these men were accompanied by their wives. They were sponsored by the Board of the Hawaiian Evangeli-cal Association, a daughter society of the American Board of Commissioners for Foreign Missions.

Ponape and Kusaie were chosen to counteract the excesses of the whalers, who had made these two islands favorite wintering places. Most of the whalers and traders and white settlers opposed the efforts of the missionaries initially, reinforcing the opposition of islander priests and leaders in the traditional religious system.

In 1854 shortly after the arrival of the missionaries the ship "Delta" with a case of smallpox came to Ponape. There are a number of versions of what happened after this. Some say that the ship set a poor sailor on the bank at night and sailed away. The natives cared for him so that he got well but thieves stole his clothes and spread them all over the island. Some stories tell how the whites on the island warned the native chiefs not to let the "Delta" come to Ponape with the disease. This, supposedly, angered the captain so much that he put the sailor ashore. Other versions give more than one case on the ship and some say that the captain merely put them ashore on a remote island thinking they might enjoy the rest there and that no natives would get to them. Later he took them back on board but it was too late, the clothes had been stolen.

It is estimated that about three thousand Ponapeans died out of a population immediately previous of five thousand. Trukese traditions suggest that the same epidemic spread to Truk Lagoon at about the same time but there is no reliable estimate of the deaths it caused there. The epidemic may have been less virulent on Truk. On Ponape only one white settler was infected . Traces of the disease remained on the bodies of about half of the natives who lived. The epidemic raged for five months and then disappeared suddenly in August, 1854.

The epidemic of smallpox brought both difficulties and success to the missionaries. They were blamed for it at times. The old spirits were supposedly angry at the people for deserting them. There were threats of killing the missionaries and a plethora of spirits around. Gulick vaccinated those who would come to him. The success of the vaccinations eventually increased Gulick's prestige and also the prestige of Western medicine in the eyes of the islanders.

Reverend Snow was first given permission to settle in Kusaie by a king known as King George. Although he thus had a sort of support from the king he often found the king trying, as when the latter used his royal authority to interrupt Snow's sermons with expressions of his own opinion. Snow was greatly angered by the trade goods (women) which the Kusaieans used to get Western articles. The king tried to keep the trade in women secret from Snow, but Snow kept his spyglass trained on the harbor. Snow was annoyed when at the first benediction he asked the people to stand, but they would only do so in the king's presence after the king himself commanded it.

In spite of his troubles with King George, Snow was much worse off when George died in 1854. At this time, Sesa, a high chief seized two pieces of George's land and people feared that he would force himself in as king. Then Sesa had a quarrel with the king's brother over another piece of land just before the funeral. At the funeral Snow stepped in and ordered all land-grabbing to stop. He told the chiefs to elect a king, but that he would leave if Sesa was elected. The king's son was elected. The new king revived many old practices. The church still had no converts and attendance fell off until at the end of 1854 there were only eleven people in church. Snow and his wife went about lecturing people they found working on Sunday.

The Ponape smallpox epidemic does not seem to have hit Kusaie but in 1855 there was a bad influenza epidemic and Snow received some blame for this. He had no specific cure or preventive to offer for this, unlike his Ponapean colleague Gulick.

Snow devoted much of his energies to trying to reform the relations of the Kusaieans with the crews of the whalers. By 1856 Snow had counted seventy-five whalers in Kusaie since his arrival. He would go on board ships to reprimand and plead and at night he would drive men from the native houses. He would write reports which were published in Hawaii naming ships and captains. Yet, whalers brought clothing to the Kusaieans, and lack of clothing was often used as an excuse for not going to church.

In 1855 the Honolulu Board increased the efforts to convert the Ponapeans. Edward T. Doane and his wife and a Hawaiian helper Kama Kahiki came to Ponape. They began work in Jokaj, but met with strong resistance. At first everything was very friendly. The Wasai of Jokaj watched to see that no one took the property of the mission family. He wanted to make a favorable impression for the sake of the ships and trade goods he felt the mission would bring into Jokaj harbor. Later, however, a regular blockade was set up around Doane and the station was given up in

1857. So little success was had that Doane went to the Ebon station in the Marshalls and did not return to Ponape until 1865. Only three people were baptized in 1860; two of these were Ponapeans and the third was the Filipino Narcissus de Santo, who has many descendants in Kiti today. Mission influence was limited to Kiti and Matolenim. In 1861 twelve Kiti people and six Matolenim people were baptized. The Christian natives of this day were persecuted by the non-believers.

The mission ship "Morning Star" became increasingly active in the Eastern Carolines following the establishment of the mission stations on Ponape and Kusaie. In 1857 the vessel paid its first visit to Mokil and in 1858 to Pingelap.

Captain Moore reported of Mokil:

> .... the boat came alongside. It was a whale boat paddled by natives and commanded by a white man, who represented himself to be a native of Massachusetts. He said his name was Higgins, that he had resided on the island three years; that the natives were perfectly friendly, and that he would be glad to have the missionaries go on shore.... Having bargained for 500 pounds of turtle, both boats left the ship together and after an absence of two hours returned, Higgins bringing 500 pounds of turtle, as a present for the mission of Ascension, 100 coconuts for the vessel and 500 pounds of turtle I bargained for. These natives were fully as much civilized as those at Strong Island, and all those who came off had on pantaloons.

Higgins had been living on the island for some time but he was by no means the first foreigner to live on Mokil. According to Mokilese tradition collected by the American anthropologist Weckler under the CIMA program it appears that four men left a whaler which visited Mokil shortly after Duperrey's visit (see above). These men were known as San, Jake, Tom, and Charlie. San married a Mokilese woman and is remembered in the genealogical charts. He "is remembered with affection and reverence on Mokil as a 'good man' who brought the people their first knowledge of Christianity". San, Jake, and Tom are said to have been killed by the Mokilese when aroused to the act by two American deserters about 1830-

31

1835. These Americans were known as Luke and Frank. Then shortly after
this the three remaining white men are said to have left and another, Jim,
to have come. It is supposed by Weckler that Jim is the man reported
drowned "by a white man who called himself Lucien Huntington" when
Commander L. U. Hammet of the "H. M. S. Serpent" decided to go to
Mokil, hoping to account for the disappearance of a number of men who
had been reported killed in the area. Weckler thinks, after some investigation, that the so-called Lucien Huntington was none other than John Higgins,
who used an alias. James O 'Connell also claims to have visited Mokil for
six months, but Weckler wonders why the people do not recall him if this
is so.

Another early resident was reported by a foreign ship to be an Englishman named James Walker. Weckler identifies James Walker as Jake
Smith under an alias. Jake had great power in Mokil for some time, advising the chief in all undertakings, until a Mokilese got to his hometown,
Liverpool, and found that no one had heard of him and that he was not the
bigwig he claimed to be. John Higgins, on the other hand, never lost his
reputation as a "big man". He was said to have been an officer on a ship
when he arrived in Mokil. His family, originally from Massachusetts, was
supposed to have become prominent in Hawaii. Higgins had one Mokilese
son, Johnny, then left for Pingelap where he had another child, Tommy.
He was killed in Pingelap.

The depopulation of Ponape and Kusaie continued for several decades after the establishment of the first missions. Depopulation was especially severe on Kusaie, where the original population was smaller to begin
with. In 1862, Snow's lack of success on Kusaie and the decline in population led him to go to the Marshalls. From then on he came back on annual
visits, leaving the church in the hands of a small band of converts and a
Hawaiian teacher.

When Snow visited in 1863 there were thirty-three church members,
none of them chiefs. "Heathenish sings and dances" were being performed
as well as an annual ceremony to the breadfruit goddess. When Christians
asked the king to stop these he was annoyed at their effrontery. He took a
piece of land from them. A week later he died suddenly. Christianity
spread spectacularly as a result of this. There were fifty converts in a year
and among them two chiefs and an elderly female priestess of considerable
status. There were forty more converts the next year. However, the next
King, Nesalik II and two high chiefs also opposed the church, but probably

from expediency the king had a change of heart in 1865. From this time Nesalik turned a pleasant front to Snow but gave Likiak Sa, the Kusaiean convert who had been left in charge of the Mission House from 1862-1867, trouble. At the end of this time Sa was ordained minister of the Kusaiean church and is remembered as its greatest. Both the king and Sa tried to exercise authority over each other.

1865 actually saw the last of the true pagans on Kusaie. In 1866 and 1867 two stone churches were built. Although Nesalik appointed seven commoners from seven districts on the main island to meet in council with the chiefs once a month it was inadequate to satisfy the people and five years later (1874) the Christians removed the king from office.

In spite of being so distant from the rest of the world, the Eastern Carolines have felt repercussions of events taking place elsewhere. Toward the end of the American Civil War on April 1, 1865 the "Shenandoah", a Confederate warship, appeared in Ponape and the natives viewed the burning of four northern whaling ships which were harboring there at that time. The crews were left on the island and it was some time before all were repatriated.

The progress of mission work on Ponape was less spectacular than on Kusaie. The greater political fractionation of Ponape undoubtedly played a part in this. If one clique or set of chiefs favored the missionaries another would automatically oppose them. The mission station in Kiti had been largely under the protection of a certain Naniken (senior "talking chief" — see chapter on Political Organization). When this man died the mission in Kiti was promptly burned to the ground and the land sold to a trader. Doane and Sturges came back in 1865, but after two years the Kiti Station had to be given up. Doane went to Kenan in Jokaj, Sturges to Oa in Matolenim. Sturges had good support from the Wasai of Matolenim, Hezekia, and Oa became the great station and remained so until its destruction by the Spanish. Today, it is again the headquarters of the Protestant Mission.

In 1870 the American warship "Jamestown" came to Ponape to measure Langar Harbor, but it influenced conditions considerably. The five chiefs guaranteed the safety of the missionaries. Further, the new Naniken of Kiti was somewhat intimidated and gave the lands of the mission back to the Christians. The "Jamestown" also gave its name for a while to the colony which was called Mesenieng by the natives. When the Spanish came the name of the colony was changed to Santiago.

The whalers had carried trade goods in order to be able to acquire supplies, enjoy themselves, and make a little extra money in the islands. As whaling declined ships whose primary purpose was trade became more important. Copra began to gain importance from 1860 on, replacing earlier products such as trepang (béche-de-mer or sea cucumber), pearl shell, and tortoise shell. Much of the trading was on a small scale and there is little record of it.

Trading, like mission work, appears to have gotten an earlier start on the high islands of Ponape District than in Truk District. However it is reported that in 1868 a Captain Alfred Tetens of the "Vesta" was attacked in Truk. The first trader on Puluwat is said to have been a Portuguese in 1870. He killed an island woman for stealing a chicken of his and was in turn killed for this himself.

Mission work was expanding through the use of islanders as mission-aries. About 1870 the first Ponapean native missionaries went to Mokil. A couple of decades before one of the foreign sailors had attempted to in-troduce Christianity and apparently even managed to get a church con-structed but Christianity does not seem to have taken a permanent hold at this time. The conversion by the Ponapean missionaries stuck, and they also introduced the latest Ponapean developments in the system of honorary political titles.

In 1873 islander missionaries went to stay on Pingelap and Ta in the Mortlocks (Satawan Atoll). Six years later, in 1879, the Ponapean mission-ary Moses introduced Christianity on Truk, establishing himself on Uman Island.

The German firms of Godeffroy, Capelle, and Hernsheim began activities in Micronesia in or after the year 1860 when a station was estab-lished on Yap. In 1874 the first major trading station was established in the Eastern Carolines on Ponape although well before this of course trading ships had visited the area and individual foreign settlers had engaged in trade on a small scale.

In 1874 the notorious pirate, Bully Hayes, lost his ship on the reef at Utwe and settled on Kusaie with his crew for a few months of rowdy living. Reverend Snow hurried to Kusaie and converted Hayes. Another ship brought forty-six pagan Ocean Islanders who were driven from home by a famine. These resisted conversion.

Toward the end of the same year the Christian Kusaieans and their supporters deposed the pagan king, Nesalik II, and installed an enthusiastic Christian, Nesu IV. Nesu did not last long however. In 1879 Dr. and Mrs. Edmund Pease arrived on the island to establish a mission school. The king granted them the tract in Mwot, using his power of eminent domain. The former occupants resented this and popular opinion supported them so Nesu IV was also deposed.

The mission school for the Marshall Islands was moved to Kusaie immediately and the school for the Gilberts was moved there in 1882. All these areas were at the time independent of European control. In 1886 a girls' school was added.

In 1878 King Nesu IV of Kusaie had left trouble for his successor Nesu V by requesting the Capelle Company to establish a trading station. A ship of Hernsheim Company arrived with a trader and the king was informed, falsely, that the Capelle Company had failed; then the Capelle trader arrived and the Kusaieans, angry at the deception, blockaded the Hernsheim trader. In February, 1880 one of the Hernsheim Brothers arrived who had been made a German consul. He ordered the king and chiefs to sign a mortgage for most of Kusaie. By the first of the following year the Kusaieans must hand over 133,000 pounds of copra and $600 for the unpurchased trade goods. This was twice as much as it was felt the island could produce. At the time the king and chiefs signed they could not read the mortgage. They managed to get the copra, but not the $600. In 1881, on a complaint, the Imperial Consul General Zemf arrived to investigate but allowed no protest.

Truk Lagoon remained unsettled at this time. In 1880 the German trader August Hartmann was killed at Sapwore, Fefen in a local war.

Reports of many of the low islands at this time are sporadic. In a report published in 1883 Captain Sir Cyprian Bridge of the "Espiegle" told of a visit to Nukuoro and Kapingamarangi. He reported that the people had firearms, indicating contact with traders.

In 1885 the American missionary Robert Logan went to Truk. He was the first foreign missionary to settle in Truk. In this same year the dispute between Germany and Spain about the ownership of the Carolines began which marked the beginning of foreign attempts to establish political control over the area, and foreshadowed the end of political independence of the islanders.

In the year 1885 the German government sent warships to raise the German flag on a number of islands in the Carolines. This action was taken to counteract Spanish attempts to regulate the activities of the German trading firms in the area. On August 26 the German warship "Iltis" raised the flag on Yap and on October 13 the "Albatross" raised the flag on Ponape. No garrison or other personnel were left on Ponape however.

In the same year Germany also annexed the Marshall Islands and turned the administration of the group over to the Jaluit Gesellschaft, which had been formed by a merger of several German trading firms.

Spain did not protest the seizure of the Marshalls but did protest Germany's claims on the Carolines. The matter was submitted to Pope Leo XIII for arbitration. On October 22, 1885, the Pope declared for Spain because of its discovery of the islands, 350 years earlier. However Germany (that is notably the Jaluit Gesellschaft) was given in effect freedom of trade in the islands and Spain was enjoined to maintain peace and order in the area.

Spanish efforts to establish a government proceeded at a moderate pace. In July, 1886 a Spanish warship visited the Eastern Carolines. The Reverend Doane at Ponape wrote on July 27, 1886;

> . . . . These are stirring, startling times for our poor
> people! A Spanish man-of-war came a few days
> ago, and a proclamation was issued that all the
> kings and chief men were to assemble on the ship,
> they went in fear and trembling and were made to
> sign away their islands to Spain. I told them
> plainly that resistance would be foolish, so they
> took my advice. The man-of-war party have been
> kind and courteous to the missionaries and to the
> natives, assuring us that we should continue our
> work as heretofore.

It was not until March of 1887 that Captain Don Isidro Posadillo arrived on Ponape as Governor of the Eastern Carolines. He brought with him the secretary of the government, Miguel Tur, the Marine Dr. Jordana, the Chief of the Fighting Battalion Candido Lozano with his wife and three children and twenty-five convicts, the infantry Lt. Diego Baena, the Ensign Ricardo Martinez,and fifty Philippine soldiers. Three fathers and three brothers of the Capuchin Order accompanied the governmental party.

While Spanish ships occasionally made official visits to the other islands in the Eastern Carolines these accomplished little and are hardly remembered by the islanders today. Ponape was the only island on which a governmental station was established and the only one on which the control of a foreign government had appreciable effect in the Spanish Period. Even Ponape was not successfully pacified, as later events showed.

Difficulties arose immediately when Doane claimed Mesenieng (the present Kolonia), the place selected for the capital as mission property. He had a paper signed by the Lepen Net and Souwenin Metipw to show for it. The paper was dated July 26, 1880.

A conference was held and it was decided that the Lepen Net had only given Doane the land on which his house and church stood and not all the land of which the document spoke. The two signers and two witnesses of the document claimed no knowledge of it. The governor gave the rest of the property back to the Lepen Net. It is hard to believe that Doane would have lied about this or even that he could have had such a big misunderstanding after having been on Ponape so long. It seems possible that the signers of the document were eager to make friends with their new governors, and considered that they had the authority to take the land back from Doane and turn it over to the Spaniards if they wished. This would have been their right as independent chieftains. However, this is pure speculation. Doane was said to have made a speech telling the natives that the Spanish would make them slaves. At any rate, he was arrested and deported to Manila for a hearing. Thus began the conflict between the American Mission and the Spanish government of Ponape.

The German anthropologist Hambruch stresses the failure of Governor Posadillo to understand the opinions of the Ponapeans. Reportedly he was over zealous to build up the colony and his subordinates on the one hand assured the governor that the Ponapeans were happy to be of assistance and provide labor while at the same time threatening the Ponapeans with physical punishment and imprisonment if they failed to work.

Finally, after repeated provocations, no workers appeared at work on June 16. Opportunely the "Manila" had just sailed away to take Doane to the court in the Philippines. The islanders undoubtedly knew that no ships were expected for a while. Officers went to Jokaj several times to get people back to work. Finally twenty-seven soldiers, led by Ensign Ricardo Martinez were sent to request the people to come. When the natives refused the soldiers fired on them. The natives returned the fire and threw stones at the intruders. The Ensign was killed as well as the sergeants and most of the soldiers. About ten managed to escape.

The Spanish priests advised that all should flee to the ship "Maria de Molina" which was lying in the harbor. The governor felt that this was not an honorable course and so did not follow the advice. Three sailors were killed out of a boatload that came in from the "Maria de Molina" the next morning. Then the captain of the "Molina" tried to come up in a boat but three sailors were badly wounded and he returned. The Spaniards were confined to the colony.

July 2, 1887 was a critical day in the colony. The Spanish were thoroughly blockaded. The house of the missionaries was obviously spared by the natives although it was near the fortifications. During a brief rest soldiers managed to get some food into the fort from the priests' house. Father Saturnino wrote the governor a letter in the afternoon in which he asked for a truce in which to try to arbitrate the dispute. The governor acceded to this request and discussions were arranged but not very fruitful. Some Ponapeans were willing to let the colony remain; others wanted the Spanish to leave all provisions behind and leave the island; still others desired to continue the battle.

A few hours later the governor signaled for the "Molina" to send a boat. It came immediately with six sailors. The missionaries carried church paraphernalia and provisions to the wharf. The governor with the help of some natives brought the government chests down and put them in the boat. He went back to the fort briefly. Meanwhile the natives became hostile again and directed weapons at the boat. The leader of the boat became alarmed and pushed the boat off. Father Augustin and Brother Benito were still standing on the wharf with the chest of provisions. They sprang quickly into the water and climbed into the boat. Sailors were wounded by the natives and one died immediately.

Things went back and forth in the colony. But, at two o'clock early on July 4, the Spanish were exhausted. They had had no food or sleep for two days. The governor and officers tried to escape to the wharf and the natives cut them to pieces with bush knives. Some Philippine soldiers were spared and some swam to the "Molina" and told the gruesome tale.

A Ponapean catechist named Edward went to the Methodist Missionary Rand to tell of the plans to overpower the "Molina" the next night. He wanted Rand to go on board and tell the captain of the ship to let the women and children go in order that they would be spared the bloodshed. Rand sent Edward back immediately to warn the insurgents against making an attack. Rand said that he would go on board but sent instead the trader Oldham. However, on the next day Rand went on board and advised that the missionaries and women be landed. He promised that they should be well-treated and sent to America at the next opportunity. The fathers, however, said that they felt safe on board and were prepared to share the fate of the others. The captain was very much angered by Rand's proposal and told him that if he or his followers came with any such proposal again he would fire on them.

Next day the leaders of Net and Jokaj sent a messenger with a letter proposing peace. It was signed by many natives and whites. So, quiet set in, but both sides were distrustful. The natives surrounded themselves with fortifications and the captain protected the ship well. During this time all that was left of value in the Spanish colony was destroyed or taken by the natives. The ship was short on food so the captain attempted to charter the Protestant Mission vessel, "Morning Star", to take his people to Manila. This wish was not granted.

On September 1 the situation improved. The "San Quintin" came in to bring Doane back with plenty of provisions. The wife of the captain of the "Molina" had been shocked by the events, so the second officer of the "San Quintin", Don Juan de la Concha took on the role of interim governor. It is said that he was an energetic officer who tried to bring permanent peace.

On October 29 three Spanish warships, the "San Quintin", "Dezo", and "Manila" came in. They brought the new Governor, Don Luis Cardarso, and seven hundred soldiers, among them two artillery batteries. On November 1 a manifesto was read to the Ponapeans in which they were given eight days to prove their good or bad will. Full pardon was promised if they would turn in weapons, munitions, and the valuables they had stolen and would produce the murderer of the governor. The natives held back on their personal weapons and gave up only three of the so-called murderers, the least guilty.

In this instance, Doane's activities gave him greater prestige than ever. His advice was followed by both Spanish and natives. Doane's local prestige led the governor general in Manila to decide the dispute between Posadillo and Doane in Doane's favor. Later, the papers to the land Doane claimed were sent to Madrid and then back to Cardarso who looked into the affair again. Cardarso found the witnesses who again swore that Doane had no property right to any land in the colony. After this the governor general wrote that he allowed Doane to return in consideration for his character, age and many years on Ponape and in the belief that he would honor the laws of the land.

This time the Spanish fortified the colony well. Fort Alphonse XIII, as it was called, included offices and houses. Both Catholic and Protestant Missions were outside its bounds. All went well until on April 24, the Nanmarki of Kiti came with gifts to the Catholic Mission in order to get a mission station erected in his state. Many months later it was built.

It was at this time that Henry Nanpei, the most prominent Ponapean in the history of Ponape, began to play a prominent role in relation to the government and to the mission. He was the son, or some say stepson, of the Naniken of Kiti. The Naniken's wife, Nalio, had an English father. Both she and her husband were ambitious for their son and the Naniken arranged to transfer to him most of the land over which he had control by virtue of his office and family position. Since Nalio was a commoner Henry owed his fortune and political position to the interest of his father, a situation which was contrary to the Ponapean custom of his day. Because of the wealth in real estate he came to have a power equal to that of his father and of the Nanmarki (senior chief or "king"; see Chapter VIII, Political Organization). Although not of the Nanmarki's matrilineal clan he received the title of Nanpei, sixth in the Nanmarki line. (His children have since used this title as a family name and his eldest surviving son Oliver also received it after his father's death.)

Nanpei was both a protégé and benefactor of the Protestant Mission in Kiti. He served it as a pastor. The Nanmarki of Kiti had also been very friendly toward the Protestant Mission but after watching the growth of Nanpei's influence the Nanmarki turned toward the Catholic Church.

40

Nanpei had been to school in Honolulu and visited the United States. According to Hambruch, who used a close associate of Nanpei's as an inform- ant in 1909, Nanpei was sympathetic to the idea of an American protector- ate over Ponape, and hoped to have a congress formed which he would lead.

Governor Cardarso erected a military post in Kiti in order that the Catholic Mission Station could be built and protected as the Nanmarki de- sired. Although the natives did not like the military post being erected in Aleniang, they did not dare battle the plan openly, but after several warn- ings, a Chamorro, Pedro, a Catholic who had married into the Nanmarki's family and who had helped in building the mission was murdered. This trouble turned attention from the building and it was only in October 1888 that a small chapel of native material was finally finished. It was located only sixty meters from the Protestant Prayer House. The Protestants dis- turbed the dedication ceremony with their loud singing. This was the last trouble Doane was mixed up in in Ponape as he became sick at this time. It was not until December 1889 that he left Ponape a second time and died a few weeks later in Honolulu.

Since it was so difficult to transport materials from the colony to Kiti the building venture was not too successful and the governor decided to build an overland route to Rohn Kiti over Wene, Matolenim, U, and Net to Mesenieng. Starting in Kiti, about fifty soldiers built a broad paved road over very difficult terrain. In Oa, which was to be a fortified point on the road, another Catholic Mission Station was put up only six meters from the Protestant Station which was the chief one in Ponape. The Father Augustin, who had figured in the Rebellion of 1887, and a brother, were sent to Oa on June 9. It was desired to dedicate the buildings on July 24, the name-day of the king of Spain. It was a difficult job at best, and wherever the natives could, they hindered the work.

The Ponapeans attacked the soldiers at the site of the new building and killed thirty-five men. The Catholic religious personnel and the sur- viving soldiers were taken to the Oa girls' school by Nanpei, who also ar- ranged for the information to be sent to the governor.

The only Spanish ship at the island was not seaworthy so the gover- nor was unable to send for reinforcements immediately. The colony had a garrison of only seventy men and the difficulties of 1887 could have been repeated, but the rebellion was limited to Matolenim.

About a month later an American schooner the "John Fowler" anchored in the harbor en route to the Marianas, messengers sent on this ship reached Manila on August 10, 1890. In between their departure and return Cardarso attempted to settle the affair himself.

The American missionary Rand came back to Ponape at the end of August and promised the governor to work for lasting peace, but relations between Spain and America were bad, foreshadowing the Spanish-American War which began in 1897. Hambruch says that Rand instigated the natives to make war against the Spanish. The mission letters indicate that the missionaries themselves urged peace on the natives but that one or more white members of the crew of the mission vessel "Morning Star" expressed sympathy with the natives' plans for an attack on the Spanish and provided practical suggestions. The Nanmarki of Matolenim said they were preparing fortifications to siege or to die. On September 1, 1890 the cruisers "Velasco", "Ulloa",and the transports "Antonio Muños" and "Salvadera" came to Ponape with five hundred men. The expedition was commanded by Isidro Cutierrez y Soto, an officer who had distinguished himself in Cuba.

Oa was bombarded from the sea and the church and mission station destroyed. Boatloads of soldiers were sent in to complete the destruction. Gutierrez y Soto also attempted to lead an expedition of troops by land but the land troops found the terrain too difficult and returned to the colony. Another plan was about to be carried out when news came that the leader of the troops, Gutierrez y Soto, had driven a bullet through his head in the night. Another report says he was shot.

However within a short time resistance ceased and most of the islander leaders sent in their weapons begging pardon.

Governor Cardarso attributed the outbreak to the incitement of the American missionaries who had protested the erection of the Catholic chapel right beside their main headquarters. Cardarso demanded the explusion of the Americans and on November 2, 1890, all the remaining American missionaries left on the American warship "Alliance" for Mokil and Kusaie. The "Alliance" had been sent to investigate the situation on complaints from the missionaries and agreed with the Spanish governor to the removal of the missionaries without condemning them, on the ground that the relations between the missionaries and the Spanish government had hopelessly deteriorated.

On the same day 251 more soldiers arrived from the Philippines to help subdue the rebels. A plan was formed to seize a Ponapean fortress at Kitam, Matolenim (inland up the Letau River from Matolenim Harbor).

Part of the force was to attack overland from Oa and Mesihso. The other part was to attack by boat from a base on Temwen Island.

Although there were five hundred well-armed men attacking the islanders those who went through the bush were shot at by concealed Ponapeans. The boats coming in from the sea side had to be abandoned sooner than had been planned at the edge of the swampy region. The battle lasted two days and after a powerful artillery barrage Kitam was stormed. Every third Spaniard fell or was wounded. The Nanmarki who was on Tol en Maraui attempted peace. After this the Spanish did not try to build a fort in Matolenim, but remained in Aleniang, Kiti, or in the colony. Spanish losses in all: 118 dead, 73 badly wounded, 14 lightly wounded.

February 1891, Julio Meras replaced Cardarso. After a year he was in turn replaced by Julio Padiman. Padiman stayed about two months and until the new governor, Fernando Claudio, arrived the government secretary Bienvenido Flandes ruled.

Catholicism began to make progress in Net and Jokaj. Governor Claudio stayed for a year and was followed by Don Juan de La Concha with whom the peace ended. His warlike nature, Hambruch says, made him disliked from the beginning. He decided to build a "more beautiful and more comfortable road to Kiti". The natives felt that the purpose of the road was only to make it easier to send soldiers to Matolenim. The leaders were invited to hear the plan in the colony. They unanimously refused and made it impossible to carry out the plan. If soldiers did the work they would be murdered by natives in the bush. So, to quiet the minds of the natives de la Concha at first withdrew his plan. The governor was fully discussed in native meetings and a new rebellion was planned in Matolenim. Net and Jokaj saved the Spanish from another disaster like 1887. The rebellion was limited to Matolenim but soldiers who wandered far from the colony were killed clear up to the end of Spanish rule on Ponape.

Before the governor left Ponape he replied in answer to a private communication from the United States Consul asking if the missionaries could return, that he would be glad to see it as he was a friend of Rand, but that he did not have the power to permit it and would write a favorable letter to the proper authorities. Then without consulting anyone, Nanpei was authorized by the governor to write a letter to Rand to tell him to come back immediately and build a house, school, and church on Mwand. This led to the devastation of schools and chapels of the Capuchins. According to Hambruch, Nanpei and his followers were eager to prove to the governor, who seemed friendly to the Protestants and on a bad footing with the Capuchins, that they had turned back more to Protestantism.

All this changed very quickly when the governor general in Manila called the plan of de la Concha lightheaded and stupid. He was immediately called away and in 1894 José Pidal began his work. On September 9 the "Morning Star" appeared to bring back the missionaries but Pidal flatly rejected them. He had no easy position with Matolenim still appearing as the victor of 1890. At times the governor was said to woo the people with such things as a yearly rent.

Nanpei got a lot as owner of great areas of land. He had a Japanese schooner in his service which brought him weapons and ammunition which he gave to the natives in payment for labor. In September and October processions and parades were held by his followers in Kiti and Matolenim. The American flag was carried and still the Spanish did nothing so that the people believed the governor to be on their side.

At about this time an argument developed between the governor and the Capuchins who had been warned not to offer provisions for sale to the colony for fear of corrupting it. The usual thing in the colony was brothels and drunkenness. Father Bernardo wrote to Governor Pidal that the colony was the dirtiest place on the island—immoral, etc. Nanpei used the situation to improve his position. He got Paul, Nanmarki of Matolenim, to write a letter to the governor stating his support of the governor's position. Nanpei delivered the letter.

The islanders got on well after this. Nanpei, with the aid of the governor, erected a school and church for the Protestants on Mwand. This policy was carried on by Don Michel Velasco (1896) and Don Jose Fernandez de Cordoba y Castrillo (1897) the successors to the office after Pidal. In 1894 the Catholic Spanish government paid under pressure from the United States a fine to the Protestant American Mission.

William of Mwand, a religious zealot, began preaching that now was the hour that the Catholic religion would disappear from Ponape and that the people of Matolenim and Kiti, united with the people of Mwand and the main part of U would drive out all the Catholics. In March 1898 the people of Mwand and Matolenim assembled on Takaiu to attack Awak (in northwestern U near the Net border) and begin the destruction of the Catholics with the mission there. On March 18 they appeared with a fleet before Awak. The people of Awak did not answer their shots, so the attackers left.

The Lepen Net came with help to Awak and the Mwand and

Matolenim fleet appeared again. The young people of Awak wanted to fight but the influence of the father held them back. In the evening as the Net canoes were going home the Mwand and Matolenim people fired over their heads. The Awak men no longer held back and a three hour sea fight followed. The cruiser "Quiros" reestablished order.

The governor appeared in Awak and sent a letter demanding that the ringleader on Mwand should come on board the "Quiros". No one appeared in answer. The attackers remained quiet while the "Quiros" was there. Nanpei's presence among the Mwand people became known to the governor and he was summoned to appear with the leaders. The day after he obeyed; everyone was surprised to see Nanpei and the leaders go free, after promising not to do it again.

A few days later a ship without a flag appeared in Kiti and Nanpei was told that the break between Spain and America was expected. The second push against Awak took place the day the diplomatic connections were broken. The Mwand people kept their promise not to attack again, and the attackers were composed of Matolenim and Kiti people. Nine hundred men gathered before Awak, which had only sixty. Word was sent to Jokaj, Net, and the colony and the Jokaj people and the "Quiros" appeared, but as no enemies were seen the governor thought it wasn't serious.

Then it became known that three hundred Matolenim men were waiting behind Awak. An attack was organized against the rebels with five hundred men from the defending states. Nanpei and William of Mwand did not obey a summons to board the "Quiros" so fire was opened at ten o'clock. The rebels fled. Nanpei tried to organize the Saladak people of U to attack without success. On April 20 Awak was fortified. With the help of the men of the "Quiros" a great wall was built. Only in Kiti did the rebels have any success. The mission station at Aleniang was destroyed and the Catholics fled to the colony

As news of the affairs in the Philippines reached Ponape the resistance grew worse so that de Cordoba ordered the cruiser "Villalobos" from Yap to Ponape. It was sent to Kiti and Nanpei was arrested along with nobles who protested his arrest. Soon after all of them were freed except Nanpei who was said by a number of islanders to have been the inciter.

It was decided that Nanpei, as the chief mischief-maker on Ponape required a great punishment, at least banishment, and this was about to be carried out when news came by way of Jaluit that the Spanish fleet had been demolished in the channel of Cavite. The governor, fearing American warships would come looking for the rest of the Spanish fleet, hid the "Villalobos" and the "Quiros" in an estuary in Matolenim where they could not be seen from the sea.

The rebels saw the opportunity and Awak was attacked again. Twenty-five soldiers were sent from the colony to protect the mission but the soldiers molested so many women that the mission had to protest against them. Though the rebels were aided by the dissension between the church and the governor, they had no great success with Nanpei in prison. At the end of January 1899 some whalers came into the harbor of Matolenim and Kiti and furnished the rebels with ammunition. On February 8 it was necessary for the "Villalobos" to come out to defend Awak. The rebels thereupon suspended hostilities and peace discussions were undertaken in which it was decided that Nanpei was to be let out on the promise not to do it again.

Spanish times were almost over. On May 31 the Spanish ship "España" appeared, under the American flag. It brought the interim governor, Don Ricardo de Castro, who replaced Cordoba until Germany bought the Carolines from Spain.

As a result of the battle with Awak, the State of U chose a new Nanmarki whose sub-clan is still in power. The old Nanmarki fought with the Catholics in the battle and this was unacceptable to the majority of the people of U, who had supported Nanpei; and to this day many U people are strong supporters of Nanpei's descendants.

There is little of note to report on the other islands in the Eastern Carolines in this period. A few Japanese firms began trading in the area at this time. However they were all expelled by the Spanish and German governments prior to 1901 for illegal trading in firearms and liquor.

On Kusaie the American trader Captain Melander made that island the center of his trading operations. His successors are still there.

In 1892 an islander missionary went to Puluwat for a while but was unsuccessful. Perhaps the opposition of the English trader living there was responsible for his failure. It is reported that the trader lived and dressed island style and was very popular with the people of Puluwat.

46

Truk Lagoon remained unsettled. In 1898 the German trader Friedrick Narruhn was killed on Uman although that island had a reputation for being especially peaceful as a result of the influence of the Ponapean missionary there.

GERMAN PERIOD 1899-1914

At the end of the Spanish-American War American missionaries in the Carolines and their supporters had hoped that the United States would take over the entire area. However America contented itself with Guam and insisted only that Spain dispose of these possessions. On September 30, 1899, in Madrid Germany paid 25,000,000 pesetas for the Carolines and Northern Marianas.

The Germans moved in quickly. On October 11, von Benningsen arrived in Ponape on the "Kudat" to be governor. The ship had also stopped at Kusaie briefly on the way. As in Spanish times Ponape was the administrative center for the entire Eastern Carolines. The interim governor, Ricardo de Castro y Gandara received the Germans and the transfer commissioner, Lt. Christobal de Aguilar. The troops were viewed and a procession took place through the settlement and the fortification in order to show the state of decay and neglect of the buildings so the new governor could arrange for the disposition of the fortifications. On October 12, the German flag was raised.

Nanpei wrote a letter to the Spanish telling them he regretted their departure but was displeased that the Spanish missionaries were not going with them, and he blamed the Catholics for the difficulties which had just been undergone. On the day after the transfer Nanpei and his followers came to Kólonia to show their respect to the new government.

Dr. Hahl was vice governor under von Benningsen, and then became governor. He forbade alcohol to the natives, brothels were driven out, the fortifications were torn down (this was regretted later), and all natives at times had access to the colony. The Spanish had not too long ago purchased thirty-five hundred Remington rifles from the trader Zarza and of these the Ponapeans had stolen a fair number before the guns had been secured. Hahl was unable to do anything about the weapons situation.

Hahl remained for two years during which the island was peaceful. For the first time the natives were able to get medical treatment from Dr.

Girschner, who was on Ponape after 1900 and wrote some reports of his work and travels in the Carolines. Hahl, himself, wrote some on the morals and customs of Ponape. Punishments of Spanish days were thrown out. Hahl knew the whole land and brought in coffee, cacao, cotton, etc. Then he was transferred and became governor of all the German regions in the South Seas.

Truk and the other islands were initially administered by periodic visits of warships as in the Spanish times. However the visits to Truk were protracted enough to settle disputes and arrest chiefs who were attempting to encourage local wars.

From 1901-1905 the Jaluit Gesellschaft had a trading monopoly in the Eastern Carolines except for the high islands of Ponape and Kusaie where independent traders were firmly established. Kapingamarangi was also omitted from the monopoly being administered from New Britain. In 1903 the Jaluit Gesellschaft opened local headquarters on Eten Island, just off Tolowas in Truk Lagoon. Sub-stations were found on other islands in the lagoon. In view of the precedent in the Marshalls it is possible that these traders may have had minor governmental powers but we have not located specific information on this point.

In 1904 the "S. M. S. Kondor" visited the lagoon and demanded that Trukese turn over their weapons. With little resistance 436 rifles and 2,531 cartridges were collected. A few protesting leaders were arrested and sent to Ponape.

On the same visit the six "flag chiefs" (see Chapter VIII, Political Organization) were instituted on the six large islands (Moen, Tolowas, Uman, Fefan, Udot, and Tol). All the formerly independent or semi-independent communities in Truk Lagoon were made responsible to these chiefs for governmental purposes.

On Kusaie the German administration had little effect, except to increase the coconut plantations. Further than this the Kusaieans were ordered to stop celebrating the Fourth of July and in 1910 a German missionary was sent to teach them German.

Perhaps the major events on Kusaie in the German period were religious. About 1900 there was so much slackening in religious interest that a revival was instituted. This resulted in bringing almost everyone into the church. In 1905 the congregation was given independence when it petitioned for it. American missionaries continued to head the school at Mwot after this but relinquished official supervision of the Kusaiean congregation.

Japanese firms returned to trade in the Eastern Carolines in 1905 after a brief banishment. These firms later merged to form the Nanyo Boeki Company (South Seas Trading), which became a government spon- sored monopoly in the Japanese period.

On Ponape Vice-Governor Berg succeeded Hahl as administrator of the Eastern Carolines area. He tried to disarm the Ponapeans, following up his previous success in Truk, but few weapons were turned in initially. A natural catastrophe came to his assistance. On April 20, 1905, a typhoon hit the island and in the hunger period which followed four sacks of rice (56 pounds per sack) or 20 dozen salmon and 20 dozen corned beef were offered for a gun and for each cartridge 10 pfennigs were given. The Ger- mans got 254 guns and 1,532 cartridges. Then word spread that the Ger- mans would attack once the weapons of the natives were gone. The gover- nor explained that hunting weapons could be obtained for a license fee. The result was that 545 guns and 3,998 cartridges were finally turned in. For every six people, they got one gun. As they were to find out later dur- ing the Jokaj Rebellion, even then there were weapons kept back. Probably the people were not quite hungry enough.

This same typhoon did more serious damage to the low islands of Pingelap and Mokil than to Ponape proper. The population of Pingelap was seriously reduced by the storm and ensuing food shortage. Two years later in 1907, a severe typhoon also hit the Mortlocks, doing greatest damage to Ta and Lukunor Islands.

When Spain lost the Spanish-American War American Protestant missionaries were permitted to return to Ponape. However German Lutheran missionaries replaced them on Ponape and Truk as well over the period 1907- 1910. American missionaries remained at the Mwot school on Kusaie. The Spanish Capuchins at Ponape were replaced by Germans of the same order before this, in 1905.

In 1907 Governor Berg died suddenly on Ponape. According to cur- rent tradition this was shortly after he had tampered with the tombs of the old kings of Ponape at the Nan Matol ruins, and before his death he was pursued by the sound of ghostly shell trumpets being blown in the mountains.

Berg's successor was Fritz who until then had administered the Marianas in Saipan. Under Hahl the leaders had all signed that none of their
fief holders would be driven from land from which they made their living.
In any case this was a rare occurence. Fritz tried to strengthen the economic position of the commoners further by restricting customs which he
considered oppressive. These infringements on custom were not initially
appreciated by many Ponapeans, who were reasonably content with conditions as they were.

This was the German plan from Fritz:

1. The present fiefs were the property of those in possession — tribute ceased.

2. The present fief holders and their relatives as far
   as they were able-bodied men from sixteen to
   twenty-five years of age should work for the district office for fifteen days a year without recom-
   pense to pay for this freeing of the fiefs.

3. This work was valued at 1 mark a day in gold and
   half of this was to go as damages for the renuncia-
   tion of the fiefs and as tribute to the present rulers.

4. With the remainder roads, bridges and canals were
   to be built for the economic advantage of the land
   and for the good of all.

Many Ponapeans would have preferred to render the traditional
forms of tribute to road work and opposed the plan on these grounds. On
the other hand Henry Nanpei and his associates had ambitions to destroy the
power of the chiefs completely and unite the five states under a common
parliament or congress to be composed of three elected representatives
from each state. While they thus did not object to the restrictions on the
power of the traditional chiefs Nanpei was also opposed to the road building
program, according to Hambruch, because he feared it would give the Germans easy access to Kiti and would facilitate their stamping out his trade
in contraband with unlicensed whaling vessels and Japanese ships.

It is hard to assess the degree to which the various Ponapean leaders
were motivated by general resentment of the foreign rule, opposition to the

road building program, sectarian religious struggle, and indigenous political feuds stemming from olden times. At any rate in the year 1908 when work began on the road to Kiti there was an attack on the property of a Ponapean family in Matolenim and a similar attack in Kiti. These signs of unrest may have been motivated partly by a desire to detract attention from the road building program but had other more important causes as well.

In Matolenim the Nanmarki had given a twelve to thirteen year old boy a high title "Kanekien Matolenim" against the custom. Some nobles did not value their leader too highly already and they made known their displeasure by destroying the property of the relatives of the boy in an old and customary manner.

Following this in 1908 the Pwaipwai people fell on the land of a Kiti noble, the Soun Kiti, and destroyed plantings and huts. According to Hambruch Nanpei had instigated this attack. Nanpei and the Naniken of Kiti wrote to the governor requesting that all Catholics be put out of Kiti in the interest of peace. The Soun Kiti was a Catholic.

One of the bases of the ill-feeling between Nanpei and the Soun Kiti was a dispute over some land in Ant Atoll. The Soun Kiti held his title by virtue of being a member of the chiefly clan of Kiti. In former times the rank of a high priest of the goddess Nahnluhk was bound up with the title of Soun Kiti and with this the possession of land in Ant. With the acceptance of Christianity the cult of Nahnluhk had disappeared but the title of Soun Kiti with its claim to land in Ant continued. Nanpei denied this claim and strengthened his position with documents from the Spanish Governor Pidal of August 13, 1896, and on the protocol of Dr. Hahl of December 16, 1899, in which Nanpei was given sole possession of Ant. The two governors had based their decision on a document of Nanpei's father, at the time Naniken of Kiti.

Hambruch believes that the culmination of this quarrel at this time was connected with the road building program. By sending messengers to the governor reporting on the resentment of the road building program Hambruch alleges that Nanpei hoped to draw attention away from his quarrel with the Soun Kiti at the same time that he cast doubt on the feasibility of the road building program— all while apparently trying to help the foreign government with wise advice.

Fritz went ahead with the road building although he wrote that he knew how sensitive and unpredictable the Ponape people were about these things. On July 17 the Mortlock workers got the warning that they would be attacked for working on the road again. A Kiti man came to the colony through Palikir and Jokaj purportedly to sell a pig and then is said to have gone through Net to Awak to stir up the land to revolt against the government. Fritz went to Kiti and on the way he met some people who were coming to calm his concern over the Soun Kiti trouble by emphasizing the trouble in the other states.

On August 15, 1908, Fritz telegraphed to the "S. M. S. Condor" "Ponape threatens unrest, please come as soon as possible." The "Condor" arrived on September 2 and on the 6th a hundred Melanesian police were landed. On the 16th the "Condor" went to Jaluit. The cannonboat "S. M. S. Jaguar" was sent to Ponape on October 15. During September, Governor General Hahl, himself, came and reported that the enmity of the Soun Kiti and Nanpei was responsible for the difficulty.

The road building went on and reached Kiti, but within a year it was overgrown. A broader road was also built from the colony to Tolonier to give access to Jokaj. Then in October 1909, Fritz went to Yap as district officer. Boeder came to Ponape. He was a man who had had experience with native government in Africa. It was rumored that he had gotten into trouble there as a result of undue harshness.

Boeder set out to continue the policies of Fritz. He planned a road around Jokaj and called in the Jokaj people to tell them about it. The work was begun on April 6, 1910 under the white officer Hollborn. Shortly after the beginning of the work the natives and the Soumatau of Jokaj, who was overseeing the job, asked if the Germans intended to keep the white overseer on watch all the time that the people were at work. According to a current tradition Hollborn had a native mistress from another district, who lorded it over the Jokaj people while the work was proceeding under him. Boeder explained to the nobles that the oversight of a European was necessary as the natives understood nothing of road building, and that he knew it was in their natures to do nothing without a white overseer.

The road building began in Denipei at the Paipalap cliff near the Jokaj mission station. In the first week difficulties arose. Soumatau received as overseer a day's pay of two marks which was raised to three marks since he was not satisfied. The road progressed briefly, then the people ceased to come to work. The work was too much for them. The life of Hollborn was often threatened. Soumatau was raised to four marks a day.

The young people aroused each other and finally decided to rid themselves of the whites. A plan was worked out by Soumatau for a push to Kolonia. Only Jokaj people were to take part. The second of June was proposed as a propitious day as Boeder was to leave with the government vessel "Delphin" for a long round trip through the Carolines. Otherwise, no visit from a ship was expected for a long time. The Germans discovered the plan but it was disavowed so thoroughly that no one was able to do anything about it. That the plan did not come off was due to the Father Superior to whom the plan was brought and to the police master, Kammerich, who directed a watch and patrol service in the colony. The schooner "Triton", of the Jaluit Gesellschaft appeared unexpectedly and took the news to Yap, so Boeder returned with the "Delphin".

He expected the East Asian Squadron, the "S. M. S. Scharnhornst" and the "Nurnberg", in July and he hoped to make a great impression on the Jokaj people. This was an error. Although a landing maneuver and parade were conducted, they made no impression. The natives laughed it off, and concealed themselves while the ship was in the harbor.

After their visit Boeder felt he could act more firmly. Corporal punishment was introduced for obstinate lies and unashamed conduct toward whites. Prisoners were henceforth made to wear special clothing which consisted of brown colored sail cloth and a hat; moreover the prisoner had his head shaved. Up to this time Hambruch claims that prison punishments had been regarded as a sort of premium since prisoners were well provided for and led an idle life. Now they came under stronger watch by the Melanesian police, performed a day's work and were shut up at night.

The sentence of corporal punishment was carried out for the first time on a Kiti man who had lied to the office. He stayed in prison. The Ponapeans felt that sooner or later his relatives would have to take blood revenge on Boeder. To touch a man's head, as was necessary if it was to be shaved, was a grave insult in Ponapean custom.

Hambruch claims to have unearthed a secret society during his stay. He said that for ten years this society had worked to do away with white rule and that it had nothing to do with religious or democratic ideas. Its members were distributed in all states. Soumatau was the leader, Lini of

Kiti his aid. The society was made up of the conservative element which wanted Ponape for the Ponapeans. It was a patriotic union for the removal of foreign rule.

The full story of these and other movements and events which led up to the Jokaj Rebellion is yet to be told. The American anthropologist Bascom has expressed the opinion that revenge for the corporal punishment of a clan member was the most important motive. Certainly this was involved, yet the political motives and island-wide movements described by Hambruch do not seem implausible to us in view of the experience of the American administration on Ponape since the war. Ponapeans are still somewhat hesitant about expressing sympathy with the Jokaj people to foreigners but much could still be learned about the Ponapean side of the story by patient investigation.

On August 2, 1910, a Japanese schooner left the harbor. The first ship expected after this was the "Germania" at the end of September. Contact with the outside world was impossible for seven weeks. The Jokaj people used this opportunity for the Soumatau to make unashamed demands on the government. They demanded higher pay and would no longer work for one mark.

Boeder explained that a mark was already too high and that he had thought of a decrease. He threatened to banish the two highest chiefs of Jokaj from Ponape if the workers did not cooperate. The warning helped and the road building progressed although Hollborn couldn't hold the natives at work except with extreme measures. Open revolt was considered and was planned for after the visit of the "Germania".

The ship came and brought the road-building master Häfner to direct the work. The two men, Hollborn and Häfner continued to oversee the work. On October 17 Hollborn rebuked a laborer who was a member of the chiefly clan of Jokaj for not exerting himself enough. The latter replied heatedly to Hollborn and was promptly taken to prison and bodily punishment inflicted on him. When the Soumatau and eighty workers saw the marks on this man's body in the evening the Soumatau urged war against the whites. A council was held in the Maluk Meeting House. Soumatau was chosen as leader.

On the 18th of October the natives refused to begin work. Words were exchanged between Soumatau and Hollborn with the result that both

of the Germans fled to the mission station of Father Gebhard at Denipei.
They were systematically besieged and threatened and the mission was
burned. Häfner tried to get to the colony by canoe. The natives threatened
him with long knives. Written messages were torn up. In the afternoon the
mission succeeded in getting three people to the office.

At four o'clock people were surprised to see Boeder and Secretary
Brauckman step out of the boat without cover and unarmed. The armed
men had disappeared from the churchyard as they feared the appearance of
the black police. Father Gebhard made the dangerous situation known to
the governor, who, with his secretary, went to the house of the Wasai.
Häfner and Hollborn stayed behind. Immediately afterwards the Father Superior of the Capuchins came.

Boeder took about two hundred steps and when a bend in the road
hid him from the view of the mission he was hit in the abdomen with two
shots. He asked Soumatau to stand by him. Instead, Soumatau gave him
the death shot in the head. The natives fell on the corpse, cut off the hands,
dirtied it, urinated on it, gave it all the insults of fallen enemies according
to old Ponape custom. Brauckman tried to reach the boat. He was hit with
three bullets and then beaten with knives as he tried to climb into the boat.
An attempt to kill the missionaries was unsuccessful. Hollborn and Häfner
who tried to flee to the boat were shot, and killed with knives respectively.
The boat crew all met the same fate with one exception. Of the five crew-
men, one got away. They had all been Mortlock people, government
workers.

In Kolonia, Girschner, the doctor, had a boat ready and got into it
with his wife on the way to Jokaj. Half way there he met the two fathers
returning to the colony. They told him to return or he would be killed.
He returned to place the colony on the defense.

If the Jokaj people had attacked that night the tragedy of 1887 would
have been repeated. Girschner, who now had to lead the fight, risked a different course. He called in the other states which came to the defense of
the colony. Net, U, Matolenim appeared immediately. The Kiti people
appeared only after three days. Reportedly Nanpei at first advised against
the defense of the colony.

The Germans armed the natives with knives and a hundred carbines.
The enemy could easily have been brought into line if it were not for the

fact that there were many people in sympathy with them in all parts of the
island. According to tradition some of the supposed defenders were actually
smuggling out arms and ammunition to the Jokaj people. The Spanish fortress which Hahl had torn down was put into condition. The first weeks are
reported to have been difficult. The natives often asked "What would have
become of you if we had not been here to help you?" Forty days had to pass
and the natives had to be fed at the expense of the government during that
time. Some thought was given to sending the government cutter to Yap,
but it appeared doubtful that an open boat could reach there at that time of
year.

Relief came with the "Germania" on November 26. Food was taken
off and the ship hurried to Rabaul to bring help. When it arrived at Rabaul
Governor Osswald was told the news. The return trip began next day with
fifty Melanesian soldiers. The "S. M. S. Planet", then in Kavieng
was dispatched with forty-two soldiers. Governor Osswald, a new secretary,
and the Police Master John went along to direct the new rule.

On December 5 the "Germania" was back in Ponape Harbor. On
December 20 the "S. M. S. Cormoran" was to come and the "Germania"
to leave. On December 13, seventy more black soldiers arrived on the
"Siar". The Ponapeans were then permitted to leave the colony to be de-
fended by the newcomers. Osswald went to Yap on the "Germania" and
cabled the chief of the East Asian Cruiser Squadron and the German Colonial Office asking for more warships. He was told that the "S. M. S. Emden" and "Nurnberg" were on the way. The "Nurnberg" stopped at Yap to
get Osswald and Dr. Kersting, the successor of Boeder. They arrived on
January 10, 1911 in Ponape.

In order to prevent the spread of the rebellion the Jokaj canal was
separated from the mainland by the "S. M. S. Planet" and the armed
schooner "Orion". The captain of the "Emden", Vollerthun, was in command. The rebels entrenched themselves on top of Jokaj and on January
13, the plateau was bombarded from 7:45 to 9:00 A. M. The rebels who
had previously had knowledge only of the less powerful guns of Spanish warships were disheartened that the German guns could reach them on the mountain top.

After this Tagert, commander of the "Nurnberg", sent in his landing crew and a hundred Melanesian soldiers on the west side of Jokaj. It
was a difficult climb and the peak was fired on about 4:30 in the afternoon.

The enemy returned the fire over a wall. There were about fifty of the Jokaj men behind the wall and these fled, leaving behind two dead. At 5:00 P.M. the position was taken but there were no captives. Next morning on search seven men and fourteen women and children were caught. Three dead were counted. The Germans had three badly wounded men, an officer and two Melanesian soldiers. One other Melanesian soldier was lightly wounded. Soumatau and his followers had gotten away to the mainland.

From the 19th to the 25th of January the Germans went through the mainland part of Jokaj and Palikir. The "Cormoran" shot in front of Tomwara to cut off Kiti from Palikir. In this period seventy-eight men and seventy-five women and children were taken prisoner. Soumatau and his aid Samuel still had about one hundred fifty men. The senior chief of Net reported that Soumatau and about one hundred men with fifty weapons had entrenched themselves in the fortress which the natives had built in Spanish times on Nankiop Mountain. The rest of the Jokaj people were reported in Pwaipwai in Kiti. On January 26 the Nankiop position was attacked but heavy losses were suffered by the Germans.

On January 29 the enemy was reported not far from Nankiop. It was difficult to reach the position and after it was encircled the enemy had already fled leaving behind bloody rags as evidence of wounded men. On February 4, the enemy was reported in Palikir. Now the people began to give themselves up. By the 11th only about thirty of the rebels remained at liberty. On February 13, Soumatau with five followers gave himself up and by February 23 all the rebels were captured or gave themselves up.

At the hearings, seventeen men were given the death penalty, the rest sent to forced labor and lifelong banishment on Palau. The death sentence by shooting was carried out publicly on February 24, 1911 at Komonlaid. A number of Ponapeans alive and active today witnessed the event as youths or children.

Practically the entire population of Jokaj Island and its more sparsely inhabited mainland possession of Palikir were exiled en masse to Palau and Yap. Later under the Japanese they were allowed to return to Ponape but their own land was gone.

The land of the rebels was taken over as government property. Some of it was given to those who had aided the government. Most of the land on

Jokaj Island was later distributed under Governor Kersting to immigrants from Mokil, Pingelap, Ngatik, and the Mortlocks in the years 1911-12. About 1,250 immigrants were brought in. As noted above, Mokil and Pingelap had been devastated by a typhoon in 1905 and the Mortlocks in 1907. Some of the population had moved temporarily to the high islands at these times under government sponsorship. The Jokaj rebellion provided a convenient way to settle these people permanently on Ponape where their descendants still live.

Developments on other islands in the late German period were overshadowed by those on Ponape. On Kusaie the king no longer had much influence and he neglected to appoint new chiefs when old ones died. People discontinued paying tribute to the king. When he died in 1910 public opinion was in favor of not electing another king but the German officials wanted someone at the head of the government and held a hasty election. A church leader, the son of a deposed king was chosen by a poorly attended meeting. He tried to restore royal privileges. The people feared him and brought tribute again. Finally in 1912 two Kusaieans wrote to the German governor, Kersting, protesting the actions of the king. The king was rebuked and rules put down for him. The German administration asked the missionaries not to allow him to hold a religious office in order to keep the two functions separate. He was given one-third of the three-mark head tax and two days' service from each man per year. The king, however, continued to serve as preacher.

In the Mortlocks a German Capuchin priest arrived in 1911 and had considerable success in converting Protestants into Catholics on many of the islands. In 1912 the Capuchins established themselves in Truk Lagoon, which up to then had only had Protestant missionaries resident.

The new governor on Ponape, Kersting, had considerable success there. Under him certificates of title were issued to all Ponapean landowners, including the immigrants from the low islands. Printed on each certificate in German and Ponapean was a land tenure code which embodied most of the reforms in land tenure and political organization which his predecessors had tried to establish (see also Chapter VI, Property). Each deed was signed by Kersting and his secretary and the cognizant local chiefs with a number of Ponapean witnesses. The land reform was on the whole in the interest of the mass of the people although it unnecessarily interfered with previous customs of inheritance. The near universal distribution which the new land code received probably went far to prevent intentional as well as unintentional misinterpretations and ensured its acceptance. The Ponapeans were also thoroughly impressed by the catastrophic fate of Jokaj and perhaps for the first time fully appreciated the strength of Western powers.

JAPANESE PERIOD 1914-1945

The Japanese period in the Eastern Carolines lasted about thirty years, equal in duration to the preceding Spanish and German periods combined. Organized open resistance to foreign rule ceased with the German period and the history of the Japanese regime is less spectacular than that of earlier periods. However important changes took place under the Japanese. Many of the younger contemporary leaders of the islanders today went to the Japanese public schools, speak fluent Japanese, and even visited Japan itself on government sponsored and subsidized tours. The Japanese invested large sums of government and private money in economic development and research in the islands. While this was intended to solve economic problems of the homeland it also raised the income and standard of living of the islanders to a new high which has yet to be attained under American rule. If this section on the Japanese period is rather short this is primarily because material in English to draw on is very scant, not because of any lack of importance of the events at this time.

The Japanese period began when in 1914 Japan declared war on Germany and immediately seized the German-owned Marianas, Carolines, and Marshalls. The military government immediately interned and eventually expelled all German citizens including trading personnel and the German Catholic and Protestant missionaries, who had replaced missionaries of other nationalities everywhere in Truk and Ponape Districts except the Americans on Kusaie.

The Japanese divided the islands into five regions or districts corresponding to the present districts except for Yap, which was created a few months later.

The Nanyo Boeki Company acquired a trade monopoly in the region which it more or less retained throughout the period, although a number of other companies were later formed for special purposes.

In 1918 the naval authorities established a Civil Administration Department to handle the affairs of the islanders.

At the Versailles peace conference the Japanese had obtained the secret consent of Great Britain, France, and Russia to annex all the German islands north of the equator. Through American efforts a Class C mandate under the League of Nations was arranged instead. This imposed fewer restrictions on the governing power than other mandates. The League of Nations mandate came into effect in 1920.

By the mandate terms Japan was obliged to permit missionary activity in the Territory. It is not generally realized that in fact the government subsidized the efforts of Japanese Christian (Congregational) missionaries on Truk and Ponape in 1920 and continued the arrangement for most of the period of Japanese rule. No Buddhist missionaries are reported for the area, although Buddhist priests did serve the Japanese immigrants. In 1921 Spanish Jesuits were allowed to enter the area where they took over the work of the German Capuchins on Ponape and in Truk District.

Also in 1921 the Nanyo Kohatsu Company (South Seas Development) was formed by the merger of two earlier firms. Its first activities were mostly development of sugar plantations in Saipan but later it was to engage in fish processing etc. in the Eastern Carolines.

In the period 1920-1922 the military forces were withdrawn from the mandate. The transfer to the civilian South Seas government was completed by 1922. Among the new organs of government established was a court at Ponape with jurisdiction over the Eastern Carolines and Marshalls.

The civilian government arranged for subsidies to the Nippon Yusen Company (Japan Mail) and Nanyo Boeki (South Seas Trading) for shipping between the islands and the homeland and between the administrative centers and the outlying islands respectively. Some contact was maintained with islands of European countries to the south (New Britain, Solomons, New Caledonia, etc.) by routes which went to these places.

In 1923 the government inaugurated its program of annual subsidized tours of the Japanese homeland for island leaders. This is a feature which is now remembered with nostalgia by many of the participants.

In 1927 German Protestant (Liebenzeller) missionaries returned to Truk, where they remained into the American period. The Ponape station was not restaffed with Germans however and the Japanese Protestant missionaries remained in both Truk and Ponape.

Also in 1927 a public branch hospital was established at Kusaie, in addition to the ones already established at the administrative centers.

In 1930 the Nanyo Boeki Company copra plantation in Matolenim, Ponape, was started. Plans for this project were said to have been laid by the Germans but World War I prevented the Germans from realizing them. This is the so-called "Metalanim Plantation" now under government control. The plantation used mostly forest land not directly on the coast and caused only minor displacement to the Ponapeans living in the vicinity.

In 1932 a town council form of government was established for the Japanese settlements at the administrative centers on Dublon, Truk and at Kolonia, Ponape. This action was symptomatic of the increasing tendency to develop the islands for the benefit of Japanese immigrants.

Another change of policy at about the same time was reflected in an increase of expenditures for harbor works of potential military value. Japan however formally denied that the islands were being fortified.

In 1934 the district administration on Ponape sponsored a revision of the internal organization of three of the petty states of Ponape: Net, Matolenim, and Kiti. The smaller sections (Ponapean kousapw; see Chapter VIII, Political Organization) in each of these states were grouped together into larger units (now called pwihn by the Ponapeans).

Also in 1934 the Nanyo Kohatsu plantation at Sapwalap, Matolenim, was started. Ponapeans report that company officials and the local police-master brought considerable pressure to bear on native landowners to sell the required land, although one man who protested was supported by the district administrator and nothing dire materialized for him. The plantation was initially devoted to cassava for the local production of tapioca starch although in 1937-38 cassava was replaced by sugar cane for use in the manufacture of alcohol.

In 1935 attendance at government schools was made compulsory for all children in range of a school. Parochial schools were no longer allowed as a substitute for a public education. One important function of the public schools was to teach the Japanese language and in general develop respect for Japanese culture.

In this same year Japan withdrew from the League of Nations because of criticism for the Manchurian War. The Japanese did not consider relinquishing their mandate as a result of this action although some Westerners opined that they should have.

In 1936 construction began on the dam at Nanipil, Net, and Ponape. This was to provide a water supply and hydroelectric power for Kolonia. In the same year the Japanese started reforestation on Ponape. A number of individuals on Ponape were making their living by cutting lumber at the time and the government was evidently concerned by the prospect of the exhaustion of timber supplies. It was probably also at this time that certain forest areas above Nanipil were reserved as watershed for the Kolonia water supply.

In 1937 separate departments of Economic Development were established at the district administrative centers. These were mainly devoted to establishing new opportunities for Japanese colonists and were not concerned with routine regulation of commerce and labor.

After withdrawing from the League of Nations in 1935 Japan had continued to submit annual reports on her government of the mandate but from 1939 on she sent no more reports. The islands were becoming increasingly isolated from the world.

Around 1939 the government Marine Products Experiment Station in Palau transplanted trochus shell to Truk. We have located no date for the introduction of trochus to Ponape but it was probably at the same time or a little later. (This shell is used in the Orient in the manufacture of buttons.)

As relations between Japan and the United States grew worse eventually culminating in Pearl Harbor, the life in the islands became more and more subordinate to the demands of the military. Japanese military personnel and civilian laborers for the military poured into the high islands and even some of the low islands (notably Satawan and Puluwat where airfields were built) in increasing numbers. Islander males were conscripted as laborers and transferred to far parts of their island or to other islands. Their pay was automatically put into postal savings or government savings bonds, except for a little pocket money.

As the Allied offensive in the Pacific gained momentum in 1944 the flow of Japanese reinforcements of men to the islands was stopped by Allied submarines and bombers. The flow of food and other supplies was stopped at the same time and the military relied increasingly on locally produced food. On islands with Japanese military personnel the military assumed possession of breadfruit trees, coconuts and other food crops of the islanders. Hungry soldiers and sailors did considerable damage to coconut plantations by removing the heart of palm for use as a vegetable. This killed the trees or if it left them half alive at times it permanently put an end to their bearing. Large areas of coconut groves were felled to make land available for sweet potato gardens and to provide logs for military entrenchments and caves. The damage to coconut trees was especially heavy in Truk Lagoon. Other coconut plantations in Truk Lagoon were felled to make room for airstrips and other military installations. On Satawan Island in the Mortlocks the greater part of the taro swamp was filled in to make an airfield.

The islanders were evacuated from potential invasion beaches. In Truk they were crowded together in restricted areas, enabling firmer control of native food supplies by the military.

Captive islanders from the British possessions to the south (Gilberts, Ocean, and Nauru) were brought to Truk and Kusaie as laborers. As the war progressed these people had an especially difficult time.

With the flow of men and supplies into the islands, the export of fish, copra, fiber, and other products stopped. All islander labor was diverted to military construction and bare subsistence. Coconut plantations which were not destroyed were badly neglected as the islanders had neither the opportunity nor the economic incentive to care for the coconut trees.

Early in 1944 the Japanese towns at Kolonia and Sapwalap on Ponape and at Dublon, Truk were almost completely destroyed by American incendiary and explosive bombing raids; some islanders were injured in these and other raids.

By the middle of 1944 American forces were established in both the Marshalls and the Marianas. No invasion of any of the Eastern Carolines was attempted however and the great base at Truk was simply rendered inactive by air attack and by-passed.

As the end of the war approached and the situation of the Japanese military grew more desperate relations with the islanders deteriorated. On Truk it is reported that one Trukese youth on Moen Island who had taken

63

a breadfruit without permission was killed and his body eaten by soldiers. Rumors began to spread on Ponape and Truk that some hotheaded officers were planning mass massacres of the islanders to conserve food supplies. Some of these rumors are said to have originated with more sympathetic Japanese officials who protected the islanders against the more hotheaded elements in the military. By the end of the war most of the islanders were violently antipathetic to the Japanese military as a whole, although they retained good will toward many civilians.

It is unclear how much resistance the islanders made to the Japanese military. Most of the islanders were certainly not enthusiastic workers, yet the Japanese were present in such great numbers that open resistance of the type which had occurred a generation or two earlier on Ponape was unthinkable. The senior Ponapean policeman under the Japanese has said that there were a few mysterious deaths of military personnel on Ponape during the war which may have been due to the actions of islanders. If so it is probable that personal grudges for beatings, insults, or stolen wives were responsible rather than political convictions. While individual islanders undoubtedly had preferences for one side or the other they did not consider the war to be their own or within their ability to affect the outcome.

Perhaps a more common reaction to the troubles of the war was a reversion to certain aspects of the old pagan religion. While there was apparently no outright abandonment of Christianity, on all three high island groups certain individuals went into trances and came forth with alleged visions or possession by spirits of the dead. One of the activities of these mediums was to prophesy the outcome of the war and the fate of individuals whom the Japanese had transported to other islands. These activities were directly related to the tension of the war and blockade and later sank into insignificance following the American occupation.

AMERICAN PERIOD 1945 -

Coverage of the American period here is brief on purpose. Since most sections of the handbook are devoted primarily to contemporary conditions there are bits of history of the American period to be found in other chapters. Also there is less practical need for a detailed account as there are official records in English available for those who need them. Where records are lacking there are still individuals both Americans and islanders on hand in the territorial government who have personally had a hand in many of the important events of the American period. Equally important, we are still too close to even the first few years of this period to pretend to take an objective view.

The occupation of the Eastern Carolines and disarming of the Japanese proceeded without serious incident. Both military and civilians were quickly repatriated. All Japanese had left the islands by the end of December, 1945. This repatriation posed problems in the case of Japanese civilians who were legally married to island women. Repatriation of these men was also accomplished and wives and children asked to determine whether they would accompany their husbands or fathers to Japan or remain in the islands without their men. In most cases the women and children decided to remain, partly because no time was available for these families to investigate by letter whether there would be any way for them to make their living in Japan and how much assistance they might expect from the men's relatives. This repatriation eliminated all but a handful of outsiders from Truk and Ponape Districts, the main exceptions being government personnel and missionaries and a few natives of islands of other parts of the Pacific. While the elimination of Japanese citizens has obvious advantages from the point of view of military security, it also meant the removal of many persons with as yet unreplaced skills and knowledge. The preparation and export of dried bonito, which flourished in Japanese times, has not been revived for this reason.

The Islands as occupied enemy territory were initially under military government by the United States Navy. In July 1947 the islands came under United Nations trusteeship with the United States as the administering power. At this time military government was replaced by civil administration, still however in the hands of the Navy.

Also in 1947 the Navy-sponsored Island Trading Company of Micronesia was established. This replaced the earlier U. S. Commercial Company. U. S. C. C. had been devised as an emergency measure to revive the island economy. Profit making was not held to be essential. I. T. C. operated on government capital and included members of the territorial government on its board of directors but was expected to operate as a normal business and show a profit.

The Naval Administration encouraged the election of local officials and in Ponape District took steps toward the formation of a congress or representative body. This first met in March 1951 in a provisional session.

In July 1951 the Territory was transferred to civilian control under the Department of the Interior. Under the Interior administration Navy transportation was replaced by private shipping and airlines under government charter. Preparations were made for the eventual dissolution of the government-sponsored Island Trading Company, its place to be taken by existing local firms. The most notable of these in 1952 were Truk Trading Company in Truk District, the Ponape Cooperative, Leo and Carlos Etscheit, and Nanpei Plantations on Ponape, and the Kusaie Cooperative and Arthur Herrman on Kusaie.

These businesses are owned by islanders with the exception of the Etscheits, who are Belgian citizens raised on Ponape and Mr. Herrman, an American citizen who inherited the interest of Captain Melander, a trader and plantation owner who settled on Kusaie in Spanish times.

The Interior administration also made early moves to increase islander participation in higher levels of government, especially in the judiciary. In both Truk and Ponape Districts several islander judges were appointed with jurisdiction over their whole district.

In comparing the American regime so far with the previous foreign regimes several contrasts appear in aim and results. With us the strategic value of the islands is the principal reason for our presence in the Eastern Carolines and the rest of Micronesia. The strategic value of the islands was also important to the Japanese but the Japanese were also very interested in exploiting the economic resources of the islands as were the Germans. It is hard to assign a motive to the Spanish occupation of the islands other than a desire to maintain national prestige, a motive which probably applies somewhat to all the foreign rulers of Micronesia.

Several differences in results flow from these differences in aim. The Japanese and American concern with military security has hindered the visit of foreign vessels and the free entry of non-residents much more than in previous regimes. The Americans and Japanese accepted responsibility to an international organization to safeguard the economic rights of the islanders and accordingly placed more restrictions on the economic activity of non-natives (for example, purchase of land) than the two previous regimes. This also had the effect of discouraging immigration.

The Japanese however were interested in economic development of the islands to supply needs of the homeland and this interest eventually came to overshadow the earlier concern for the economic position of the islanders. Toward the later part of the Japanese period there resulted a considerable immigration to Truk and Ponape of Japanese nationals. This immigration was later and less extensive than in the Northern Marianas and the Palaus but it was still extensive enough so that by the time of the block - ade civilian Japanese nationals barely outnumbered islanders on Ponape. With the numerous military forces in both Truk and Ponape islanders were outnumbered by several times. With the American emphasis on mobile striking forces however military garrisons have not been felt necessary in the Eastern Carolines after the immediate post war stage of disarming and repatriating the Japanese.

The interests of both Germans and Japanese in economic develop- ment and research led to an expanding economy for the islanders as well as foreign residents, although the islanders remained at the bottom of the heap. The low economic value of the islands to the United States makes it seem unlikely that the real income of the islanders will easily regain its heights of the Japanese period. A certain amount of disillusionment of the islanders with the idea of economic progress has been inevitable under the Americans. Economic progress is still held desirable but conceived to be nearly impos- sible to attain. A return of interest in old ways has resulted in some places, especially, where the economic decline has been greatest.

Some of the differences between the American and other regimes are attributable to recent technological advances. Air transport did not develop until the later part of the Japanese period. German, Spanish, and Japanese doctors lacked antibiotics such as penicillin, a quick cure for yaws.

The advance in technology has raised the living standards of the foreign officials and families. The average American employee now ex- pects some kind of automobile transport if his work requires it and in his home he expects hot and cold running water, electric stove, flush toilets, etc. This necessitates plumbers, mechanics, electricians and other Ameri- can employees whose foreign counterparts were largely lacking in the Span- ish and German regimes. The American personnel are thus considerably more numerous than the German but probably do not have many more man hours per month to devote to actual government of the islanders. The Japanese government personnel were the most numerous of all four regimes but this is partly balanced by the fact that much of their effort went to governing and assisting Japanese immigrants and businessmen.

With the development and application of new technological improvements life in the Eastern Carolines and Trust Territory as a whole will probably show further changes in the future. Radio communication with all islands seems likely in the long run. Helicopters for flights between the administrative centers and outlying islands may increase the efficiency of government services. At the same time increased efficiency of communication presents the possibility of more detailed supervision of island life which could mean increased dependence of the islanders on American officials, slowing down the advance toward self-government.

Other differences in the four regimes stem from differences in the national character of the administering powers. Both the Germans and Japanese were firm and at times harsh in their governing of the people. The Germans with their small number of officials used a system of indirect rule through traditional and appointed officials. The Japanese encouraged the development of democratic forms around the administrative centers but in practice the numerous Japanese police had considerable power over the detailed actions of both elected and traditional island leaders. Americans have been more lenient in their dealings with the people than previous regimes but have sometimes been characterized by island leaders as encouraging the concept of individual rights without a proportionate emphasis on the corresponding concept of individual responsibility.

CHAPTER III

NATIONAL RESOURCES
AND THEIR CONSUMPTION

The purpose of this chapter is to give an outline of the major natural assets and deficits of the Eastern Carolines, along with factors affecting these. The question of marketing is however considered in the chapter on Economy.

SEA

The main economic resource of the sea in the Eastern Carolines is fish. The islanders exploit mostly the shallow water fish of the lagoons and reefs. There is a great variety of these. The islanders on the more densely inhabited islands (Pingelap, Kapingamarangi, Truk Lagoon, low islands south of Truk) appear to exploit the supply of reef and lagoon fish near their homes fairly thoroughly. The Trukese complain that their waters were overfished during the war when numerous Japanese military were also dependent on the same supply of fish. The fish supply was undoubtedly reduced by explosives and burning oil which covered the water around some of the islands during the American bombings.

The open sea around the islands contains large amounts of bonito and some tuna which were exploited during Japanese times but are little caught now. To catch these fish on a large scale appears to require power boats and fishing equipment which the islanders as yet only partly understand and lack enough capital to acquire. Some of the low islanders however catch enough of these fish in sailing canoes to constitute an important supplement to the supply of reef fish in the diet of their communities.

Hawksbill turtles were important in the last century as a source of tortoise shell. Tortoise shell is now of little value because of the ease of simulating it in plastic. Although in many parts of the world the hawksbill

turtle is considered inedible the islanders eat it and the green turtle whenever they can find them, in the water or on the beach at breeding time.
They also eat eggs when they find them. Sea turtles are not common a-
round any of the inhabited islands, high or low. They do breed a little
however on the uninhabited reef islands of the larger atolls. Islanders who
have visited Oroluk and East Fayu say that turtles are numerous there.
Oroluk is an atoll with a small land area between Truk and Ponape. East
Fayu is an isolated low island between the Halls and Namonuito. According to tradition Oroluk was inhabited long ago until most of the land was
washed away in a prehistoric typhoon. Later it was a stop for sailing canoes
on their way from Ponape to Truk. After sailing canoes stopped making
this trip the island was little visited until Japanese times when a Japanese
planted some coconuts on it and caught turtles for sale to the Japanese colonies on Ponape and in Truk. East Fayu has been traditionally considered to
be a possession of the people of Nomwin and the people of the Halls have
continued to visit it for catching turtles and turtle eggs. In view of the
scarcity of turtles near the inhabited islands it would appear that this abundance on these two uninhabited islands is mainly a function of a relative
difficulty of access, not of traditional practices of conservation which are
often found in primitive communities. There is also little reason to believe
that the islanders pay much attention to the laws promulgated for the conservation of turtles.

Shellfish and other bottom dwelling sea animals constitute an important marine resource for daily subsistence and have been of some importance for export. From the nineteenth century through the Japanese period
some trepang (bêche-de-mer, sea cucumber) was exploited for export.
There is a shallow water black variety which is very numerous but appears
to have no economic value. The valuable varieties have not been harvested
in the American period and may have increased. The supply of trepang is
probably great enough for it to become a minor export again if markets can
be found but it is not comparable in potential value to ocean fishing.

Japanese and American investigators have noted the existence of
commercial grade sponges in the Eastern Carolines and other parts of American-administered Micronesia. Apparently the quantity is not encouragingly
large but could be increased by cultivation.

Some pearl shell was obtained from the waters of the Eastern Carolines in the nineteenth century. Apparently it is only found on some of the
low islands in any quantity. In Japanese times pearl shell seems to have

70

been produced only in Palau District which suggests that there is little on most of the islands of Truk and Ponape District.

Trochus shell was formerly limited to the Western Carolines but was introduced by the Japanese into Truk and Ponape Lagoons and also Kapingamarangi. The supply increased enough by natural reproduction to enable commercial harvesting by 1950.

EARTH

The main earth resource is agricultural soil. On the low islands this is coral sand and humus in varying proportions permeated by a more or less brackish ground water. On the high islands a greater variety of soils is found but most of the soil contains relatively little humus and is leached of soluble plant nutrients by the heavy rains. The soil on the high islands is subject to quick exhaustion if the land is cleared and planted in field crops but is maintainable indefinitely if planted in tree crops with suitable ground cover.

It is possible that on Ponape and the other high islands there are low grade deposits of clay suitable for firing. These have never been exploited so far and are probably not extensive.

The high islands have supplies of basalt and coral rock useful in building roads, piers, etc. The low islands have only coral rock. Coral rock is also used to produce a little lime. Natural basalt gravel is not found but, the Japanese had rock crushing machines on Truk and Ponape to produce basalt gravel for the roads. Supplies of basalt and coral rock are both inexhaustible but the coral rock is found near or below water level. Supplies of natural coral gravel and sand are variable. Sand is abundant except on Ponape.

On Ponape the Japanese prospected extensively for bauxite, iron ore, and other minerals. They found low-grade deposits of bauxite and iron ore but did not exploit these in contrast to Palau.

NATURAL VEGETATION

Cultivated trees and plants are considered under agriculture in the chapter on Technology. Several zones of vegetation may be distinguished. On the low islands the natural vegetation is mostly replaced by coconuts,

71

breadfruit, pandanus, and in the swamps, taro. The lower areas of the high islands mostly contain the same plants.

Isolated specimens of the indigenous wild trees are found on some of the low islands and in the lowlands of the high islands. The islet of Elei (Alet on charts) in Puluwat contains perhaps the best example of unculti-vated virgin forest in the low islands of the two districts.

The undisturbed forests on the high islands are limited to the moun-tain tops and higher elevations. In Truk Lagoon only scattered patches re-main except for Tol, which contains the highest mountain. Larger areas are found on Ponape and Kusaie. On the tops of the highest mountains on Ponape where the plants are exposed to constant winds there are only shrubs and dwarf trees. At somewhat lower elevations there are full-sized trees, some of which would be useful for lumber if they could be removed. Cul-tivation has been expanding up the mountain slopes on Ponape and in the process potentially useful lumber trees have sometimes been cut down and let rot because of the difficulty of taking the trees to a sawmill.

On Ponape a native species of palm (Exorrhiza) is very common at higher elevations. The Japanese used the terminal buds of this as a green vegetable ("heart of palm") and collected it for sale on the island. The quality is as good as coconut heart of palm and it is a popular food with Americans who are acquainted with it. A related species is found on Truk but there undisturbed forest is smaller in area and nearly all the mature trees were chopped down by the Japanese during the war. Japanese con-sumption of Exorrhiza heart of palm on Ponape reduced the number of eas-ily accessible mature trees but did not destroy a very large proportion of the total number on the island.

Relative to determining the management and disposition of remain-ing forest areas in the future it may be noted that the needs for more ag-ricultural land and lumber tend to be opposed to the needs for maintaining watershed areas, habitats for wild birds and other animals (some of value in the island diet, others of value scientifically for their uniqueness), and scenic areas for a potential tourist industry.

The high islands contain good sized mangrove forests along the la-goon shores and estuaries, although these have been seriously depleted by the Japanese in places especially on Truk. In sheltered places in the man-grove swamps of Ponape and Kusaie some kinds of mangrove reach heights comparable to land trees. Some of the low islands also contain small belts of mangrove trees on the sheltered sides of the lagoon. The leaves need some protection from salt spray for the tree to flourish, although one genus will grow with its roots in pure sea water, as is shown by its presence on the southwest part of the barrier reef of Ponape.

Mangrove wood is a favorite source of lumber on Ponape and Kusaie since it is hard and heavy and more resistant to termites and rot than are the common land trees. Smaller trees found in more exposed sites are useful to supply poles for native-style buildings and to supply firewood. Mangrove burns long with a hot flame. In Japanese times mangrove wood was also used to produce charcoal. The bark contains tannin but this has not been exploited locally.

Another important function of the mangrove forest is to protect the low lying coastal lands of the high islands from wave erosion. In a few places in Truk where the forest was completely removed from a stretch of coast by Japanese woodsmen the coast has since been washed away rapidly and is lined with coconut trees in various stages of falling into the sea.

The Ponapeans and Trukese before contact both recognized the importance of the mangroves as protectors of the shore line. One of the esoteric names of a common species on Ponape means "Fastener-of-the-Shore". According to Ponapean legend mangrove trees were introduced to the island by the first settlers to prevent wave erosion. Whether this is true or not it indicates a traditional appreciation of this function of mangroves which still partly survives.

However with the Japanese example of indiscriminate cutting before them and with the growing disrespect of many of the more acculturated islanders for their own culture the islanders are probably less careful about cutting mangrove than they once were. Since mangrove lumber is sawed up for modern type houses on Ponape and Kusaie consumption of the mangrove forests on these islands is proceeding more rapidly than in pre-contact times. There appears to be danger of exhaustion of high grade mangrove lumber on these islands if a forestry program is not introduced.

On the high islands areas covered with a wild cane related to sugar cane (but inedible) and other grasses are found. These grassy areas are especially extensive on Ponape and on the larger islands of Truk Lagoon. In some places these grasses have taken over formerly cultivated areas,

including gardens cleared by the Japanese before and during the war.
Some of these grassy areas are old however according to the reports of the
islanders. The soil of some of these tracts is said to be poor and unable
to support trees. The islanders, especially on Ponape, have been in the
habit of burning over some of these areas in the dry season to "keep them
clean" Small tracts of burned over land are used for gardens. The islanders feel that the grass is too thick to clear economically without burning, that the ashes form good fertilizer and that burning controls pests,
notably the giant African snail. Burning over grassland is also practiced
on Truk but not on Kusaie or the low islands. Even in the dry season these
fires stop at the edge of the grass and do not penetrate surrounding forested
areas. They do however damage trees on the edge of the area and prevent the forest from encroaching on the grass which it otherwise might do
in places. Attempts by local authorities to control burning in the interests
of soil conservation have not met with much success as far as is known.

Land which is simply burned over does not develop gullies as a
rule since the soil is held together by grass roots until new grass covers
over the area again. Considerable soil may be washed away however
where the surface of the ground is broken for garden plots.

The types of grass most commonly found have limited uses. The
common wild cane is used in the construction of copra drying trays and in
native house construction. It is in fact likely that it may have been introduced into the islands prehistorically for use in house construction. The
new shoots of the common grasses are eaten by cattle but they are not the
best cattle feed. Somewhat better as cattle feed are some tracts of Napier
grass on Ponape. This grass was introduced by the Japanese to provide a
source of paper pulp and has become naturalized. It is used elsewhere
for cattle feed. Carabao can eat tougher grass than the local cattle.

Some formerly cleared land on the high islands is covered with
secondary forest growth. This includes some smaller specimens of the
trees found higher up in the mountains but an especially common tree is
the wild hibiscus. The wild hibiscus grows especially rapidly along the
edge of streams and in wet places but is common on well drained soil as
well. According to Ponapean belief and Japanese investigations as well it
improves the fertility of soil in which it grows.

The most important use of the wild hibiscus is as a source of fiber.
The inner bark constitutes a readily available source of temporary cord to

74

tie burdens, etc. The wild hibiscus may have been introduced to the islands originally by early settlers for these reasons. The fiber was also developed by the Japanese as a major export but this use has not yet been revived to our knowledge. The trees recover rapidly after their branches have been stripped.

The trees are also of some value as a source of lumber. The young branches produce carrying poles which are freely cut and when discarded in damp shady places sprout and form new trees. The wood of older trees is used for constructing parts of canoe outriggers, whaleboats, paddles and other purposes.

On Ponape much of the secondary forest has been invaded by the weed pest lantana. This is said to have been introduced from Hawaii as an ornamental plant by the Ponapean leader, Henry Nanpei. Lantana is spread by birds which eat the fruit. It is difficult to eradicate since it springs up readily after being cut down and cut segments will take root again unless burned. It is thorny and difficult to handle. It invades cultivated areas where it chokes out more desirable plants and impedes access to them.

So far lantana is not found on Kusaie or any of the low islands in either Truk or Ponape Districts. A fairly small infestation was detected on the east side of Moen Island, Truk early in the American period. It is not known whether it was successfully eradicated or not. On Ponape lantana has been combatted with some success by insect parasites introduced from Hawaii.

On the high islands some turmeric grows wild in the secondary forest and cultivated land. Turmeric was formerly cultivated primarily as a cosmetic but is also used in food somewhat on Ponape. It has not been exploited as an export.

The sensitive plant (Mimosa pudica) is a common plant in cleared areas on Ponape. It is a legume which harbors nitrogen-fixing bacteria and was reportedly introduced by the Germans as a ground cover under coconut plantations to improve soil fertility. Unfortunately it also possesses sharp thorns and makes collection of nuts difficult for anyone not wearing shoes. Ponapeans regard it as a weed.

ANIMALS

There are a large number of insect pests in the Eastern Carolines, especially on the high islands. These form obstacles to the introduction of new cultivated plants but do not seriously affect the existing traditional varieties, except on occasion locally. Perhaps the most serious insect pest is a white fluted scale which attacks breadfruit and other tree crops. On the high islands it is kept well in check by natural enemies but it has on occasion multiplied seriously on the low islands, where it can spoil most of the breadfruit harvest if unchecked.

Local coconut beetles and other pests of the coconut sometimes kill young trees and reduce production especially on the high islands. These pests attack trees planted in unfavorable locations most severely and do not appear to threaten the elimination of the coconut industry as do the rhinoceros beetle in the Palaus and the Marianas coconut beetle on Saipan.

It is of course possible that if adequate quarantine regulations are relaxed these and other pests will become established in the area. Another serious pest which threatens the Carolines generally is the Oriental fruit fly, now established in the Marianas.

The most serious agricultural pest now in the area is the giant African snail (Achatina). This is found on Ponape and several islands in Truk Lagoon. As yet it has not become established on any of the low islands, nor apparently on Kusaie, thanks to luck and quarantine. Investigation of biological controls are progressing but as far as our information goes parasites and predators have not yet been introduced into Truk and Ponape districts.

In some areas on Ponape where the snails were formerly common they have since decreased or even disappeared (e.g. Wene, Kiti in 1952). The reasons for this disappearance are not clear but Ponapeans claim to have observed that some pigs have adopted the habit of eating the live snails and that the decrease is associated with this.

The snails were originally introduced for their supposed medicinal values on Ponape by an Okinawan. They escaped captivity and rapidly multiplied. In the war they were used as a supplemental protein food by the Japanese military and this appears to account for the spread to Truk.

Islanders and Americans, except for a few isolated individuals, are not interested in eating them. The islanders cite the snails' habit of feeding on human and animal excreta as particularly objectionable. The snails have been used for pig and chicken feed however.

The snails interfere with introduced vegetable crops more than with the traditional island agriculture. They prefer young shoots or sickly vegetation. Right after the dry season when they have been estivating they are extremely voracious and are more destructive than at other times. The snails do practically no harm to breadfruit or swamp taro, except that they often destroy young shoots of breadfruit if these are not protected. Breadfruit groves often have more shoots than are needed anyhow.

The most serious damage to island crops is that to yams on Ponape. The snails are fond of the young shoots and the Ponapeans must now protect these by screen fences or covered stone enclosures. Once the shoot puts forth leaves, it is no longer tempting to the snails however.

The snails are also fond of papaya leaves. If a papaya tree is healthy the snails do not seriously damage it and feed mainly on the yellowing leaves. However in the dry season the trees are not growing as vigorously and the snails begin to eat away the bark and may invade the hollow trunk, in which event the tree is gone.

The land bird fauna of the high islands of the Eastern Carolines is of special interest to scientists and naturalists as many of the species are restricted to a single island. At least two species have become extinct since foreign contact: the native rail and starling on Kusaie. Other species are reported to be threatened, especially on Truk where the natural forest was smaller to begin with and has been more severely disturbed.

Native doves have traditionally been a source of protein on the high islands. On Truk the damage to the natural habitat and intense hunting by the islanders and Japanese military during the later part of World War II have seriously reduced and perhaps exterminated these species. They are still common on Ponape although the widespread purchase of firearms by Ponapeans in 1951 threatened to deplete the dove and pigeon population seriously. Later the district administration collected the firearms and this danger was eliminated.

On Ponape a native species of parakeet is also sometimes eaten.

Young birds are also captured and raised as pets. Several other birds are also eaten occasionally but apparently have never formed an important part of the diet of the islanders.

Of mammals rats are present on all islands. On the low islands they are serious pests at times. The main damage they do is to gnaw the young nuts of coconut palms. The native rat is a fairly small variety. It was probably introduced on large sailing canoes long before the islands were discovered by Westerners. On Ponape rats were formerly caught in pit traps and eaten according to tradition. Apparently they are no longer considered as a source of food.

Wild pigs found on Ponape, Kusaie, and occasionally on Truk constitute a minor source of protein food. Also found on Ponape are wild deer said to have been introduced by the Germans and wild carabao descended from tame animals owned by Japanese farmers. The deer and pigs are kept under reasonable control by islanders hunting with dogs and killing the animals with machetes. The carabao are not easily killed and may be expected to multiply unless special measures are taken. Pigs, deer, and carabao all invade gardens of islanders occasionally although they are shy of men and stay back in the mountains most of the time.

These animals so far do not appear to be numerous enough to threaten seriously the forest cover of uncultivated areas. Due to the high rainfall natural recovery of plants is rapid and there is an abundance of seedlings on the forest floor. The experience of other islands in the Pacific, however, suggests that serious damage to the natural forest cover may be expected if either the deer or carabao are let to increase without control.

AREAS OF SCENIC AND HISTORICAL INTEREST

A number of places of scenic and historical interest are found in the Eastern Carolines. The most outstanding prehistoric site is Nan Matol in Matolenim, Ponape. This is a group of about fifty artificial islands built up on the reef off Temwen Island. One of the islands contains a large enclosure with walls of lengths of columnar basalt built up in crib work. This site was reserved for public ownership by the German and Japanese administrations. A similar enclosure is found at Lele, Kusaie, but the site here is privately owned. On Ponape, Kusaie, and Truk there are a number of other prehistoric ruins of historic and scientific interest which have not been adequately described (see also Chapter on The Past, section on Prehistory), and are not now being preserved from the forces of nature or from those who wish to tear them apart and use the material for modern construction.

Several places on Truk and Ponape were recognized by the Japanese to be of scenic value. School teachers would take their pupils to these places on picnics and visiting officials and other travelers would make tours of these spots. On Ponape there are several waterfalls in this category. Especially notable is the great cave of Pahn Takai in U, which was formerly a ceremonial place before Christianity. Certain large pools in the mountain streams and vantage points on the mountains are also favorite visiting spots. On the high islands good saltwater beaches are limited in number. On Ponape there is a temptation to use the sand in them for construction. The Japanese completely demolished one sand island on the southwest part of the Ponape reef in this way.

At present these historic and scenic sites are of value mainly to the islanders themselves as places of recreation and reminders of their past. There is also an important scientific value in preserving archaeological sites and representative natural areas. However when and if world conditions become more settled and if the efficiency of means of transportation continues to improve the islands of the Eastern Carolines and the rest of Micronesia may one day develop an important tourist industry. In this event these historic and scenic sites could become an important resource if they are properly maintained.

HUMAN POPULATION

The adequacy of all the natural resources discussed above is dependent on the size of the human population using them. In Ponape and Truk Districts at present the population is increasing as it is in the Trust Territory as a whole. (Official figures for the Territory as a whole indicate an increase of about five to six thousand from 1948 to 1952 starting with about fifty thousand and ending with about fifty-seven thousand. Increase in Truk and Ponape Districts on the whole is roughly proportionate.)

Throughout the Territory World War II had a depressing effect on the birth rate. On the high islands the Japanese military competed with the local people for the food supply and venereal disease was spread by the military. On all islands many local men were conscripted for labor and separated from their wives. Some of the early postwar scientific investigators felt pessimistic about depopulation in Truk Lagoon, parts of the Mortlocks, and Ponape Island. The restoration of diet and family life plus American medical care have since resulted in increases in the populations of these areas.

Considerable differentials in birth rate still exist among different communities within the two Districts and both increasing and decreasing populations are still found. In Ponape District Kusaie and Pingelap are both undergoing rapid growth. The population of Kusaie has increased about tenfold since 1880. The population of Pingelap now seems to be increasing at about the same rate but has not maintained this rate for such a long period. The population of Ngatik on the other hand seems to be about stationary. The population of Kapingamarangi appears to be increasing more rapidly than that of Nukuoro, the other Polynesian atoll. Official figures for the atolls in Ponape District have sometimes been misleading as to birth rate. These islands all have colonies on Ponape Island which have sometimes been counted with the home islands, sometimes with Ponape, and sometimes not at all.

In Truk District the greatest proportionate population increase has been in the low islands south of Truk. Here again emigration to Ponape and Truk makes it difficult to assess the exact rate of increase. The low islands north and west of Truk have been about stationary in population and some have shown decreases but an eventual improvement is indicated as the fertility of young couples appears to be increasing, although still low.

The pattern of population increase appears to bear little relation to population density in the Eastern Carolines. In Ponape District Pingelap has the highest density (about nine hundred per square mile) and also the highest or second highest birth rate. On the other hand Kusaie has the lowest density (about fifty per square mile) with an equally high birth rate.

In general the high islands have lower densities than the atolls. Losap atoll and Nama Island in Truk District have a reported density of nearly two thousand per square mile, while Kapingamarangi and Pingelap in Ponape District have about nine hundred per square mile. The median density for the low islands of both districts appears to be about six hundred per square mile. This high density is at first sight surprising since the high islands can support a greater variety of crops and receive more rain. However nearly the whole surface of the low islands is cultivable while large areas of the high islands are not suited to existing crops because they are too steep and rocky or at too high an elevation where they are covered with

80

clouds most of the time. This is especially true of Ponape and Kusaie.

The low islands also generally have a greater proportion of reef and shallow water fishing grounds in relation to land area than the high islands. Here again the contrast with the low islands is greater with Ponape and Kusaie than with Truk.

Even so population density on the high islands is lower per area of cultivable and cultivated land. This is perhaps attributable to somewhat more unhealthy living conditions. The high islands have suffered more from introduced diseases. A recent study of human parasites on Kapinga-marangi by Dr. Ralph Miller of Dartmouth indicated that hookworm did not spread on that island because the newly hatched worms did not survive in the dry surface coral gravel and sand. All cases of infestation on the island had spent time on Ponape. The relatively more sanitary conditions of the low islands may affect the incidence of other parasites and diseases as well. Before foreign administration imposed peace the high islands of Truk Lagoon and Ponape were less settled politically than the low islands and warfare may have helped keep the population down. The people of Kapingamarangi on the other hand had so little contact with outsiders that they are reported to have lost the art of making weapons when discovered by Westerners. There are some indications that abortion is sometimes practiced by unmar-ried girls on many of the islands. If any of the herbal abortifacients used are effective it may be that the effective ones, like many other plants, are found only on the high islands.

Not all the low islands in the two districts have greater population densities than the islands of Truk Lagoon, although all are more heavily populated than Ponape and Kusaie. Namonuito and Puluwat Atolls and Pulusuk Island are reported to have densities of around 200 per square mile as against the Truk Lagoon average of about 275. Some of these islands are reported to have had low populations a hundred years ago.

Famine has been important in controlling the low island populations in the past. Typhoons have occasionally devastated most of the low islands causing many deaths at the time and destroying the food supply so that many of the survivors starved subsequently or have succumbed to disease, weakened by malnutrition. The typhoon in the Mortlocks and the one in Ponape District in the German period resulted directly and indirectly in hun-dreds of deaths on the low islands. Although Ponape and Kusaie were hit by the same storm that hit Pingelap and Mokil, the damage to the high islands

81

did not result in much loss of life there. It seems possible that in some unknown way the high birth rates on some of the low islands are connected with
the periodic decimation of the population by typhoons.

Kapingamarangi is in a lower latitude than all the other atolls and is
out of the path of the storms but it is subject to serious droughts which stop
the growth of all food plants. Famines have resulted from these droughts in
the past. Droughts on the other islands are not such a problem.

Most of the known factors formerly limiting population growth in the
Eastern Carolines and in Micronesia as a whole have been reduced or eliminated by the successive foreign regimes. Some of the islands are already
populated so heavily that nearly all resources go to maintaining a minimum
subsistence level. For a time the surplus population from these islands can
be accommodated by emigration to the high islands of Ponape and Kusaie.
Ponape and Kusaie are both somewhat underpopulated with their present
economy and methods of agriculture. There have been signs that some indigenous leaders of these two islands want to reserve most surplus land for
their own expanding populations and resent the prospect of the uncontrolled
alienation of what they consider to be their own tribal lands to people with
different dialects or languages and cultural backgrounds.

All things considered the balance of population and resources seems
likely to take an unfavorable shift in the future unless population growth
stops or economically feasible new techniques of exploiting existing resources can be developed to keep pace with the population growth.

CHAPTER IV

TECHNOLOGY

This chapter is intended primarily to give an outline of the more important technological aspects of daily living in various communities included in Truk and Ponape Districts at the present time. As such it discusses both native and introduced objects and processes. Special attention is given to agriculture and the food quest since this occupies such a large part of the time of almost any people with a weak cash economy. No attempt has been made to give complete coverage. For obsolete or obsolescent objects and processes of little practical importance in the present day the reader should consult the works listed in the bibliography (especially Hiroa, LeBar, and the German authors). No attempt has been made to do more than mention introduced objects and processes in most cases.

AGRICULTURE

Cultivation of plants, mostly for food, has probably been carried on in Micronesia ever since the islands were first permanently settled. The number of kinds of plants cultivated was never large and even now few of the introductions made by Europeans have been adopted on a large scale.

In Truk and Ponape Districts the breadfruit, coconut, wet-land taro, and bananas are found everywhere on both high and low islands, and everywhere are of some importance.

Also found on some or all islands and of varying importance are yams, pandanus, arrowroot, dry-land taro, kava (a mild drug), and sugar cane. Introduced plants which are cultivated by the local people to varying extent include the cassava, sweet potato, pineapple, mango, lime, orange, watermelon, squash and pumpkin, chili pepper, eggplant, green onion, cucumber, and green bean.

83

Trees

The breadfruit tree is of great importance to the people of Truk and Ponape Districts.

The main use of the tree is as a source of starch food. The fruit is usually eaten cooked just as it is about to ripen. Ripe fruit is preserved by fermentation in pits where it keeps indefinitely. The method of drying and packaging ripe breadfruit practiced on Kapingamarangi is not found in the Truk or Ponape areas.

The breadfruit tree is also everywhere important as a source of lumber since the wood is easily worked and reasonably strong. The two uses are somewhat opposed, since the best tree for lumber is a mature but vigorous one whose trunk has not yet begun to rot. On Ponape, where there are more other trees available for lumber, the breadfruit is less used for this purpose.

Formerly the inner bark of the breadfruit was beaten into bark cloth on Ponape and Kapingamarangi but this is no longer true.

The greatest number of varieties of breadfruit is found on the high islands of Truk. Most of these varieties will not grow on the low islands except in very favored locations. A seeded variety of breadfruit flourishes on the atolls however and trees are larger than on high islands.

The coconut is of importance as a source of food, drink, cordage, fuel, thatch, and cash (through the sale of copra or dried coconut meat). Grated coconut or the "cream" squeezed from it is used in many local recipes. The "milk" of the green nut is drunk, especially on the low islands. The young flower stalk may also be tapped for its sweet sap which may be drunk as is (in which form it is especially suitable for infants), or condensed into a syrup tasting like a light molasses, or fermented to make "coconut toddy". (This term is also sometimes used to refer to the unfermented drink.) Cordage is handmade from coconut husks and used most notably in canoe building and construction of native style houses. Husks and shells are also used as fuel for slow burning fires. Bound dry fronds provide torches for night torch fishing, which is especially popular in the Truk Lagoon. On Ponape the fiber from the unfolded new fronds is still used for "grass" skirts worn by some men on occasions of native ceremony. Fine hats are also made from this fiber. Green fronds are quickly woven into baskets which are generally regarded as very disposable. Plaited fronds are used as thatch "shingles", but coconut thatch is inferior to pandanus, nipa or ivory nut palm and not used if these others are available. It is used most in the low islands of the Truk area where there is less pandanus, and no nipa or ivory nut palm. Copra (dried coconut meat) is produced for export and is a source of oil for soap, margarine, etc. It is the main source of cash income for the people of all these islands.

The local people distinguish several varieties of coconut, mostly by the color of their fruit and frond stems (red, yellow, green), and the number of nuts on a stalk. There is one variety used especially for drinking which bears many small nuts on a single stalk. Some trees, surprisingly, have edible husks. Husks of normal trees are both too tough and too astringent to eat. Dwarf trees which come into bearing rapidly are found on Nukuoro and have been carried into the Truk and Ponape areas since foreign contact by visiting natives. These may have the disadvantage of aging more rapidly as well. Foreigners familiar with copra production have been trying since the German times to improve the quality of the nuts planted but evidently production could still be improved by further care in selection of nuts for planting.

Bananas grow better on the high islands than on the low, although they are found everywhere. A number of varieties are found, both cooking and "eating" (eaten raw). Neither type is highly regarded as food and eating bananas are apparently regarded as a luxury to be eaten between meals only, giving little nourishment. A nutritionist would probably find them of considerable importance as a source of both calories and vitamins. Some islands in the Truk Lagoon use cooking bananas as a major food during the season when there is little breadfruit. In Ponape, the man who has to eat cooking bananas often is considered a poor man, and one who is to be pitied.

Both native and introduced varieties of banana are found. Cooking bananas are eaten either ripe or green. Americans usually prefer the ripe fruit.

Pandanus is grown more on the low than on the high islands in both areas. It is more grown for its leaves, which are used to make sleeping mats and for thatch. Varieties grown for leaves often do not have edible fruit. Varieties with edible fruit are known but of little use. Unlike the Marshalls, Gilberts, and some other parts of the Pacific, pandanus is not used as a main food by any community in Truk or Ponape Districts. Use as

85

a supplementary food and the number and quality of varieties appears to de-crease from east to west.

The ivory nut palm is used mainly as a source of thatch although in the past the nuts were sold for export to Japan and elsewhere for the manu-facture of buttons. It is sometimes planted. It grows best in wet ground but will grow anyplace on the high islands. It is not found on the low islands.

The nipa palm grows in the inland edges of high island mangrove swamps in brackish water. It is well known that it makes very durable thatch, but is little used since it is not abundant enough. Farther east, on Kusaie, the nipa palm is of more importance for thatch. It is not purposely planted at present in the Eastern Carolines but the mangrove is cleared away from it while gathering the fronds, and new seedlings start in the cleared area — a sort of unconscious cultivation.

The lime is an introduced tree which grows mainly on the high is-lands although occasional trees are found on the low islands in good soil. Oranges are restricted to the high islands and are more common on Ponape than Truk. Kusaie is noted for its large production of oranges. A few pom-elos (a sort of primitive grapefruit) are also found on Ponape. They are prized by the American population but have not been planted widely by the islanders.

Mango trees are found only on the high islands. They were brought in by the early missionaries. At least four varieties are found on Ponape, of poor to good quality. Many natives, especially children, eat them in great quantities in season, green as well as ripe.

An introduced variety of mountain apple (no relation to the true apple) is sometimes grown on the high islands. A wild variety grows on both low and high islands and the fruit is sometimes eaten.

The wild hibiscus (Hibiscus tiliaceus) is found on all islands, high and low. Its bark is widely used as a readily improvised cordage. The inner bark was formerly a source of fiber for native cloth and later under the Japanese fiber was exported from Ponape as a cash crop. The wood is also used wherever too large pieces are not required. The tree is amaz-ingly hard to kill: if it is growing in a moist shaded location most of the bark can be stripped from a branch and in a few months the branch is cov-ered over with bark again.

Root crops

Two varieties of swamp taro are grown on all islands in the two
areas: the true taro (Colocasia, a fairly small plant), and the giant swamp
taro (Cyrtosperma). Some kinds of true taro are also grown on hillside plots
in the high islands. True taro is more tender than the giant taro and matures
more rapidly but is apparently less productive than the giant taro. Also the
giant taro may be left in the ground indefinitely while true taro is said to
become wormy after a time. The giant taro is especially popular on the
low islands where the people are especially concerned about producing as
much food as possible on their limited land. The amount of taro produced
in a community depends partly on the area of swamp available. Some communities lack enough swamp to produce as much as they would like. On
the other hand partly empty swamps are found on Ngatik, some of the islands west and north of Truk, and some of the high island communities in
Truk, Ponape, and Kusaie.

A wild variety of giant dry-land taro (Alocasia) is found on all islands. This is bitter and must be boiled or leached before it can be eaten.
It is considered a reserve food in case of famine. Cultivated varieties of
better quality are found in the Truk area but are unknown in the Ponape
area except where they have been recently introduced.

Yams are of great importance on Ponape, where they provide the
main starch food between the winter and summer breadfruit seasons. Many
cultivated varieties are known and new mutations are prized. Wild varieties are found on all the high islands. One is poisonous and must be grated
and leached before eating, and is only used as a famine food. The yam
(Dioscorea) should not be confused with the sweet potato, some kinds of
which are often called yams in the United States. The flavor of the yam
is very mild and not sweet. The flesh is coarser than the white potato and
often appears fibrous but the fibers readily soften in cooking. Nutritionally
it appears to contain less supplementary food elements than breadfruit, wet-
land taro, bananas, and sweet potatoes, the other main starch foods.

Yams are also fairly important on Kusaie but not on Truk or any of
the low islands. Apparently the Trukese have also cultivated yams on Truk
from prehistoric times, but this cultivation has been limited to a very few
people. Some Trukese say growing yams is too difficult, although the
climate of Truk is actually better for yams than that of Ponape, since Truk
has less rain. The difference can only be understood in terms of the

importance of large "prize" yams in Ponapean feasting customs.

Most varieties of yams on Ponape do not do well on low islands although a few yams are grown on at least one of the low islands in the Ponape area (Ngatik).

Arrowroot grows on both high and low islands. It especially flourishes on the low islands under coconut plantations. If harvested with care it maintains itself without cultivation. The root of the common variety is poisonous and the islanders grate and leach it before using it. Arrowroot starch is an export of some tropical countries but has not been exploited in Micronesia. On the high islands of Truk a sweet variety of arrowroot is found which is cooked whole without elaborate processing. It is little used probably because the harvest season coincides with the winter breadfruit season. Trukese say this will not grow on the low islands.

Cassava (manioc or tapioca) is an introduced plant which has become of considerable importance on the high islands. The Japanese also grew it commercially on Ponape as a source of starch. Both sweet and poisonous varieties are found. The poisonous varieties are more common on Truk and are leached before consumption.

Sweet potatoes are found in both areas, but are especially important on Ponape and Truk. The Kusaieans have reportedly abandoned the Japanese plantings on their island. The greatest use of sweet potatoes is made in Truk. They will grow on the low islands but require a cleared sunny space on well-drained land to produce tubers. Usually no one wants to cut down trees to plant sweet potatoes. The varieties preferred by the natives have firm, starch-filled tubers with a lower sugar content than those common in the United States. In color they are purple, white or light yellow. Sweet potatoes were not native to the area but their introduction was apparently quite early in the contact period. In Truk, where the Spanish administration never established a post, the native name is of Spanish derivation. An early report from Ponape mentions both sweet potatoes and yams. Introduction may have been from Guam in the early nineteenth century by way of the Central Carolines. Improved Japanese varieties were introduced by the Japanese government agriculturalists.

Miscellaneous crops

Sugar cane is found mostly on the high islands although low

islanders sometimes plant small clumps on mounds in the taro swamps. It is used mostly as a between-meals snack. The stalk is chewed and the juice sucked out.

Kava is a variety of large pepper found only on Ponape and Kusaie in Micronesia. It is widespread in Polynesia and parts of Melanesia. It will not grow on the low islands, however. A drink containing a mild drug is prepared from the pounded roots. (Some students claim that kava in moderation is mildly beneficial in its effects on the human body.) The local varieties bear no fruit and are reproduced by cuttings. The use of kava on Kusaie was stopped by the missionaries but on Ponape it has continued to the present and even spread to many of the immigrants from other islands.

Pineapples are an introduced plant found on the high islands which have the advantage of growing in very rocky soil. They tend to bear fruit seasonally along with the breadfruit trees. Existing varieties are of good quality.

Watermelons are grown mainly on the high islands but even there not in large quantities. They appear to grow better on Truk than Ponape, probably because they get more sun. Watermelons may have been introduced along with sweet potatoes, but are less popular.

A few cucumbers are grown on the high islands, mostly Japanese varieties.

Large squashes or pumpkins are occasionally grown on both high and low islands. They are perhaps a little more common in Namonuito than any place else.

Small, very hot, red peppers are grown mainly on the high islands where they are used locally as a condiment. None have been exported.

On Ponape a few green onions, long green beans, and eggplants are grown. Ponapeans acquired familiarity with these from Japanese gardeners.

A little corn has also been grown by some people on the high islands. A Guam variety is usually grown. No other grains are grown in the Truk or Ponape areas at present. The Japanese successfully grew rice on Ponape on a small scale but the Ponapeans were not interested in continuing cultivation, preferring to get their rice by purchase.

The Ponape Agricultural Station, started by the Germans and continued by the Japanese, contains a number of other introduced plants which
are potentially useful locally or exportable but most of these have not been
taken up by the islanders as yet. One exception is cacao. The American
administration has recently been distributing seedlings from the fruit of
selected trees planted by the Germans and Japanese. As of this date cacao
is not yet produced in exportable quantities.

A few basic types of cultivation are used with all the plants listed
above. These are swamp, tree and garden culture. For all of these an
imported machete and a digging stick or crowbar are used. Imported shov-
els, hoes, axes, picks are also sometimes used.

Fire is often used to clear uncultivated land, even in the swamps
during dry periods if needed. Most uncultivated land is on the high islands
so fire is rarely used on the low islands. To prevent them from sprouting
again a small fire is often built at the base of trees which have been girdled
or felled.

On the high islands swamp culture (for wet-land taro) merely involves
planting and weeding of the existing swamps, mostly on the coastal plains.
Little purposeful irrigation of the type seen in Hawaii and elsewhere in the
Pacific is practiced, although ditches are dug for drainage and an attempt
may be made to keep brackish water out by small dikes. No fertilization
is practiced.

On most of the low islands the wet-land taro culture is more complicated. The existing swamps were evidently not large enough in a number of cases and the people have laboriously expanded the swamp area by
excavation and have also dug smaller taro pits here and there throughout
the larger low islands. To build up the soil of the swamps and also provide
a mulch which helps keep down weeds the low islanders constantly collect
leaves from certain wild and cultivated trees and place these around the
taro plants as a fertilizer. The people have learned by experience that
certain trees produce better leaves for this purpose than others. Investigation as to which these are and a chemical analysis of the leaves might provide a lead as to which chemical fertilizers would be useful for taro cultivation on the low islands. Even with the extra care the taro grows more
slowly on the low islands and does not grow as large as on the high islands.

Tree culture mainly involves periodically clearing the undergrowth and preventing vines from strangling the trees. Coconuts must be replanted on passing bearing age -- but if a large breadfruit is cut down for old age or for lumber replacements usually spring up from the roots. Breadfruits are usually planted only on new land or if a different variety is desired. Shoots springing from the roots are planted.

Seedlings of fruit trees such as the mango, citrus, or soursop may be transplanted from wherever they are found to a desired location but the seeds are not usually planted.

Bananas are often planted and they do best if replanted every few years. On the low islands bananas are fertilized and may be planted on high places in or around the taro swamps or beside pits used to dispose of the leaves falling in the house yard.

Garden crops are planted mostly on the high islands, usually in very small plots (a fraction of an acre) which are cleared by felling most of the trees and burning the brush and branches. These plots are generally abandoned to brush after a few crops. They are fairly often on rather steep hillsides subject to erosion.

Two exceptions to these statements about garden crops are yams and kava on Ponape. Large trees are rarely cut down to grow either of these crops and land is never burned over as far as I know. Kava grows well in shady, damp places. Yams need good sized trees to climb on according to Ponapean belief. To produce large specimens Ponapeans sometimes kill trees by girdling. This reduces the competition of the tree roots with the yam roots, may give fertilizer through decay of the tree roots, and the yam leaves receive much more sun when the girdled tree loses its leaves.

Ponapeans often mix decayed coconut stumps or other organic fertilizer with selected soil in large holes in which they then plant yams. The tubers are protected from roving pigs by circular enclosures of boulders. Since the introduction of the giant African snail (Achatina) the chinks are often filled with smaller stones and pebbles and the whole covered over with closely fitted sticks or boards to keep the snails out while the shoots are young and tender. After the vines are a few yards high and trained up on strands of hibiscus bark there is no longer serious danger from snails.

Some high islanders in planting sweet potatoes bury leaf mold in the

91

rows. Leaf mold from under wild hibiscus trees is supposed to be especially good as fertilizer. This practice was learned from the Japanese.

Harvesting of food plants

Root crops, dry land and wet land, are generally pulled out with the aid of a digging stick or crowbar. When the Ponapeans remove yams for display at feasts, however, they carefully dig all around the tubers so that they can remove them uninjured.

In harvesting bananas the entire fruit bearing shoot is cut down with a stroke of a machete. This does no harm since each shoot dies after bearing fruit.

Fruit and nuts from small trees and plants may be collected by hand. Ripe coconuts for food and copra-making are usually allowed to fall although sometimes they are picked. Green coconuts for drinking can only be obtained by climbing the tree. Notches are often cut in the trunk to provide footholds in climbing. These notches hasten decay of the trunk and reduce the yield of the trees but the islanders are little aware of this.

Harvesting breadfruit from large trees is quite an exercise, especially on the low islands where the tallest trees grow. Men must climb up the smooth trunk with the aid of a climbing rope thrown over a limb many feet above the ground and then climb around in the branches picking the fruit with a long picking pole. The fruit is then tossed down to a partner waiting below.

In the Truk area and possibly elsewhere there are men in good health who refuse to climb breadfruit and other trees because they are afraid. Accidents are not unknown and give native bonesetters a good part of their practice.

Storage

Storage of food plants is principally in the form of pit breadfruit. This is practiced on all islands in the Truk and Ponape areas whenever the harvest is abundant enough. On Ponape the breadfruit is sometimes peeled and soaked overnight in sea water before being put in the pits. If the pit linings are renewed periodically the preserved fermented breadfruit will last for many years.

Of the root crops yams keep best after removal from the ground. According to one old Ponapean, people formerly coated yams with powdered lime to preserve them better after harvest. The flavor is said to deteriorate with age, however. Mature but not ripe bananas and the giant swamp taro will also keep for a week or so after harvest. Other crops spoil more rapidly and no methods of storage are practiced in these areas.

In a sense a form of living storage is practiced with plants like the giant taros which can remain unharvested for years after reaching optimum size without becoming inedible.

Food preparation

Native ways of food preparation are relatively the same on most islands. The recipes for many of the "native" dishes presented to foreigners were actually learned from American or European missionaries or from the Japanese.

The poverty of native recipes is not entirely attributable to the lack of varieties of food. The nearby Polynesian atoll of Kapingamarangi has fewer foods than the high islands of Kusaie, Ponape and Truk but more ingenious ways of preparing these.

The two principle native ways of cooking, still frequently used, were the stone oven and open fire broiling or roasting. Fish, fowl, and meat may be cooked in either of these ways. In the stone oven method, widely used in the Pacific, stones are placed on top of fuel and heated thoroughly. As the fuel is consumed the stones are spread out in a pit (or simply on the ground, in Ponape). Food is wrapped in or laid on leaves and placed on top of the hot stones and more leaves are put on top of this to retain the heat and steam. The black basalt stones from the high islands are best for stone ovens. The coral rock of the low islands crumbles with excessive heat. Low islanders sometimes take back basalt rocks from the high islands for this reason.

Fires were originally lit by the "fire plow" method: a hard stick is rubbed back and forth rapidly in a groove of a larger softer piece of wood until the friction ignites the sawdust produced. The art is still known, but matches are mostly used.

Pounders may be bell-shaped made from coral rock (used more in

Truk and all of the low islands) or whittled on the spur of the moment from a green stick of wood and discarded after use (especially on Ponape). Some of the stone pounders cannot be distinguished from similar pounders found in distant parts of Polynesia such as Tahiti. A board may be used as a pounding slab. On the high islands flat basalt rocks are sometimes used, especially on Ponape where they also serve as slabs for pounding kava.

The cooked food may be eaten as is. Breadfruit, taro, bananas and cassava are often pounded into "poi" which may be eaten as is or served with coconut cream.

Pottery was used for boiling in Yap and western Micronesia but is not found in the Truk or Ponape areas. Stone boiling (putting heated stones into wooden or shell containers filled with water and food) was formerly used somewhat in Truk and Ponape Districts but it is not now used. Boiling foods in imported metal pots and pans is now a common way of cooking which has been introduced. Pork fat, coconut oil, or imported cooking grease may be used. In addition to native foods, doughnuts made of imported wheat flour are fried.

On most of the islands, except probably Namonuito and the Puluwat group, there are people who know how to bake bread with imported flour. Coconut oil is often used as shortening and some places know how to use fermented coconut toddy as a yeast substitute. Coconut molasses may be used in place of sugar or other syrup.

If a family has enough cash from copra and the local store is well supplied part of the meal is likely to come directly from a can: canned meat or fish.

Beverages

Since the introduction of metal roofing, fuel drums, and concrete cisterns, rain water collected from house roofs is widely used for drinking and cooking. On the high islands water from springs and small streams is also used for drinking. Ground water on the low islands is used mainly for bathing and laundry. If rain water is not available the people drink coconut "milk" and toddy, each superior to plain water from a nutritional viewpoint.

On Ponape a sort of herb tea is made from the bark of a tree closely related to cinnamon known locally as madeu. The Ponapeans consider this a mild tonic. The taste resembles sassafras.

Imported coffee and tea are also drunk. Coffee is made very weak by our standards with plenty of sugar.

Techniques of producing alcoholic liquors are known on all islands although many native political and church leaders as well as some foreigners strive to control or suppress these with varying degrees of success. Fermented coconut toddy (the sweet sap from the coconut flower stalk) is the most common. According to tradition in the Truk area this may have been introduced from Guam via the Central Carolines before direct contact with Westerners. Originally it may have been drunk only fresh. On Ponape proper toddy is subject to contamination by the blister bug (cantharides, related to the so-called "Spanish fly") which may fall unnoticed into the collecting container. Drinking contaminated toddy can cause painful damage to the urinary system. Closely related species of blister bugs are found on other islands but are apparently much less potent. The British administrator Grimble has reported personally experiencing similar trouble in the British-administered Gilbert Islands in southeastern Micronesia.

Various other techniques are known by some individuals for making fermented liquors out of bananas, green coconuts, pineapples, soursops, etc., but are little used. On the high islands there are a few individuals who understand the principal of the still and have made stills with military scrap and produced potent raw distilled liquor.

A fermented drink known as "yeast drink" was supposedly learned from American soldiers on Truk at the end of World War II. Baker's yeast is mixed with flavored sugar syrup which quickly ferments. Coffee flavor has been especially popular on Ponape. Administration attempts to control excessive consumption of this have been reasonably successful.

DOMESTIC ANIMALS

Domestic animals in Truk and Ponape Districts include the pig, dog, cat, goat, carabao, cattle, chicken, and duck. All of these are eaten in one place or another in the area. The cat appears to be eaten only in Ngatik occasionally. Dogs are especially popular as food on Ponape where dog meat is ceremonially valued but they are also eaten elsewhere. Goats, carabaos, and cattle are limited to the high islands. Carabaos and cattle are also used for draft purposes on the high islands, especially Ponape. Hen's eggs are rarely eaten, more because they are hard to find than because of any distaste for them.

Of these animals only the dog and chicken were found in these areas before contact with Europeans. The dog was apparently limited to the high islands. Dogs are reported to have been absent from most other islands in Micronesia before introduction by outsiders. The Mortlockese word for dog is kamwia, said to be derived from the English words "Come here!" with which English-speaking sailors called to their pets.

The pig and cat were evidently introduced on the high islands by passing Western ships before foreign control. Elaborate feasting customs reminiscent of parts of Melanesia have grown up on Ponape in connection with pigs, although pigs do not appear in the mythology.

Most native domesticated animals are of mongrel or scrub varieties and are of small size. The immediate reaction of a foreigner is to introduce larger new varieties. The local varieties have the advantage of being hardy in the local environment, however. Larger size is no doubt desirable for chickens but is questionable for pigs. Large pigs are more destructive of native gardens, and the quantity of meat is more difficult to dispose of and storage facilities are almost entirely lacking. More useful to the islanders than increased size would be increases in the proportion of usable parts of the animal to unusable, in rapidity of maturation and growth to full size, in the efficiency of the animal as a converter of vegetable feed into protein, and in the average number of young in a litter. None of these characteristics have any necessary connection with size.

Some domestic animals have escaped and gone wild. Wild pigs are now found on Ponape and Kusaie and have been found on the larger high islands of Truk. Wild cats are occasionally found on both high and low islands. Wild carabao originating from tame animals owned by the Japanese and abandoned at the end of World War II are now found in the interior of Ponape. They descend periodically into cultivated areas and damage gardens and young trees. Wild fowl are found on the high islands. Domesticated dogs, goats, cattle, and ducks have not gone wild on any of the islands.

Little care is taken of domestic animals as a rule. Pigs, dogs, cats, and fowl are usually fed enough to keep them from wandering too far from home but they must forage some food for themselves. On the low islands pigs are usually more carefully controlled if present. They may be kept in pens and fed regularly or restricted to certain areas. Thus on Murilo in the Halls in 1950 all pigs were kept on an islet separated from the residential island by a narrow channel. On the low island of Ngatik the people have recently built a wall of coral boulders around the circumference of the island. Pigs are kept on the beach outside the wall while people live on the inside in the center of the island. On the high islands where pigs are let run free rings or wires are often put in their noses to reduce damage to crops. The owner is held financially responsible for damages if the pig can be caught and identified. A fairly recent attempt on Ponape to restrict pigs to pens was abandoned when the number of pigs decreased drastically without an opportunity to forage.

On the high islands dogs are valued as watchdogs as well as a source of occasional meat. On the low islands many people consider them nuisances since they tend to chase chickens and snap at neighbors. Since Micronesian dogs are usually underfed one can hardly blame them for these tendencies. The people of Mokil have recently eliminated all dogs from their atoll. The people of Nukuoro have done the same thing independently. Perhaps similar action in prehistoric times accounts for the widespread though not universal absence of dogs in Micronesia at the time of first European contact.

Small numbers of cattle and carabao are allowed on Ponape to graze untethered as long as someone representing the owner is nearby to keep an eye on them. Otherwise they are usually tethered, although the principle of fenced pasture areas is known to the natives from government and foreign example.

Special shelters are rarely if ever built for domestic animals. Pigs often take shelter under the raised floors of houses, feast houses, etc. Chickens roost in the nearest suitable tree.

Pigs, dogs, cats, and chickens are all given a similar diet consisting of leftover food and coconut meat. Pigs sometimes are given surpluses of the main starch foods, especially the less favored varieties: pit breadfruit, giant swamp taro, cassava, extra ripe breadfruit, bananas. On Ponape some people gather an aquatic morning glory which they feed to pigs as raw greens. Some pigs on Ponape have learned to forage for the giant African snail and eat it raw. Many snails in a pig's diet are alleged by some to spoil the flavor of the pork but we have not personally been able to detect a snail flavor in any Ponapean pork.

FISHING

A wide variety of fishing techniques is known in the Eastern Carolines. Not all of these are found on every island. Most of the uncommon ones are omitted here.

In general the low islanders know more techniques and are better fishermen than the high islanders. When typhoons or irregularities in rainfall reduce the plant crops on the low islands the inhabitants become especially dependent on fishing.

Techniques Using Hook and Line

Fish hooks made of the shell of molluscs or turtle shell were formerly found in the area but are now entirely replaced by imported metal fishhooks except as an item for the tourist trade. Imported fishline is also generally used.

Fishing with a pole and line from the shore or edge of the reef is widespread. On Truk and probably elsewhere people fish in the same locations by simply throwing a baited hook on a line into the water and drawing it in. The same equipment may be used from a paddling canoe in deeper parts of the lagoons or even outside the reef.

Trolling from a sailing canoe for large deep sea fish outside the reef is now limited almost entirely to certain low islanders, as is deep line fishing in the open sea. However on Ponape and Kusaie immigrant low islanders now catch fish by these methods for sale to some of the high islanders.

Nets

A large variety of nets are found in the area. In Truk the framed hand nets used in pairs by the women are especially important. A group of neighbors wades over the fringing reefs, forms circles around schools of fish and closes in and scoops up the fish. The nets are also used individually at times. Similar nets are also found in Ponape and probably many other places in the area.

An important type of fishing on Mokil involves the use of framed nets with long handles to catch flying fish. These are especially abundant at night in a certain season of the year. The fish fly in toward torches carried on the canoes and are scooped out of the air with the nets. The Mokilese dry much of the abundant catch.

Throw nets have become popular in recent times in Truk Lagoon, Ponape, and some of the low islands. This technique is said to have been introduced by the Japanese. The islanders make the nets themselves out of purchased string and lead weights.

Modern seines also introduced by the Japanese are used on Truk and Ponape. Older types of seines without floats were used on Truk to catch turtles and some fish. These nets were used on the reef and supported by poles.

Basketry traps

These are used mainly on the low islands. Many high islanders do not even know how to construct them. They are sunk on the bottom of the lagoon and picked up after several days have passed.

Basketry fish traps are considered especially important in the Mortlocks. To be able to set out traps was considered a mark of adulthood for a youth.

Spears

Wooden fish spears, some with multiple points were formerly common throughout the area. Now small metal spears, often propelled by a strip of inner tube have largely replaced older types of spears. Goggles of local manufacture are also used with these.

Fish spears are used both in day and night fishing. Night fishing with dry palm frond torches is especially popular in Truk but known generally throughout the area.

Fish Weirs

Fish weirs are found widely on suitable areas of fringing reef. Several designs of the walls have been described. On the high islands they were often made of basalt boulders, which are relatively immobile in storms.

Elsewhere coral boulders are used. On the high islands at least fish weirs are little used now and are falling into disrepair. On Ponape the Japanese appear to have had some dismantled for piers and others for landing obstacles during the war.

Fish weirs of cane fences are built near Dekehtik (Takatik) Island, Ponape, off Kolonia, by immigrant Yapese fishermen. This technique was not known to natives of the two districts.

In Truk at least and probably elsewhere long coconut leaf sweeps are made to use in fish drives. These may be used to help drive fish into the mouth of a weir or simply to drive fish into shallower water where they may be caught.

Other methods

Fish poisoning is used occasionally. The Derris plant and Barringtonia nuts are used.

A spectacular method of catching sharks has been reported for Kapingamarangi. A shark was enticed alongside a canoe, a noose slipped over its head and the fish pulled partly out of the water and killed with a blow on the head. On most of the other islands sharks are not eaten and there is little reason to catch them.

In Truk and probably elsewhere the bow and arrow was formerly used to catch fish in shallow water but this was mostly considered a child's sport.

In Truk a barbed harpoon is now used for catching turtles in the water and is said to have replaced the old turtle net. The harpoon is re-ported to be a Japanese introduction. Turtles are also caught in Truk by lying in wait for them to come up on the sand of uninhabited reef islets.

Collecting Shellfish

A good part of the protein diet of the islanders comes from shellfish. Just how much is hard to say since the islanders regard shellfish as inferior food to fish and do not serve it to foreign visitors. Shellfish collecting is everywhere primarily women's work. To a certain extent it can be carried on along with fishing on the reef although the best opportunities are when there are very low tides in the daytime.

ARCHITECTURE

Types of Building

The most important native types of buildings classified by use are dwelling houses, cook houses, feast or meeting houses, and canoe houses. Important introduced types include churches, community offices, stores, school buildings, and copra drying sheds.

Dwelling houses are everywhere of rectangular floor plan. They may contain from one to several rooms. There is usually no distinction between sleeping rooms and living or dining rooms. Foreign style houses often have a porch. Houses are usually small and one story although one foreign style house observed on Mokil in 1952 had three stories and two story houses are not unknown in some other communities where foreign construction is popular.

Less pretentious garden houses are common in some communities where land holdings are widely scattered, that is, on the high islands and the larger atolls. Some of these resemble the simpler types of dwelling house while others are simply crude thatched shelters.

Cook houses are small sheds usually separate from the main dwelling house although with foreign construction a cooking shed may be attached to the back of the house. The people usually eat in the cook houses except on special occasions. Large cook houses contain a place for a stone oven.

In some communities, especially in Truk District, a single cook house may serve several small dwelling houses. This is especially characteristic of the more acculturated communities which were more responsive to the attempts of the Japanese government and other foreigners to relieve crowded housing conditions by encouraging each married couple to have its own house.

Feast or meeting houses vary somewhat in function from island to island. In Truk Lagoon meeting houses are now most commonly section ("village") or island ("municipality") structures, although formerly each large lineage had its own meeting house. The meeting house was formerly the place of residence for the young unmarried men of a lineage, who were not supposed to sleep in the same house with their sisters. With the shift of the meeting house from a lineage to a community structure it is much less a place of residence for single men than it used to be, although meeting houses still are used to put up visitors (especially male) from other communities and some have unattached men living in them. More important now is the use for community meetings where public labor is assigned and new laws promulgated by the American administration and other news is disseminated. The meeting houses are also places for the old men and others to while away the time of day. Some meeting houses in Truk Lagoon also double as schools during the workday.

On the outer islands in Truk District large canoe houses serve many of the functions of the meeting houses in Truk Lagoon, although on some of these at least (e.g. Puluwat) there have also been community ("island") or section meeting houses which were the site of dances and community meetings. These meeting houses proper are less cluttered up with canoes, fishing gear, and living equipment.

On Ponape feast houses similar in function to the Trukese meeting houses are possessed by every important family. Feast houses belonging to the senior chiefs of the petty states and the sections (subdivisions) of these states are often used for public meetings as well as for the public feasts so important in Ponapean life. The smaller feast houses are used for family celebrations, kava and palm toddy drinking parties of friends and entertainment of guests. As in Truk, feast houses often double as living quarters. On Ponape the smaller feast houses sometimes double as cook houses, and, if on the shore, as canoe houses. Small canoe houses are also found on Ponape (and some other islands) which are used mainly as shelter for canoes.

The distinguishing mark of a feast house on Ponape is a platform across the far end from the door on which visiting chiefs and other guests are entertained. Feast houses of any size also have platforms along each side for less distinguished guests. Actually seating arrangements are highly irregular as the guests usually try to evade the place of honor even if pressed. On formal occasions however the highest ranking chiefs are nearly always seated on the platform against the back wall near the center.

On the other islands of Ponape District native-style feast or meeting houses are less important. Pingelap has had a single meeting house. Mokil has had none recently used as such although the Mokil school erected in the American period is in the style of the old meeting house with partitions for schoolrooms. The school has been occasionally used for island meetings. The Mokil and Pingelap structures lack a chiefs' platform but the people of Ngatik after several years lapse without an island meeting house constructed one in the American period on the Ponape model, with a chiefs' platform. Kusaie appears to have lacked community meeting houses and family feast houses in recent years.

As on the outer islands of Truk District canoe houses on the low islands of Ponape District commonly are used as sleeping and living quarters as well as for the storage of canoes, boats and fishing gear.

Most of the introduced types of buildings are kinds which serve a community or local group rather than a family.

Churches, community offices, and stores are built on Western plans. Some of the churches are of respectable size by American standards. The largest appears to be the new Protestant church at Lele, Kusaie, which is said to seat one thousand people. On most islands there are also smaller buildings which are used during the week for prayer meetings, meetings of laymen's groups and other religious functions which do not require the presence of a minister or priest.

Community offices as of 1952 were found in the more heavily populated communities of Truk and Ponape Districts. These have contained one to several rooms and are used as places for storage of community records, as places for meetings of community officials and leaders with each other or with American visitors and as places of work for the officials. Community offices are sometimes combined with meeting or feast houses used for community meetings, e.g., the Moen Island meeting house and office at Moen Village, Truk. But until recently at least the community office in many communities has been used mostly for "official" functions—that is, those functions of government prescribed by the American or other foreign administrations—and the islanders have not deemed these important enough in themselves to justify constructing a large meeting place in addition to the working places of the officials.

Stores are mostly small one-room buildings and are often attached to a dwelling house. The only commercial buildings of any size belong to the wholesale firms on Moen, Ponape, and Kusaie. Some of these are surplus quonsets made available by the naval government. Others have a timber frame covered with galvanized iron sheets on the side and the roof.

Methods of Construction

Several different methods of construction are now used in the types of building listed above: The principal ones are native style thatched buildings, poured concrete made with burned coral lime or imported portland cement, and foreign style with sawed lumber and galvanized iron roofing.

Original native style construction was everywhere roughly the same and involved a wooden frame lashed together with sennit cord (made from coconut husk fiber) and covered with thatch. Sennit cord is still used in native style construction but there is an increasing tendency to use nails in all timbers large enough not to be split by them.

In Truk District buildings were usually constructed directly on a well-drained piece of ground, but on Kusaie and Ponape platforms of basalt rock and earth were usually constructed. On Kapingamarangi and Nukuoro the floors of native style buildings as well as the surrounding yards are covered with small coral pebbles. Sleeping platforms constructed of canes or reeds tied together were apparently used some on the high islands but are now no longer constructed. Raised board floors or platforms serve the same purpose and are sometimes found now with native construction.

The walls of native houses in Truk District were low. Dwelling houses had low walls of thatch or plaited coconut frond matting. Meeting and canoe houses usually lack permanent walls, but the roofs are low all around and temporary walls may be constructed on the side if the building is being used for dwelling. Nowadays scrap sheets of galvanized iron are a popular siding, either permanent or temporary.

In Ponape a siding constructed of reeds or canes lashed together was used at times, perhaps usually. Native style houses are no longer constructed on Ponape. The feast houses are usually partly in native style but this type of siding is seen now only occasionally.

In Kusaie a somewhat similar siding was used for house walls but hibiscus poles or mangrove roots replaced the canes used in Ponape. A similar style of wall is reported to have been used occasionally on Truk but is now obsolete. Old native style houses are no longer made on Kusaie.

On Nukuoro and Kapingamarangi house walls are somewhat higher than in the other islands of the two districts. The walls have a permanent

104

framework of posts and cross pieces. Coconut frond matting is fastened to the outside of walls at night and in bad weather, but normally the matting is removed during the day to allow free ventilation and light.

The type of construction of houses in these two atolls appears to the Western observer to be better adapted to the tropical climate than the darker, ill-ventilated types of the other islands. It seems likely that typhoons are rarer on both Kapingamarangi and Nukuoro than the more northerly islands. The more open native style house may be connected with this.

Early missionaries have introduced a form of solid wall construction using burnt coral lime, sand, and coral boulders. The cement formed from the lime and sand may be poured into wooden forms into which unshaped boulders are also set, or it may be used as a mortar with shaped coral blocks. Dead coral lumps are soft and can be shaped with axes, machetes or even wood saws. Walls of shaped coral boulders with lime-mortar are stronger than walls of poured lime, sand and gravel with boulders but the poured walls are faster to construct, since the labor of dressing the stone is more difficult than that of making the extra lime needed.

Lime is usually made by burning branch coral which is gathered by hand in fairly shallow water of the lagoons. Branch coral is preferred because it permits a good draft for the underlying fire. It seems likely that the wholesale removal of branch coral for burning may seriously damage the habitat of young and small fish and render them easier prey to larger fish. No studies have been made testing this however.

This type of construction has been used mainly in Truk District, especially in the Hall Islands where many houses as well as community buildings have this type of construction. It is most practical where supplies of sand and coral are readily available. This means on any of the low islands or on certain spots of the shores of the high islands. Ponape is the least convenient for concrete construction of any sort because of the poor supply of sand on the mainland where most of the people live.

Imported portland cement is sometimes mixed with lime to give the resulting concrete greater strength. More often it is used with sand and gravel alone to make concrete. The Japanese built a number of private and official structures of poured concrete and some islander laborers have learned the technique from them. Poured concrete has been used so far mostly for churches and, on some fairly acculturated islands, the first floor of houses. On Ponape two Japanese-built poured concrete school buildings are still in use.

Buildings of sawn lumber are now used by most of the population in Truk and Ponape Districts for dwelling houses, stores, and other important structures. These buildings are raised on piles and usually have galvanized iron roofs, although thatch roofs are also sometimes reluctantly used. Much of the lumber in use recently has been scrap from Japanese buildings but where this has been lacking local sawmills on the high islands have provided some local lumber and other lumber has been sawed by hand.

The widespread use of these foreign style houses must be attributed primarily to Japanese example and encouragement. Many of the better examples have been built by graduates of the former Japanese carpentry school on Palau. In 1952 the only communities lacking an appreciable number of foreign style houses were Kapingamarangi and the islands of the Puluwat area and Namonuito.

Near the two district administrative centers a few buildings owned or used by islanders are quonset huts obtained from the military government. Island laborers learned how to set these up in working for the American government. These quonsets have mostly been used by islanders for commercial purposes: stores, warehouses, and one movie theater each on Truk and Ponape.

TRANSPORTATION

Land Vehicles, Roads, and Paths

Wheeled vehicles were unknown in Micronesia before foreign contact and those which exist now are mostly owned by the American government and foreign residents. Near the administrative centers and on the high island of Kusaie islanders have maintained a few miscellaneous motor vehicles since the end of World War II. Islander mechanics have learned how to keep the vehicles going by working for the government. The greatest use of motor vehicles by islanders in Truk and Ponape Districts has been on Kusaie and Ponape. On Ponape a number of carabao carts were also taken over by the islanders following the war and are used somewhat for hauling firewood and agricultural produce into Kolonia. On Kusaie much of the copra is brought to Lele Harbor by truck and the trucks are also used in a sort of bus service between the capital of Lele and the other three towns.

106

As far as is known motor vehicles are not in use on any of the low islands. It is questionable if extensive use would be economically warranted. The main conceivable use would be for collection of copra and transport to a central warehouse on each island as is done in the Gilberts. The islets in the Gilberts where trucks are used are larger in area than most of those in the Eastern Carolines however and the atolls in the Gilberts contain on the average fewer separate islets.

In pre-foreign times there were no large roads or bridges as there was no need for them. Even today footpaths suffice for the land transportation now used by the average islander (except on Kusaie) and there is little immediate reason for the islanders to construct or maintain on their own initiative anything more than simple footpaths, although on a long term basis it would seem that the larger high islands could benefit by the example of Kusaie.

However all the foreign administrations have been concerned about building roads on the islands near the administrative centers. The Germans and Japanese considered that roads would aid in bringing the islanders under political control and aid in economic development. Later the Japanese built a number of military roads on the high islands. Local American officials after World War II continued to stress the desirability of roads.

The high point of the island road systems was reached in the Japanese period when community labor put in regular work on road maintenance and the Japanese military commandeered further island labor (with nominal pay) for construction of new roads for military purposes. During the Japanese period many of the high islanders owned bicycles and the roads and paths were in good enough condition so that bicycles could effect great savings of time.

While these roads and paths were a convenience to the islanders as well as the Japanese they required much manual labor to maintain. Without the combined incentives of pay and threat of jail held out by the Japanese the islanders have not in general considered that the gain was worth the effort needed to maintain the road systems.

Some of the military roads did not go anyplace of importance to the islanders in their daily life; for instance, the road into the mountains of Moen Island, Truk, from Peniesene village, or the roads to gun emplacements on the top of Jokaj and Net mountains, Ponape. In most places motor vehicle roads have reverted to footpaths and the smooth coral gravel covering on the bicycle paths has been washed away and not replaced.

One exception to this generalization is Kusaie. The Japanese road system there was not as large as on the other high islands. The Kusaieans with American encouragement and technical advice have actually expanded the Japanese road system. Four reasons may be given for this effort: the interest shown by the U. S. Commercial Company representative in the early Navy period; the strong interest of the Kusaieans in becoming "Americans"; the economic utility of the roads in the transportation of copra; the relative ease of building and maintaining roads on the flat coastal plain where the people live and most of the copra is made.

The last point is one that deserves emphasis. Roads on Ponape and some islands of Truk are on slopes with a subsoil which when cleared of vegetation does not absorb water easily. In the torrential tropical rains the ruts become little streams which rapidly erode the surfacing. Vegetation grows up in a matter of weeks to block the drainage ditches and culverts. This funnels the water down the center of roads and paths.

On Ponape there are a number of good sized streams which are difficult to bridge with local materials. Most bridges constructed by the Japanese have not been replaced as they have deteriorated. Some of the streams are impassable at high water without bridges, although high water usually does not last more than a day or so at the most.

On the low islands and on the sandy coastal plains of Kusaie and parts of Truk (for example, the west coast of Moen, northeast coast of Fefen) there is much less trouble with rain erosion, although mudholes developing from puddles in heavy showers require filling periodically. Moreover where this sandy land is in coconuts the trees provide shade which keeps down the grass and weeds which interfere with road drainage in the interiors of the high islands.

Canoes and Boats

Island style canoes are still used on all islands in Truk and Ponape Districts but foreign style boats are also used on the high islands and some of the low islands. The government chartered field trip ships are at present essential to the economy of all islands but details of their operation will not be considered here.

In former times sailing canoes made periodic trips between all islands of the Eastern Carolines except Kapingamarangi and Nukuoro, which also received occasional visitors. Ocean-going sailing canoes are still found in two areas of Micronesia today: the low islands between Yap and Truk, including Puluwat, Namonuito and the Halls in Truk District, and the Marshalls. Ocean-going canoes were also found in Truk and the islands south of Truk up until the German and Japanese periods.

To say that ocean-going canoes are no longer found on the other islands does not mean that the people elsewhere never venture into the open sea in small sailing and paddling canoes. On all the atolls the people often use canoes to fish in the open sea in favorable weather, but they do not as a rule use these small canoes for trips to distant islands.

The Puluwat area sailing canoes have a centrally located mast which is normally fixed while under way. Smaller sailing canoes all over Truk District have the same arrangement. The Puluwat sea-going sailing canoes have a platform opposite the outrigger with a small thatched hut on the outer end of it. In this the navigator sleeps and some of the trade goods are stored. The rest of the crew sleeps in the open hull.

In Ponape District a lateen type sail is used on all islands. Masts are set at an angle in the front of the canoe. They are easily dismounted and tacking is effected by moving the mast to the opposite end of the vessel, thus making the back into the front.

There is considerable variation in the shape and details of construction of canoe hulls and outriggers from island to island over the two districts. Some of these differences are dependent on different local conditions while others are simply historical accidents.

Canoes with very shallow draft and with short outrigger booms are found on Ponape. These canoes are well adapted to being poled through narrow shallow channels in the mangrove swamps in which Ponape abounds. The canoes of the other islands have deeper drafts and longer outrigger booms.

The canoes of Ngatik have an especially large capacity and deep draft. The larger ones can easily carry a ton of copra. These are particularly suited to carrying food and copra from the agricultural islets at the east end of the lagoon to the main inhabited island at the west end. The Ngatik Lagoon is large and its islets are far apart compared to most other atolls in Truk and Ponape District. (The large lagoons in Truk District contain more than one community.) So, on Ngatik, there is a special premium on canoes that are seaworthy in the waves of a large lagoon and can carry a big load in one trip.

Kusaiean canoes are used mostly in protected waters or on the fringing reef at high tide. Accordingly the outriggers are more simply constructed and appear weaker than those of other islands.

But a number of other differences in types of sails may be listed which appear to have no functional explanation, such as the fact that outrigger floats of Trukese canoes are removable and regularly removed for ease in beaching while those in Ponape District are not, the fact that Nukuoro canoes (now also used on Kapingamarangi) have sides which curve in at the top while canoes elsewhere do not, and the fact that the three low island communities of the Greater Ponape area (Mokil, Pingelap and Ngatik) paint their canoes with black, white, and blue or green longitudinal stripes while elsewhere islanders paint canoes red or not at all – on Kusaie.

Western style pulling whaleboats are now used in large numbers on the islands of Mokil, Ponape, and Pingelap. A double ended type was formerly the usual type and is used with oars or sail. These boats are made mostly by men from Mokil, Pingelap, and Ngatik. They are made and used on the first two islands and by immigrants from all three islands on Ponape. The Ngatik people have been slow to take up the use of these boats on their own island however.

The lumber is local but the hardware and paint are imported. Traditional style paint can be made from local materials but is said to be inferior to imported paint. Lumber supplies on Mokil and Pingelap are inadequate and lumber must be imported from Ponape. The lumber is worked mainly by hand tools. These whaleboats have the advantage that they can carry more than the traditional canoes and still have a fairly shallow draft. They are especially well suited to loading copra and unloading trade goods at visits of the field trip ships.

Similar boats with transom sterns (straight, blunt) have now become common on Ponape since these are better suited to use with outboard motors. Outboard motors are also used with traditional style canoes on Ponape. The motor is attached to the outrigger platform and a paddle is used to steer with. Outboard motors by 1952 were not yet common on other islands in

Truk and Ponape Districts but they may be expected to spread with the example of Ponape as a stimulus if copra prices continue to provide sufficient cash with which to purchase them. Outboard motors will probably not replace sails, paddles, and oars entirely but they are of obvious assistance when one wants to travel into the wind or travel during a calm.

Larger boats with inboard motors are also under islander operation and ownership, especially around Truk Lagoon and Ponape. These are mostly of Japanese or U. S. military surplus origin. They are especially important in transporting copra within Truk Lagoon. Some of these boats have made trips to the low islands to carry copra and passengers. As far as is known the capacity of these boats does not promise to be able to take care of all the copra and passenger traffic from all islands in the near future, but at times they have alleviated the passenger backlog for the government field trip ship.

The people of Ngatik and Mokil each built Western style sailing schooners in the Japanese period and possess the technical skills to do so again, preferably with a little advice from competent Americans. The main obstacle to building small schooners with auxiliary motors locally again appears to be financial. With the effective buying power of the money received for copra lower than in the Japanese period the people cannot save enough to buy the necessary imported supplies and support the carpenters while they are doing the work. There are also organizational problems since the people on these two islands are extremely individualistic. Shareholders in the vessels in Japanese times were reportedly dissatisfied with the management of the vessels.

CLOTHING

Native style clothing has been mostly replaced by imported clothing on most of the islands for a long enough time that it could not be revived during the shortage of imported clothes in the blockade in World War II. Traditional dress has been worn up to the American period in the Puluwat area but even there imported clothing is being used increasingly.

Weaving was known on all the islands in the two districts. The fiber was made from the inner bark of the wild hibiscus or from the trunks of special varieties of banana (probably closely related to Manila hemp). On most of the islands the technique has now been forgotten or is known only to a few older people. Weaving was very time-consuming and the resulting fabric was coarser than imported cloth and the colors were not as bright, so that there has been a tendency to abandon the use of local fabric even where the traditional style of clothing has been maintained.

Bark cloth is reported for Ponape and Kapingamarangi and may have been found elsewhere. It was made by soaking and beating the fibrous inner bark of the breadfruit tree. Large saplings were used. Plaited skirts made with the same technique as pandanus sleeping mats are reported for Kapingamarangi.

Throughout the Eastern Carolines the standard dress for men was originally a form of loincloth. This varied in width and design of textile from island to island. On Kusaie loincloths were of narrow width and the weaving was especially fine and of complicated design. In the Puluwat area loincloths were fairly wide and were used folded over. On Kapinga-marangi loincloths were made of bark cloth. Japanese style loincloths made of imported cloth are still used fairly widely as an undergarment and in Truk Lagoon as a work garment. On Ponape a length of imported cloth is now used by the men as a sort of wrap-around skirt on informal occasions.

"Grass" skirts (actually made of fiber from the unopened frond of the coconut palm or from the inner bark of the wild hibiscus) were used on Ponape as dress for men. These were worn over the loincloth and are still worn by some men on the occasion of traditional feasts and for leisure wear around the home. They are now worn over cloth wraparounds or imported undershorts.

The description here of men's clothing in pre-contact times on Ponape is not entirely certain as it does not agree with some statements in the literature. One report states that "grass" skirts were worn by men without a loincloth underneath; another that at times men wore nothing at all.

Capes and poncho-like garments are reported for Truk District and Ponape. On Ponape these were made from bark cloth and on Truk from woven cloth. These were not worn at all times however. In the Puluwat area rain capes made of strips of hibiscus bark (on the order of the Ponapean "grass" skirts) are reported.

Special decorative belts were worn on festive occasions on many of the islands. On Ponape and Kusaie some kinds of belts appear to have been considered especially valuable.

Women throughout the area wore wraparound skirts. Variations in the women's costume are not reported to have been extensive.

At present imported clothes are generally used throughout most of the area. Men wear trousers and shirts while women wear a dress on more formal occasions.

The voluminous "Mother Hubbards" introduced by the missionaries for the women are no longer in vogue on any of the islands.

At work around home on many of the islands the men and women simply wear undergarments. These are cloth wraparound skirts for women and loincloths, undershorts, or cloth wraparounds for the men, varying according to the island and individual. Kusaieans are the most heavily clothed of the people in the Eastern Carolines and the people of the Puluwat area and Kapingamarangi the least.

CHAPTER V

FAMILY RELATIONSHIPS

This chapter discusses first the islanders' terms for different relatives, then the events which ultimately determine all kin relationships (birth, a-doption, marriage, divorce) and some of the patterns of rights and obliga-tion between different relatives. However, inheritance and the economic aspect of kinship are discussed later under property and economy.

KINSHIP TERMS

To a person who is not familiar with anthropological writing on kinship it usually seems that there ought to be little to say about the kin-ship terms a people use beyond giving the translation into English. Actu-ally among the many small societies of the world with their own special cultures there is a wide variety in the applicability of even such obvious kinship terms as those used for father, mother, brother, sister, and wife. A term which means the same thing as an English term in reference to one relative may be applied to a number of other relatives which to us seem quite distinct, and categories of relatives which to us are the same may be broken up into several distinct categories by peoples of other cultures. To give an example, which is explained below more fully, in Trukese and Ponapean the term for "father" is also used to refer in part to one's grand-fathers, father's brothers, and what may be more surprising, certain first cousins (one's father's sister's sons). On the other hand other first cousins (one's mother's brother's children) are spoken of as one's "child" and still other first cousins (mother's sister's and father's brother's children) are classed as brothers and sisters.

Such ways of classifying relatives seem at first preposterous to peo-ple of Western cultures and we may want to dismiss them as savage or childish notions of little consequence. But relatives are usually much more important to people in small societies than to us so it would be unlikely that these peculiarities would be meaningless.   In fact anthropological investigation has established that kinship terms are important indicators of similarities and differences in relations between people.   There are almost always important similarities in customary behavior toward all relatives grouped together by a single kinship term, while there are usually important differences in behavior toward two groups of relatives called by two different terms.   In the example given above this means that in Truk and Ponape one behaves differently toward one's father's sister's sons and father's brother's sons (both first cousins to us) but that in some important way one's father's sister's sons are like one's own father and grandfather.

In addition to the general knowledge of the workings of the society which a study of kinship terms helps provide, such a study also is of direct use to alerting one to mistranslations likely to be made by islander interpreters in court work, such as cases relating to inheritance, claims for compensation, and other official matters where an understanding of kin relationships between people is important.

All of the cultures in Truk and Ponape Districts have simple kinship systems as far as number of terms go.   In Trukese there are eight terms and in Ponapean ten under which all recognized relatives may be classified. The kinship terminology of Truk, Ponape, and the Mortlocks have been well described as a result of the postwar Coordinated Investigation of Micronesian Anthropology and are rather similar.   Information on other islands is more limited but it appears that the kinship systems of all the low islands in Truk District are essentially like Truk proper while Kusaie and all the low islands in Ponape District, both Micronesian and Polynesian, have a somewhat different type of kinship system.

The main difference between the two types of kinship terminology is in whether there is a special emphasis on relatives through the female line or not.   In the simpler type of terminology relatives on both mother's and father's sides of the family are called by the same terms.   This is the type which appears to be found on Kusaie and the low islands of Ponape District and is also found widely on many other islands of the Pacific.   It is sometimes called the Hawaiian type because it was used by the natives of Hawaii. It is also called the "generation" type because in it all or most relatives of the same generation and sex are called by a single term.   That is, the word for "father" is also used to refer to one's father's brothers and his male cousins, the husbands of one's mother's sisters or of her female cousins.   The words for "brother" and "sister" are applied also to male and female first,

115

second, or even farther degrees of cousins respectively and the children of any classificatory brother or sister are referred to as "sons" and "daughters" with one's own children.

This type of kinship system has only one basic difference from our own: we have separate words for ancestors and descendants in the direct line of descent on the one hand and other blood relatives on the other hand (for example, parents versus uncles and aunts), and a generation type system does not. It lacks separate words to distinguish father from the different sorts of uncles, mother from aunts, brothers and sisters from cousins, children from nephews and nieces, etc.

Such a system usually means that the number of relatives with whom people maintain close ties is great: cousins are relied on as "subsidiary brothers", uncles as "subsidiary fathers" (that is, become acting brothers and fathers when there is need for it such as in making a feast). Often the household group contains several related couples so that the social distinction so apparent to us between cousins and brothers, uncles and fathers, and other direct or immediate and more distant relatives is minimized in everyday life. Even where more distant relatives are not living in the same household they are usually living nearby and frequently visit each other and cooperate on important tasks such as thatching houses, making feasts, hauling logs for canoes, and so forth.

Keeping up a relatively large number of kinship ties is characteristic of all the peoples in Truk and Ponape Districts, as well as of the Marshallese and Gilbertese and apparently of the peoples of the low islands in Micronesia as far west as Yap. The range of kinship seems to be narrower in Western Micronesia (Yap, Palau, and especially the Marianas). Dr. Alexander Spoehr's study of Chamorro and Carolinian communities on Saipan discusses this contrast in range in considerable detail. The Carolinians of Saipan are descended from people emigrating from the low islands between Truk and Yap and continue to have more to do with their relatives outside their immediate families than do the Chamorros, who are the descendants of the original inhabitants of the Marianas plus considerable admixture.

In terminology as well the Chamorros have a system mostly taken over from the Spanish which is quite similar to our own. Cousins, uncles, aunts, nephews, and nieces, are all distinguished from the immediate relatives: brothers, sisters, parents, children. The terms for immediate relatives are thus used much more narrowly than in the generation type or

Hawaiian terminology described above, or in the other type (Crow type) to be described below. The people of Yap have a different sort of restriction on the use of some of their terms for immediate relatives: for instance, the term for "father" can be used for one's father's oldest living brother but only after the death of one's true father. While one's true father is still alive a man's father's brother is not referred to by a kinship term and has little authority or responsibility for him.

A relatively broad use of the terms "father", "mother", "brother", "sister", "child" for more distant relatives is found in all cultures of Truk and Ponape Districts on which there are adequate reports regardless of the exact type of terminology found. This does not mean that the islanders cannot distinguish between a "real" father and an "uncle" who is called father, nor that the islanders cannot describe the biological relationship of any kinship as adequately as we can. If there is need to do so the islanders can easily and do make such statements as "He is not my true father, he is my father's brother". We are liable to forget that our own system is not too accurate for some purposes and that we must use more explicit circumlocutions at times, such as "He is not my blood uncle, he is my father's sister's husband".

One case of a genuine confusion of relatives has been reported by Dr. Kenneth Emory for Kapingamarangi. The people of this island formerly sometimes practiced polyandry (two or more men marrying one woman) and the woman often did not know which of her two husbands was the father of her children. In this event the two or more men shared responsibility for the child. But this confusion did not occur because Kapingamarangi children used the same word to refer to father and mother's other husband in ordinary speech. The confusion was caused rather by two men having intercourse with one woman within a short period.

The second type of kinship terminology found in the Truk and Ponape districts evidently developed historically from the first. The local forms are variants of what is known technically as the Crow type, named for the Crow Indians of the Great Plains of the United States. This type originates in societies with emphasis on the female line. Its characteristic feature is that it draws more attention to membership in matrilineal groups than to generation. Certain people of different generations are called by the same term if they are in the same female descent line, while others of a single generation are called by different terms if they are of different female descent lines.

Roughly, all persons, regardless of age, descended in the female line from the same female ancestor form a matrilineal descent group and are considered to be equatable for certain important purposes.

On the other hand a man and woman of the same female descent group are forbidden by custom to marry, so the men's wives must all come from other female descent groups. Also the children of the men of one female descent group must themselves belong to other female descent groups. These children are by no means equatable to any member of a man's own female descent group but he does have some cause for classifying them with his own children and this is in fact what happens: all the children of the men of a female descent group, including a man's brother's children and a man's mother's brother's children (who are one kind of first cousin) are classed with his own children. The classification of a man's brother's children with his own children is not so surprising and is also found in the generation system discussed above. The peculiar characteristic of a Crow system shows up in the terms for a man's mother's brother's children which are the same as the terms for his own brother's children in the next lower generation. In effect the terms for one's mother's brother's children are "lowered" a generation, that is they are the same as the terms applied to some members of one's children's generation, although biologically they are of one's own generation.

Equally diagnostic are the terms for a man's father's sister's children, again a kind of first cousin. These are in effect raised from one's own to one's father's generation. A man's father, father's sister, and father's sister's children are all necessarily of the same female descent line, and therefore all equatable for certain important purposes. Father's sister's children and their descendants in the female line are classed with father and father's sister depending on sex. On Truk and Ponape as a survival from the generation system one's father's sister is referred to as "mother" so this means that certain first cousins are referred to simply as "father" and "mother"

Other usages flow from these terms for father's sister's and mother's brother's children. Anyone in the father's female descent line, even down to father's sister's daughter's children of men in a man's own descent line, even up to one's mother's mother's brother's children, are referred to as "children".

The following chart sums up the wider use of terms for immediate relatives for some of the more distant relatives in the cultures in Truk and

118

Ponape District as far as these cultures are known. This includes good information on Truk proper, Ponape, and the Mortlocks and fragmentary information on the remaining islands. The left hand column indicates the biological relative referred to and the middle and right hand columns indicate the native term used to refer to the relatives in the first column. The second column applies to Kusaie and the low islands of Ponape District, the third column to usages common to all islands, and the fourth column applies to Ponape proper and all of Truk District. To save space, terms for grandparents' and grandchildren's generation are omitted.

There would be no practical value in giving a list of native equivalents in each dialect for the above terms. Administrators in the islands either know or can easily find out the native words if they so desire and professional anthropologists would want a fuller description of the terminology than given above, and should consult the works listed in the bibliography. The main purposes in discussing kinship terms in this handbook are to give the reader an understanding of some of the possibilities for mistranslation by local interpreters in this field and to use the differences from our own terminology as a way of calling attention to some of the underlying differences in relationships between people in response to which these terminological differences have historically developed.

A few other differences in terminology for immediate relatives will be noted here for these reasons. The difference in sex is less emphasized in the islander terminology than in our own. Parents are distinguished by sex in the basic islander terms but children and spouses are not. Instead of saying "my son", for instance, islanders must say "my child" and qualify this by adding "male" in order to specify that a son is meant.

In Ponape, Kapingamarangi, and probably Ngatik brothers and sisters are not distinguished by sex in basic terms. A single word means either "my brother" or "my sister" according to context. This term is the equivalent of the English anthropological term "sibling" which means children of the same parents without reference to their sex. In Truk District and probably on Pingelap and Mokil a single term means "my brother" if spoken by a man and "my sister" if spoken by a woman. This term may be defined concisely as "sibling of opposite sex" ("my brother" when spoken by a woman, "my sister" when spoken by a man). In Truk proper and also probably on Pingelap and Mokil there is one term meaning "brother of a woman" and another meaning "sister of a man".

TERMS USED FOR UNCLES, AUNTS, COUSINS, NEPHEWS, AND NIECES UNDER
THE GENERATION AND CROW TYPE KINSHIP SYSTEMS IN THE EASTERN CAROLINES

Biological Relatives by Generation	Generation Type (Ponape District except Ponape proper)	Usage Shared by Both Types	Crow Type (Truk District and Ponape proper)
Uncles and aunts			
father's brother		father	
mother's brother	father		father or special term
wives of the men in above			
two lines		mother	
father's and mother's sister		mother	
husbands of women in the			
preceding line		father	
First Cousins			
children of father's brother or			
of mother's sister		brother, sister	
father's sister's children	brother, sister		father, mother
mother's brother's children	brother, sister		child
Nephews, nieces, and children of first cousins			
man's brother's child		child	
man's sister's child		child or special term	
child of father's sister's daughter	child or special term		father, mother
child of father's sister's son	child		brother, sister
child of mother's sister's			
daughter or of father's			
sister's daughter		child or special term	
child of mother's sister's			
son or of father's brother's son		child	
child of mother's brother's			
daughter	child or special term		child
child of mother's brother's son		child	

The term for spouse was also used in a special way in the Eastern Carolinian cultures and still is in places. While there was no question as to who was the real wife or husband of whom, a man would also refer to his wife's sisters and his brothers' wives as wives or "spouses". No other term corresponding to sister-in-law existed to denote these relatives. Similarly a woman would refer to her husband's brothers and her sisters' husbands as "spouses". The missionaries have endeavored to discourage this usage with its implications of wider sexual rights and it seems to be on the wane. It is still quite customary in much of Truk District however. No substitute term for these relatives by marriage has been reported to have taken hold as yet, so where they are not called "spouses" any more they are simply considered as "relatives" without any more specific term.

A single term is generally used to refer to the brother-in-law of a man or the sister-in-law of a woman on all islands.

On Ponape proper there is a special term used to refer to one's mother's brother and mother's mother's brother, and another term referring to a man's sister's child. Interpreters usually translate these into English as "uncle" and "nephew". This is not too misleading, except for the sex of nieces. When the translation is reversed, from English into Ponapean, trouble arises if the interpreter succumbs to the temptation to translate all "uncles" in English as "mother's brother" in Ponapean and all "nephews" as "sister's son". Similar troubles are likely to arise wherever special terms for "mother's brother" or sister's son" exist and where interpreters understand the European kinship system little better than the average white man understands the native system.

EVENTS DETERMINING KINSHIP:
MARRIAGE, DIVORCE, BIRTH, ADOPTION

Native marriage ceremonies appear to have been fairly simple on most islands in the Eastern Carolines. On Ponape, Truk, the Mortlocks and perhaps elsewhere in the area infant betrothal was formerly practiced. This involved a formal agreement between the two families and an exchange of food and presents over a period of years. On Truk and Ponape at least it is said that couples could break these arrangements when they became of age if they were very determined about it. The practice of infant betrothal was discouraged by the missionaries (and the German administration) and is now extinct. Marriages arranged by the families of a boy and girl are still found, although in the minority on all islands as far as is known. Prior approval of

121

a proposed marriage by the families of the boy and girl is almost universal. Where approval by one or both sides is lacking the marriage is often abandoned or if entered into may easily break up.

The purpose of arranged marriages is often political or economic. On Ponape and in the Mortlocks, and occasionally on some islands of Truk, marriage between certain types of first cousins was arranged (a boy would be encouraged to marry the daughter of his father's sister or mother's brother). This had the effect of keeping land and other property within the family, by eliminating the need for marriage gifts to non-relatives. On Ponape, where each district had two chiefly clans each with its own line of duties, continued intermarriage between the two clans helped cement the political solidarity of the district. Such intermarriage often took the form of a boy marrying his father's sister's daughter. Marriages with one's father's sister's daughter are found on Lukunor and probably elsewhere in the Mortlocks. Marriages between other types of first cousins (a boy and the daughter of his mother's sister or father's brother) was and is strictly forbidden and considered incestuous. On Kusaie marriage has been prohibited between all cousins as far as third cousin. This restriction evidently came from the missionaries.

Native marriage ceremonies are no longer practical on most of the islands but Christian ceremonies have not entirely taken their place either, except on Kusaie where missionary influence has been longest and strongest in the area. So called "common-law" or "civil" marriages remain fairly common on all islands except Kusaie, although probably nowhere a majority. (This is in contrast to the Marshalls where Spoehr reported that on Majuro only a minority of the marriages were validated by the church.) On the basis of incomplete surveys it would appear that about three-fourths of Ponapean marriages have been validated in the church and probably somewhat less in Truk Lagoon. The proportion of functioning church marriages on the various low islands is probably higher on the whole than for Ponape as the low islands are especially amenable to missionary influence because of their small concentrated populations.

A fairly large minority of non-church marriages is not a true measure of the likelihood that an islander will fail to get married eventually in the church. This is because the non-church marriages are more common among young childless couples who stand a good chance of breaking up later and eventually getting married in church. In fact probably most couples married in the church on most of the islands have lived together more or less openly for a while before their church marriage. Certainly nearly all

122

have slept with each other and virginity as such is little valued except among those most fully indoctrinated in Christianity.

On the other hand the picture some Westerners have of the South Sea Islands as an idyllic savage paradise where everybody spends his time making love with everybody else is mainly a daydream. Even in pre-marital affairs faithfulness is valued and openly promiscuous men or women, especially the latter, are censured and held in low regard by the community. And while many parents condone some pre-marital sexual activity in their children they usually disapprove of any that does not involve a potential spouse for the child, especially if the child is a daughter.

By no means all older married people have had their marriage validated in the church. In general the islanders' criterion for a common-law marriage is similar to our own. If a couple live together openly for a while and behave toward each other as man and wife they are considered as married by the community. It is usual for the families of both to be consulted first and to give their consent to such an arrangement but if the families fail to do so at first the couple may persist if they can find a place to live. The families are usually reconciled eventually. A common-law marriage becomes more stable when the couple's families approve and when children are born but at least on the islands of Truk and Ponape it has been generally recognized by the community as a marriage without these two conditions.

DIVORCE AND ADULTERY

Divorce was apparently initiated aboriginally simply by one party leaving the other or chasing him or her away. It became final on remarriage of either of the parties. In spite of the emphasis on female descent and inheritance the father on Truk and Ponape, and perhaps on other islands, was said to have the right to the children. This notion was probably reinforced by the Japanese administration. On Kapingamarangi Dr. Kenneth Emory reports that both sides had rights to children.

While divorce appears to have been frequent on all islands and still is on Ponape proper and in Truk Lagoon it was and is not always a smooth process, especially when the grounds are adultery as they usually are. In general the double standard prevails and women object less to their husbands' affairs than men do to the affairs of their wives. The women are by no means always acquiescent to their husbands' philandering and insist that the husbands be reasonably secretive in their affairs. And because of the sex ratio women are always in demand for marriage. When divorce is imminent one partner generally accuses the other of an extra-marital liaison and may attempt to fight with the third party. Relatives on both sides rally to the aid of the two antagonists. Before foreign rule fights over women or men were an important cause of feuds, and still may become an instigation for brawls. Hard feeling may also exist between the families of the husband and wife on the grounds that the other party failed to fulfill his part of the marital contract.

Another common way of satisfying honor and holding on to one's spouse at the same time, on Ponape and Truk, is counter-adultery. To give an example, if one man, A, commits adultery with B's wife then B or a close relative can take revenge by committing adultery with A's wife or with the wife of a close relative of A.

On Ponape the senior male in the female descent group of the adulterer would sometimes take the initiative in formally begging pardon of the relatives of the offended spouse. This was done in order to avert a feud. If the adulterer's relatives failed to apologize a chief might summon both sides and force an apology to preserve the peace.

In some parts of Truk District, especially in the Mortlocks, but probably also in Truk Lagoon, the adulterer's relatives sometimes gave the offended spouse's relatives land or other valued goods for the offense. Land is no longer used for this purpose today. Ponapeans appear to have set greater value on the formal apology than land or goods in this connection, however. A reliable Puluwat informant has denied that any such payment was ever made on his island.

Divorce and adultery caused more trouble when involving people of high rank than commoners. Since Ponape and Kusaie had the greatest political development they probably had the most stringent rules on divorce and adultery for people of high rank. The Irish sailor O'Connell stranded on Ponape for several years in the early nineteenth century reported that divorce and adultery were practically non-existent then for the nobles. But noble males on Ponape and probably Kusaie had the out of polygyny: if they could not lightly divorce their principal wife they could take on additional wives or concubines. With the decline of polygyny on Ponape the stability of chiefs' marriages appears to have declined as well. The divorce, or threatened divorce, of a chief is still something that shakes and splits the community however. On Kusaie the problem does not exist since almost no one

124

now gets divorced. Divorces are also reported to be uncommon in the Mort-locks, although they do occur.

BIRTH

On all the islands in the two districts most births are legitimate. Abortion is occasionally practiced to prevent illegitimate births on Truk and Ponape and probably elsewhere but is practiced rarely if at all during marriage. The common technique is by vigorous massage although alleged abortifacients are also taken by mouth. One of these on Ponape is said to be green mangoes, which are also eaten anyway in great quantities by nearly everyone for their taste.

The position of illegitimate children is nowhere very bad. On all islands people are eager to adopt children so that an unwed mother need not worry about physical support of the child. In most of Truk District, where there is a strong emphasis on inheritance and descent in the female line the child is in almost as favorable position without a father as with a father. In Ponape District, where there is a stronger emphasis on inheritance in the male line children without fathers are in an unfortunate position but they usually acquire them by adoption. The fate of a child depends more on whether he is adopted or kept by his true parents and on the intentions of his adopting parents than whether he is legitimate or not. Legitimate children are also often adopted.

On Ponape proper all children born to a married woman are presumed to be her husband's children as well for purposes of care and inheritance, regardless of whether some other man is known to be the true father. This is very likely true of the other islands although specific information is not available.

As the time for birth approaches, especially the birth of a woman's first child, the prospective mother on Truk and Ponape and related low islands usually wants to return to the home of her own family, if the couple is not already living there. This is because childbirth is feared and the woman wants to die with her family if she is to die. Delivery at the district hospitals is becoming more popular.

ADOPTION

Adoption on a large scale is widespread in Micronesia and other

125

areas of the Pacific Ocean as well. Islander adoption differs from our own in that legitimate children in fairly easy circumstances are often adopted and there are usually close ties of kinship or friendship between the foster parents and the true parents. In Truk and Ponape District the adopted child usually knows who his true parents are and keeps up contact with them throughout his childhood. The true parents may demand their child back if they think he is being mistreated. On Ponape proper and in Truk District adopted children retain the clan membership of their true mother although they also gain a sort of provisional membership in their foster mother's clan.

A small scale survey of the biological kin relation of adopting parents to currently adopted children on Ponape did not show any significant preference for adopting relatives of the man or his wife. Cases are reported from Ponape of a sort of false adoption where a man would notify the Japanese authorities that he had adopted a younger relative to whom he wished to leave land. The relative would not necessarily live with the supposed foster parent in actual fact. This device arose from the desire to follow the original custom of inheritance in the female line, which meant that property held by a man would go to his sister's or maternal aunt's children instead of to his own children. Genuine cases of adoption of a sister's son or daughter also occur. There appears to be no restriction on who may adopt whom, so long as there is a sufficient difference in ages. Cases of grandparents adopting grandchildren and older sisters adopting a much younger brother or sister are reported for Ponape.

The common reasons given for adopting children are: to get children if one has none, to get someone to care for oneself as one grows old, and to relieve a friend or relative who has too many children. In a subsistence economy children acquire value as laborers at a fairly early age. On the other hand, with a limited area of agricultural land available to each family for subsistence, a family can as easily have too many children as too few. Adoption serves an important function in equalizing the distribution of labor and land in relation to each other and the islanders themselves recognize this.

Adoption has more than an economic aspect: The meaning of adoption in the life of individual people is also of great importance. From the individual's point of view adoption is often unpleasant. He is taken away from his mother immediately after weaning and weaning may be hurried up to enable the separation. If his foster parents later give birth to other children of their own the adopted child is often in fact slighted in favor of the

126

true children, although this is not considered right by the community. One gets the impression that adopted children show more personality disturbances than children kept by their parents.

On the island of Mokil a form of adoption especially injurious to the interest of the children has been reported. Men with much land and not enough workers in their family "take care" of children without actually adopting them and make the normal use of their labor but then later refuse to give them a share of the family inheritance. Similar situations probably occur occasionally on Ponape and some of the other islands. The emphasis of foreign traders and officials on the accumulation of privately owned land for copra plantations may have increased such abuses.

The above facts should not be taken as a plea for trying to make adoption complicated and difficult so as to reduce its frequency. Even with the abuses and disadvantages mentioned above adoption on the whole has its functions in providing for care of children who would otherwise be an undue economic burden on their parents and in providing children to care for otherwise childless couples in their old age. In a subsistence economy having too many children for one's land and resources can easily mean malnutrition, not simply a less expensive car or smaller rooms in one's house. Severe malnutrition can easily arise also in old people from not having children to work their land and resources for them.

True adoption, in the islander sense of the term, is carried out in infancy. When the parents of older children die relatives take over their care. This is not considered adoption in the narrow sense. On the other hand the relatives taking care of the children have in most cases been referred to as parents and to a certain extent acted as extra parents in the past. The obligations of these substitute parents to their wards are probably as strong as those of adopting parents. The difference is not in the type of care rendered but in the original cause of the obligation. A deceased brother's or sister's children are taken care of with little question, while an adoption is voluntary.

GROUPINGS OF RELATIVES

It is important to keep clear the difference between two kinds of groups of relatives. The first kind of group is that based on living in the same house, and includes the spouse and children of the household head regardless of the rules of inheritance and descent, and may also include a number of other relatives of the household head or his spouse and children. This residence group is technically known as the extended family.

The second kind of group relatives is based on descent from a common ancestor. When descent is reckoned through one sex, either female or male, the result is a lineage. A matrilineal lineage, based on female descent, includes the children whether male or female of a woman and the children of her daughters and female descendants but not the children of her sons and male descendants. The children of the men belong to their wives' lineages. A lineage thus includes on the average the children of only about half of its members: in a matrilineal lineage only the children of the females but not those of their brothers; in a patrilineal lineage only the children of the males.

Native words are of little help in making the distinction between lineage and extended family. Both Trukese and Ponapeans have words which depending on context can mean either, although more commonly refer to lineage rather than extended or simple family. Trukese has even taken over the English word "family", which is used mostly to refer to lineages.

The main thing a lineage system does is to establish in a community a series of clearly-defined, mutually exclusive groups of relatives within which various kinds of property and social and political rights and duties are held and transmitted from one generation to the next. At birth the individual's lot is clear: he is tied to a single lineage and barring something special, will remain a member of that group of relatives until he dies.

A lineage system does not mean that a man recognizes only members of his lineage as relatives and ignores all others. Even though lineage membership is determined by the lineage membership of only one parent and the other parent ignored for this purpose, the other parent is also counted as an important relative. Again, only certain first cousins will normally be members of a single lineage yet all first cousins are counted as relatives in nearly all societies in the world. The lineage members are not the only relatives a man has but they have a special significance for the purpose mentioned above.

In most societies with lineages the marriage of two members of a lineage to each other is forbidden and it is never required as a general practice in any society. This means that lineages can never constitute the customary residence groups, since outsiders will be brought in to marry some of the children, while others of the children will leave their family home to live with their spouses' families. While all the members of a lineage do not customarily live with each other they do normally keep in contact with each other and meet from time to time to share and work the property which they own, and to assist each other on important occasions. Examples of such occasions in Truk and Ponape Districts include first-fruit and other feasts, housebuilding, marriages, funerals, and sickness of lineage mates, etc.

If each couple in a community produced one boy and one girl who each grew to maturity and begat children then the number of lineages and the size of each lineage would remain constant and each lineage would go on forever. Obviously this does not happen. The random variation of proportions of sexes of children born within a family may make the lineage expand or vanish completely, depending on how many children of the right sex are born. If the women of a matrilineal lineage bear no daughters the lineage becomes extinct. If they bear many daughters it grows, regardless of the number of sons. The opposite is true for a patrilineal lineage, of course.

If a lineage keeps expanding it tends to become unwieldy in a couple of generations and breaks up into two or more new lineages. The original tie to the common ancestor will still be remembered and the members of the smaller lineages may keep up some contact with their more distant relatives for a time. However after several generations special contact, common property and the memory of the exact genealogical ties are likely to disappear although the memory of common ancestry may persist longer. A group of lineages tied together by little more than a vague assumption of common ancestry form a clan (or according to more recent technical anthropological usage a sib). Clans, like the lineages which compose them, may be formed on the principle of male descent (patrilineal) or female descent (matrilineal).

In Truk and Ponape Districts matrilineal clans were formerly found on all islands except the two Polynesian atolls. Matrilineal clans were found at one time on all the other islands of American administered Micronesia in fact, from the Palaus and Marianas to the Marshalls. Marriage with a clan member was generally prohibited, reportedly under strict penalty. A traveler visiting a strange place could usually rely on local clan mates for hospitality.

129

Many of the clans were found in different communities scattered over Truk or Ponape District. A few were found in both Truk and Ponape Districts, such as the "Under-the-Breadfruit-Tree" clan. The number of clans varied from place to place. Four are reported for Kusaie, fourteen for Mokil, about twenty for Ponape, perhaps thirty-five for Truk Lagoon.

Each clan has its own name and on Ponape and Kusaie some of the sub-clans also had their names. Most of the names with intelligible meanings appear to refer to the place where the clan started. The component lineages of the clans lack special names. They are referred to either by the names of the clan at large or of the living head of the lineage.

Under foreign contact matrilineal clan ties have probably been weakening throughout Micronesia and can be expected to continue to weaken gradually if acculturative pressures remain strong. The rate and degree of change have varied considerably from place to place. On Kusaie and Mokil and possibly Pingelap many people cannot tell what clan they belong to if asked. In Truk District and on Ponape Island clan membership is still known to all.

Where clan membership is known the ban on marriages within the clan is still generally observed although it has been broken in a few instances here and there. Even where people have married within a clan however it has been between two distant branches as far as is reported. It is hard to say with certainty that such marriages did not take place occasionally in ancient times as well. The prohibition on marriage within a clan was related to the supposed social solidarity of the clan and was not a rational attempt to prevent biological inbreeding. This is shown by the fact noted above that marriage with certain first cousins out of the clan has been encouraged by parents in some parts of the area, especially in the Mortlocks.

On Nukuoro a special type of descent group is found. The people are divided into five groups (some authorities say more) which formerly had religious and political significance. No restrictions on marriage have been connected with these groups. Where both man and wife are members of the same group their children are also members. Where man and wife are members of different groups the first child and all odd-numbered children belong to the man's group, while all even-numbered children belong to the woman's group. The result is a unilineal descent group (that is, the child is grouped primarily with one parent, one of his grandparents, one of his great grandparents and so forth) which is based on a random alternation of female and male ties.

It is not known what functions these groups now have, if any. They are still remembered by at least some on the island. A former island secretary of Nukuoro made a census of the number in each group in 1952.

The typical residence group throughout Truk and Ponape Districts has been some form of extended family: several related couples with their children. These people all live in a single house or in a group of small sleeping houses with shared cooking facilities. The manner of formation of the extended family varies from place to place depending on where a couple goes to live on marriage. If the couple goes to live with the man's father the core of the typical extended family is a man, his sons and grandsons. This core is then the members of the household group who live in the same place from birth to death, surrounded by blood relatives in their daily work. Their wives are brought in from other households however and their daughters move to strange households on marriage. Extended families formed on father-son ties were found before contact on Mokil and probably Pingelap and are now common on these islands and Kusaie, Ngatik, and Ponape as well.

On Mokil the male core of the extended family also forms the core of a patrilineal lineage. Note that the lineage consists of this male core, plus the daughters and sisters of the men while the extended family consists of the same male core, and the men's wives. The men's daughters are also included in the extended family before marriage but not after.

In pre-foreign times on many of the islands, especially in Truk District, a man would most commonly go to live with his wife's family on marriage. Most marriages were within a community so marriage did not mean a complete break for a man, although it did mean he was in more frequent contact with his wife's relatives than his own. With such marriages the core of the extended family is a woman, her daughters, and granddaughters. The other members are the husbands of these women and their unmarried sons. These women also constitute the core of a matrilineal lineage but in the case of the lineage the other members are the brothers of the women and girls, not their husbands. The matrilineal clans widespread in Micronesia and other more primitive parts of the world are believed by some authorities to have originated in matrilineal lineages which in turn developed originally around the core of women in extended families of the sort just described.

Extended families with a core of women continue to be the typical form of residence group on all the low islands of Truk (except Losap which is described further below), and are not unusual although of varying frequency on the islands within Truk Lagoon and Ponape proper.

On the larger islands of Truk Lagoon and on Ponape proper there is at present considerable freedom in where a couple will live and no very clear rule can now be given for the formation of the extended families. On Ponape and on the island of Fefen in Truk Lagoon a father-son core appears to be somewhat more common than either mixed or mother-daughter cores. On the other islands of Truk the balance is about equal or somewhat in favor of mother-daughter cores.

On Losap atoll southeast of Truk a special form of extended family is found where the core consists of a man, his sister's sons, and their sister's sons (the man's sister's daughter's sons). This core amounts to the male members of a matrilineal lineage. Under this system the men must move to their maternal uncle's house at or before marriage, while the women of course leave all their relatives behind. In this arrangement the women still constitute in a sense the core of the lineage since it is they, not the men, who produce new members, but the men constitute the core of the residence groups. There are some signs that this type of residence group may also have been found on Ponape, but it is not now common there.

Another aspect of extended family organization which probably varies from island to island is the average size of the extended family, regardless of the composition of its core. Foreign contact appears to have tended to reduce the size of the residence group, and on the high islands of Truk and Ponape households containing only one married couple and their children are found fairly frequently. There are indications that even in the past Ponapeans had smaller extended families and more independent families than other cultures in the area but this tendency must certainly have been reinforced by the German and Japanese emphasis on individual enterprise and ownership of land.

Kusaie and the low islands of both districts had few or no foreign governmental officials during most of the preceding regimes, and the size of the extended family on these islands has probably been less affected than on Ponape and the more acculturated parts of Truk Lagoon. Statements on the comparative average size of the extended families on the different islands are made on the basis of personal impressions. No meaningful figures are reported for most of the islands.

RIGHTS AND OBLIGATIONS BETWEEN RELATIVES

Some rights and obligations between some relatives are practically world wide, for example, the mother has primary care of her infant children. This section will pass over these and point out some of the differences from our own culture in the relationship between relatives.

The tendency throughout the area for several related couples to live together means for one thing that women can share the care of their children with their sisters or sisters-in-law. This makes time available for other kinds of work, such as fishing, agriculture, and cooking. Since care of children is spread among several women children consequently have less concentrated relationships with their mothers. This sharing of care of children is less characteristic of Ponape than other islands in the area but even on Ponape women usually cooperate considerably with relatives by blood or marriage in this and other respects.

The relation of a father to his children varies considerably from island to island depending on the degree to which matrilineal lineages are important in the inheritance of property and are responsible for the behavior of their members. In many matrilineal societies a child's maternal uncle (mother's brother), who is his lineage superior, has considerable authority over the child and is the prime male disciplinarian, while the father is more lenient and tends to "spoil" his child. This contrast between the roles of fathers and mother's brothers is also somewhat evident throughout Truk District and to a lesser degree on Ponape proper, where matrilineal lineages remain important in daily life. Greater formality is considered proper with one's mother's brother and other relatives than with one's father or father's relatives.

These sentiments are manifested in a number of rules of etiquette. On Ponape, for example, a chief's sister's son or other lineage mate is not supposed to be on the platform of the feast house with the chief on formal occasions and must in general be very respectful to the chief in public; the chief's son however may sit beside him on the platform and fail to perform a number of marks of respect for the chief which his maternal nephews and the public at large customarily observe.

At the same time this contrast between the role of a father and mother's brother is not black and white. Both share authority over the children and both can be relied on for help. In Ponape the nature of the relationship is sometimes even reversed: a man may protect his nephews and nieces against their fathers' wrath.

This reversal of role may be partly a recent development caused by foreign contact and especially by the German land reform of 1912. This reform established private ownership of land and prescribed that a man's sons should have highest priority in inheritance rather than his sister's children. This change must have given fathers more power over their sons and also made them feel a greater need for controlling their sons' behavior.

The tie between brother and sister is especially strong throughout Truk District, on Ponape proper, and probably on the other Micronesian islands in Ponape District. It is characterized both by a strong affection and obligations to help each other on the one hand and by a strong taboo against close contact on the other. Formerly in Truk District and on Ponape a woman and her brother could hardly talk to each other and a woman could not remain standing in the presence of her brother. This latter custom is still observed at last report only on Puluwat and nearby islands and is probably vanishing there. These taboos were and are strictest when the brother and sister were close in age. These strong brother-sister avoidance taboos were not found on Kapingamarangi according to Dr. Emory. The obligation of a man to care for his sister seems to reach its extreme on Losap Atoll where a man is supposed to provide more food for his sister and her children than for his own. Elsewhere a man's responsibilities for his own children appear to be stronger.

Ties uniting two or more brothers or two or more sisters are likewise strong. Where brothers form part of the core of the extended family (see above) ties between brothers become especially strong; similarly for sisters. In general the oldest brother and oldest sister receive special respect, are responsible for their younger brothers and sisters, and may manage any property owned jointly by the group of children. It is reported for Ponape and Mokil that the age hierarchy of brothers and sisters is sometimes undermined by parents who select a younger child as favorite and give him special privileges. This does not make for harmony among the children. The ties between brother and brother or sister and sister seem to be stronger in the Truk District than on Ponape proper and perhaps the other islands of Ponape District.

The strength of the ties between brothers, sisters, and brothers and sisters shows up when compared with the relative weakness of the tie between husband and wife. An argument or split between brothers has been traditionally considered more serious than the divorce of a married couple. In Truk it is reported that a man living with his wife's family will often keep his most valued possessions locked in a box in his sister's house.

The importance of brothers- and sisters-in-law also shows the importance of ties between brothers and sisters. An islander cannot easily marry a woman and ignore her brothers and sisters. When a man and a woman marry each party establishes important relations with the brother and sister of the other as well. The old joke about marrying a woman's family is more appropriate in Micronesia than in our own country, since the islanders are more concerned than we are about maintaining ties with brothers, sisters, and other blood relatives after marriage. The relations between two brothers-in-law or two sisters-in-law were and are characterized by great respect and mutual help. On Truk and Ponape the obligations of a man are reported to be greater to his wife's brother than to his sister's husband.

In former times in Truk and Ponape and probably throughout the two Districts a man had secondary sexual rights in his wife's sisters and brothers' wives, a further manifestation of the solidarity of brothers and sisters. These rights have been derogated by missionaries and other foreigners and are probably less exercised now than in the past but by no means extinct. Their exercise was always supposed to be with the consent and knowledge of all parties but secret affairs between a man and his brother's wife or wife's sister were also readily forgiven, if still cause for argument or jealousy. Probably it was unmarried men who most commonly had sexual relations with their brothers' wives, while sexual relations with one's wife's sister appears to have been most common during the long taboo on intercourse for a woman after giving birth to a child.

When a man died it was considered appropriate for his brother to marry the widow, although not absolutely necessary. On Ponape widows were not supposed to remarry any one outside of their husband's clan without special permission. For widows of high chiefs this prohibition was absolute. These limitations on remarriage are no longer enforced but it is said that permission of the deceased husband's brothers or lineage mates is still sometimes asked.

Relations with parents-in-law are not uniform throughout the area. In Truk proper a man has mild respect for his mother-in-law but it is said that even the occurrence of sexual relations between the two is not censured severely. On Ponape on the other hand, the mutual respect between son-in-law and mother-in-law is much more marked and the two must keep out of each other's way. A man's respect for his mother-in-law is also marked in Kapingamarangi. The Mortlocks appear to be intermediate between Truk and Ponape. Relations with the parent-in-law of same sex are less variable and marked by considerable but not exaggerated respect in Truk and Ponape. No information is available for the other islands in the two districts.

Relations of children with grandparents do not differ strikingly from many other societies in the world as far as reported (Mortlocks, Truk, and Ponape). The grandparents tend to treat the child more indulgently than its parents and leave most of the work of disciplining the child to the parents. In the Mortlocks it is reported that the grandparents often protect the child against punishments which its parents wish to impose. In general grandparents are more important than in the average American family. This is because old people are more likely to live in the same settlement and even house as their grandchildren and married children, and also because, as in most small societies, great respect is paid to old age.

CHAPTER VI

PROPERTY

OWNERSHIP

Before foreign rule individuals, groups of relatives, and communities each held title to certain types of property. In our culture popular talk about "primitive communism" is sometimes heard. If communism is given its usual sense of involving state ownership then the island peoples of Truk and Ponape Districts were farther removed from communism than we are ourselves. The property of the independent political units consisted mainly of uncultivated land within a community's boundaries on the high islands (all land was probably cultivated on the low islands). The chief's feast or meeting house and some sacred places on some islands might also be considered community property but little else was. Even favorable fishing grounds in the lagoon were privately owned. There were no community-owned schools, prisons, treasuries, hospitals, highways, armories, and so forth.

The main contrast in ownership between these peoples and ourselves lay in the type of private ownership. Among the island peoples families and groups of relatives were and are more important as owners of property than among ourselves, while individuals and specially formed corporations were less important. In fact corporations in the Western sense are a recent introduction, although some groups of relatives (lineages: see section in Chapter V on groupings of relatives) have some of the characteristics of Western corporations. A further contrast with Western societies is that the ownership of some kinds of property, especially real estate, has traditionally been much more stable among the islanders as a consequence of ownership by groups of relatives. These groups usually persist much longer than the life of any one of their members so that death is not a cause for transfer of ownership, and the kind of property needed by the group has not changed from one generation to another so that there has been no reason for the group of relatives to liquidate their holdings of one kind to invest in something else.

Under foreign rule there has been increasing emphasis on individual ownership of all kinds of property and a corresponding weakening of family ownership, but the contrast with our own concepts of ownership still holds. This development has both benefits and disadvantages for the islanders. Individual ownership encourages initiative and facilitates concentration of resources for economic expansion. On the other hand family ownership gives security to those too young, old, or otherwise incapable of participating in active management and to those who meet with misfortune and accidents. Old age pensions, life insurance, orphan and insane asylums, savings banks, unemployment insurance and the like are not needed where sizable groups of relatives work and share property in common, including the land on which they live.

In weighing the advantages for the islanders of a preponderance of the two systems of private ownership, individual and family, it would appear that individual ownership will become preferable when the cash economy expands enough to enable the formation of vigorous private insurance companies and banks and to enable the government to siphon off enough money in taxes to take over many of the welfare services now largely in the hands of groups of relatives.

Since the beginning of the American administration the idea of native stock companies for trading has been officially encouraged. Truk Trading Company and the Ponape Cooperative are results of this program in Truk and Ponape Districts. (The Ponape Cooperative is not a true cooperative and differs from an ordinary stock holding company only in that each stock holder has only one vote regardless of his number of shares.) Yap Trading, Western Carolines Trading in Palau, and the Marshalls Import=Export Company are similar enterprises in the other districts of the Territory.

It was a new experience for the people of Truk and Ponape Districts to participate in owning such an enterprise. The companies would not have succeeded without their competent American managers, who were selected with the assistance of the Naval Administration. As it was some of the islanders were disappointed and had hoped to get larger dividends (say 50 or 100 per cent) and turned their stock back in. Some unsupervised attempts of islanders to form further companies on their own initiative have resulted in the disappearance of funds of investors.

THINGS OWNED

The principal types of property recognized by the islanders can be categorized as real estate, movable goods, cash, lore, and skills, and mainly in Ponape, honorary titles. Islander ideas about what is and is not owned are different from ours in some respects and it is these differences which will be the main subject of this section.

Real estate traditionally included reefs, mangrove swamps, and shallow areas of the lagoon as well as land. During the Japanese regime the government claimed title to all such areas using homeland precedent. The only exceptions to this ruling appear to have been certain mangrove swamps on Ponape which the German government had previously explicitly recognized as belonging to the Etscheit family (Belgian plantation owners) and the Ponapean landowner, Henry Nanpei.

During the early part of the American regime official policy vacillated at the district level as to whether lineage and individual rights to underwater fishing areas should be recognized, although the islanders themselves in the areas around the administrative centers at least had already largely accepted the edict of the Japanese administration. An advantage of private ownership is the fact that the owners in former times instituted taboos on fishing periodically to allow the fish to multiply. Potentially at least this was a valuable conservation practice. A disadvantage of private ownership is the inequality of rights to an important natural resource which inevitably results from the fact that the ownership of shallow water is bound to be uneven. It is said on Truk at least permission for others of the community to fish on one's fishing grounds was never withheld except when the owner invoked a general taboo which applied to himself as well. But this sharing of the resources of the sea did not apparently extend to more remote communities. A further argument against private ownership is that our own precedents happen to be against private ownership of any part of a body of navigable water, even the unnavigable parts.

The shallow reefs are the site of two kinds of construction: fish weirs (an arrangement of stone fences used in fish drives) and rock heaps which are used to attract certain kinds of fish which like to feed on the algae growing on the rocks and hide in them. The fish weirs seem to be going out of fashion both in Truk and on Ponape although it is not clear that the government claim to ownership of all reef areas has anything to do with this.

The principal types of land are dry agricultural land, taro swamp, residence sites, and uncultivated land (jungle or waste land). On the low islands agricultural land is further divided into coconut land near the shore and breadfruit land farther inland. This division is also found on the high islands but is not as clear cut. A more significant division in the high islands is that between mountain land used for shifting cultivation and other land used for tree crops. The ownership and transfers of these different kinds of land vary somewhat. For instance, it is reported that on Kapingamarangi only taro swamp is exchanged at marriage. Where transmission of property in the female line is important residence sites are more likely to be transmitted to females or at least used most by females with an interest in them. There is a general sentiment that children should receive some of each of the major types of land necessary for subsistence.

In Western cultures the owner of the land usually acquires ownership automatically of any fixed improvements such as trees or buildings which an occupant makes. In the Truk and Ponape Districts this acquisition of ownership of permanent improvements by the landowner is not automatic in native custom. For one thing, no buildings are as permanent as ours. Since buildings are made of wood they are usually taken down by the builder and reconstructed elsewhere if he has occasion to leave the original building site.

With regard to trees, clear cases of separate ownership of land and trees are reported only from Truk District. In former times a property owner or property owning group never voluntarily relinquished full rights to land but might give away either general use rights to a specific plot or specific valuable trees such as a breadfruit or coconut. In the local phrasing one man or lineage would own the "soil" and another "trees". The interest of a party acquiring the use rights would persist without limit with a right to replant, but the interest of a party acquiring specific trees would only last as long as the life of the tree, which could not be replanted. Some aspects of this system are further discussed below under the section on transmission of property within the family. It is still in existence although there is a growing tendency to treat certain occasions formerly resulting in divided ownership as transfers of full ownership.

Ownership of land in Truk is not quite as exclusive as in the United States. In general the owner or occupant is little concerned about trespass. People may collect wild medicinal herbs wherever they find them. On Ponape however trespass has been regarded as a serious offense, especially if the owner suspects the trespasser of trying to find out how many yams or kava plants are growing on the property.

On both Ponape and Truk the people are careful to respect the ownership of plants and trees useful as a source of food or lumber. They will not
as a rule cut a drinking coconut or pick a breadfruit on another family's
land without asking for permission, although when accompanying a foreign
official a local guide may use this as an excuse to cut down a neighbor's
drinking coconuts.

Ownership of livestock, tools, clothes, ornaments, fish nets, canoes,
cash, and other movable goods is much like in Western culture. With some
kinds of productive goods such as livestock, canoes, and fish nets it is customary for a borrower to pay the owner a portion of the product for their use.

The complex systems of native "money" and finance found in Yap
and Palau in the Western Carolines were not found in the Truk and Ponape
Districts. However shell bead necklaces were generally considered to be a
form of valuable especially appropriate for offering at marriages and funerals, paying indemnities, and paying for certain services. In Truk District
large red wooden bowls constituted a further kind of valuable used on the
same occasions. Other kinds of goods, such as canoes, sennit twine, and
foreign and native made textiles, have also been used for the same purpose
on some or all of the islands.

Certain types of lore and magical and technical skills are considered
valuable intangible property in Truk District, on Ponape, and on at least
some of the low islands in Ponape District. Included are house and canoe
building, native navigation (now limited mostly to the low islands of Truk
District), yam cultivation (on Ponape only), native medicine, magic and
sorcery, clan and local history. An islander cannot learn any of these
things unless he pays an expert to teach him or unless a close relative of
his is an expert and willing to teach him free. These skills are considered
valuable because they enable a man to receive compensation for services
rendered or goods produced. The historical lore is valuable for the prestige
and political influence which its possession gives. A person who is familiar
with historical lore can cite precedents to support his proposals. Simple
skills such as plaiting pandanus floor mats, are not considered valuable and
no attempt appears to be made to keep them secret.

On Ponape native titles bestowed by the senior chief constitute a
further important type of intangible property. An individual's right to his

title is somewhat analogous in our own society to the right to a copyrighted product name. The title always remains partly under the control of the senior chief however. These titles are discussed further in Chapter VIII, Political Organization. The three outlying atolls in the Ponape area—Mokil, Pingelap, and Ngatik, also had a simple title system originally but under the influence of foreign contact a modified Ponapean system of titles has been introduced to these islands.

INHERITANCE AND TRANSMISSION OF PROPERTY BETWEEN RELATIVES

The most important property which is transferred from one generation to another is real estate—land with its improvements—since it is land which plays the most important part in the subsistence economy by which nearly all islanders still live.

With land held by groups of relatives and lineages a sharp transfer of ownership from one individual or generation to another does not occur. All children acquire an interest in the lineage land on birth or being adopted into the lineage. As they grow older they may be assigned specific plots for their own use and in any case have the right to use lineage land for getting food and making copra under certain conditions and subject to the rights of other members of their lineage.

To avoid the multiplication of technical terms we may refer to these acquisitions of rights by juniors from seniors as inheritance. The term inheritance is used here very broadly to mean any transfer of property or rights in which a difference of age between old and new possessors is crucial, and in which the older person relinquishes in part or entirely something to the younger with the understanding that the latter will continue to enjoy it after the former's death. Thus if the members of a lineage by custom allow each child of the women an undivided share of the lineage land on its birth this is here considered as a form of inheritance. It is likewise considered to be a form of inheritance if the lineage head assigns the child use rights for life to a certain agricultural plot as he comes of age.

Land owned by groups of relatives is usually under the control of the senior competent male member even on those islands where inheritance in the female line is emphasized. Where inheritance of land in the male line is emphasized (Mokil, Kusaie, Pingelap, Ngatik, and Ponape, and incipient in parts of Truk Lagoon) the senior relative is in the position of elder brother, paternal grandfather, uncle, or great uncle relative to the younger men. Where inheritance of land in the female line is emphasized (Truk District in general and formerly Ponape) the senior relative is in the position of elder brother, maternal uncle, or maternal great uncle.

On Ponape proper the German land reform of 1912 purported to establish a sort of individual ownership of land and patrilineal inheritance of land. The German land program for Ponape was evidently intended to provide each married man with land of his own to develop as he saw fit. In general the person actually using a piece of land was given a deed for it. The rights of other relatives in the land were recognized to the extent that "all male relatives who have no property of their own and all unmarried female relatives have the right to live on and use the property along with the owner" (article III of the Land Certificates). Moreover the rights of dependent relatives were further protected by a provision that both the Nanmarki and the German District Administrator had to approve of any alienation of any part of the land holding. These same officials were to approve of any heirs designated by the owner in the absence of the legally prescribed patrilineal heirs. In view of these restrictions the system devised by the German government for Ponape can be termed a mixture of individual and family ownership.

The German government was replaced by the Japanese within two years after the issuance of the first land deeds so that the land laws were put into effect more by the Japanese than by the Germans who wrote them. The Ponapeans were aware of the German laws, however, since they are printed in both German and Ponapean on the back of each German land certificate. (The two versions are not quite identical at a few critical points, it should be noted.) The Germans also prepared supplements to the land certificate rules in Ponapean clarifying certain unclear points and distributed these in quantity. The Japanese officials on Ponape did not enforce the German land laws in all respects but did continue to protect the rights of other members of the owner's family.

Property holding groups of relatives tend to split up easily on Ponape now. Children most commonly split any joint holdings after the death of their parents, if the parents have not already arranged such a division.

In Truk Lagoon the Germans also issued land certificates and attempted to institute patrilineal inheritance but the whole reform was pressed less vigorously than on Ponape. Whether due to these efforts or other factors, at present on the larger islands of Truk Lagoon (which are also the ones most subjected to foreign influence) the land holding and working groups tend to be composed of both male and female sides of the family. It is now becoming more important where one lives and works for purposes of inheritance. If one lives and works on land of one of his parents he is able to pass this on to his children. If one lives and works on the land of his parents-in-law he has a harder time claiming land from his parents for his children and is likely to get a smaller share.

A sentiment shared by all the islands for which there are reports including most of Truk District, Ponape, Mokil, Kusaie, and Kapingamarangi is that all children deserve some land of their own, regardless of whether inheritance in the female or male line is emphasized, and regardless of the fact that on all islands men have the most to say about how land is used.

In the low islands of Truk District where inheritance in the female line is heavily emphasized, it is reported that while much of the land is owned by matrilineal lineages there are other plots which are owned individually by men, who have received these from their own fathers or who have acquired full title to them as the last surviving members of their lineage. The men in turn usually pass this personal property on to their sons, providing that the lineage of their children (and wives) contains enough land to support the daughters adequately. The same division of property into that owned by individual men and that owned by matrilineal groups of relatives is also found in Truk Lagoon but it appears that on the larger islands of Truk proper there is a growing tendency for more land to be held by men and transmitted from father to son than on the smaller islands of Truk Lagoon and the outer islands of Truk District.

In any of these communities a man who goes to live with his wife's family is not entirely dependent on them economically nor is he necessarily an economic burden on the women of his lineage if he decides to leave his wife; he can help support himself and if need be, his children on his own personal land for a while.

In parts of Truk District, (the exceptions being most of the Mortlocks) if a man does not have enough of his own land to give his sons he may ask his lineage (mother's side) to let him take part of the lineage land to give to his sons or even daughters. Actually according to custom full title to the plot was not transferred to the man's sons but only usufruct rights: the "trees" but not the "soil" in Trukese terms. Normally the plot involved is land which he has cared for, planted, and used himself. But unless permission of

144

all the other members of the lineage with an interest in the land is given, transfer of any plot of lineage land to a child of a man of the lineage has been traditionally invalid in native custom. Even so, strong-willed male lineage heads sometimes try to take advantage of their senior position to alienate unduly large amounts of land from their lineage to give to their own sons. This is primarily at the expense of their sisters, sisters' daughters, and sisters' daughters daughters. A man with a strong personality may be able to make such unapproved transfers stick while he is alive but when a new lineage head succeeds him the sons are liable to be evicted and public opinion will support the man's lineage against his children, who are adequately provided for under custom by their mother's lineage.

In Truk proper the German land certificates are sometimes given as justifications for such arbitrary action by a lineage head. Unlike the Ponapean certificates, those issued on Truk are said by Trukese to be written entirely in German and thus incomprehensible to the great mass of people. The authors have not been able to locate a sample certificate for determination of their purported significance. Whatever the German government intended by these certificates they did not succeed in making these intentions public effectively.

When a Trukese arranged to give lineage land to his children it was formerly customary for the children and their heirs to make token payments of first fruits to the original ancestor's matrilineal lineage. The original owner's lineage (and all successive lineages if several transfers were made) also retained reversionary rights to the land. If the children's lineage became extinct the last previously occupying lineage would get the land back again.

The custom of rendering first fruits to the father's lineage for land received from it is said to be dying out in Truk Lagoon because people have come to feel that "fathers ought to provide land for their children" even at the expense of lineage mates. This is evidently connected with a decline of interest in the lineage system under acculturation. On Puluwat also it is said that first fruits are no longer rendered for land received from the father's lineage, although they once were. The reason for this change is obscure, but the lineage system does not seem to have declined there much. Instead the recipients of land from another lineage are obligated to make especially large funeral gifts when any member of the donor lineage dies. This custom may prevail on Pulap and Pulusuk which are culturally similar to Puluwat although there is no specific information on this point.

145

In all of the Mortlocks Islands except Namoluk, Etal and since about 1937 Lukunor, it has not been customary for the lineages to allow men to give land to their sons without "payments". Nevertheless in the Mortlocks too it is common for a man to arrange to give lineage land to his sons, with the understanding that the lineage of his wife and sons will "repay" this later by giving the father's lineage another equivalent piece of land in exchange. In this case neither side gains anything but there is presumably a strengthening of the ties between the two groups of relatives as a result of the exchange. The custom probably also serves a socially useful purpose in appealing to the pride of each side to put its plots of land in good condition before offering it to the other side. Even the son has gained nothing by this transaction since his own lineage considers that they own the new plot jointly with him by virtue of paying for it with one of their own plots. While the son will have special use rights in the plot he will still have to share it with other members of his lineage and consult them if he wishes in turn to "trade" it to his own son.

There is still land owned individually and unconditionally by men in the Mortlocks. This is land which men get who are the last surviving members of their lineage. Since they have no sisters or sister's children to provide for when they die their own children normally inherit full title to the lineage land.

In Ponape District at present matrilineal lineages exist on Ponape where they retain some importance in succession to political titles and as work groups but they no longer hold real estate as such. On Kusaie and the low islands of Ponape District matrilineal lineages are either now absent or have no important functions with respect to property.

In Ponape District the main emphasis on inheritance of land now is in the male line on all islands on which there is information. Available information is best on Ponape and Mokil, next best on Kusaie, and frag-mentary for the other islands. On Ponape in fact according to the German land laws only men could own land and this land was supposed to go auto-matically to their sons if they had any. Elsewhere in the District the Ger-man and Japanese administrations did not prepare local land laws but due to acculturation or local developments a similar sentiment has developed on the low islands and Kusaie.

With all the emphasis on inheritance in the male line the women on Kusaie and the islands in the Greater Ponape area still receive consideration and in effect possess land in their own right. According to Weckler, on Mokil women have recently received actually more than half of the total number of plots transferred from one generation to the next, although less than half of the area, since the plots given to women tend to be small. Another difference between men's land and women's land is that the residence plots are usually given to men on Mokil and probably elsewhere in Ponape District while women usually get purely agricultural plots. (In the communities of Truk District with emphasis on female inheritance it is the lineage core composed of women who most commonly retain the residence plots in case of division of land between men and women in a lineage.)

Where inheritance of land in the female line is emphasized (Truk District, especially the low islands) it was noted that land automatically is inherited by the males if the female line becomes extinct. Conversely in Ponape District where inheritance in the male line is emphasized land is automatically inherited by the females if the male line becomes extinct. This was not true on Ponape proper under the special German land laws for that island but the Japanese retracted the limitation on inheritance of land by daughters on Ponape and most Ponapeans at present consider that a person's daughters should take precedence in inheritance of land over any relative except sons.

In Truk District land inherited by a group of brothers with no sisters is usually quickly divided by them while land inherited by a group of brothers and sisters or sisters only is often held and worked jointly. In Ponape District it is the land inherited by groups of brothers which tends to be held jointly while land inherited by groups of sisters tends to be more quickly divided among them individually.

In Truk District, it will be remembered, men gain a certain degree of economic independence from their sisters and female relatives and from their wives' families by the plots of land which their fathers try to give them. Conversely on Mokil at least the land that women receive from their parents, especially from their mothers, gives them a certain degree of economic independence from both their husbands and their brothers. The Mokilese explicitly recognize that this land owned by a woman gives her greater prestige and security when she marries and is living with her husband's family. Marriage is therefore a common time for a Mokilese girl to receive land from her parents. If a woman is living with her husband's family her land is used by them as long as the marriage lasts but she can give it to whichever child she wishes and in the event of divorce takes the land back.

On Ponape during the end of the German period and earlier part of the Japanese period only men's names were officially recorded on land certificates. Persons wishing to leave land to female relatives resorted to family arrangements and pseudo-adoptions. A man would instruct his sons to leave certain plots for the use of his daughter and daughter's children, even though the name of a son would be recorded as official owner. If a man came to live with his wife's family on marriage the woman's parents sometimes "adopted" the man into the family, that is, had him registered as a family member by the Japanese policemaster, and turned over land to their daughter's husband with the understanding that it was "really" the daughter's land. If a man had few children and much land and wanted to give land to another relative not in the officially prescribed line of inheritance the land owner sometimes "adopted" this other relative. Some of these adoptions were not adoptions in native custom, it is said, and did not always even involve a change of residence, but since they were honored by the foreign officials this was all that mattered.

After the Japanese and American governments recognized the right of women to be recorded as owning land such subterfuges were used less often. A feeling still persists on Ponape however that it is best to have a man's name on the land certificate. This may be partly a persistence of the old pre-contact idea that men should manage land for their sisters.

The general pattern of inheritance of land from parents throughout the greater Truk and Ponape areas may be summed up by saying that everywhere children of both sexes ideally acquire some sort of rights in land from their parents, and that in general boys tend to get their interest in land from their fathers and girls from their mothers but this is adjustable according to actual needs and numbers of children of both sexes in the family. The principal variations are in the type of rights—full title or a share in lineage land—acquired by each sex.

In certain communities, places in Truk and Ponape districts, land is transferred between two families to validate a marriage. This practice is most highly developed in the Mortlocks at present though it is reported from Kapingamarangi, the Halls, and the Puluwat area also. It is reported that formerly land was sometimes given at marriage in Truk Lagoon but this seems to have been restricted mostly to marriages of persons of high wealth and rank. In the Mortlocks several pieces of land may be exchanged, along with other valuables. The husband's side usually gives more than the wife's. In Puluwat each side is said to give the other a small plot of roughly equal value. On all these islands in the event of divorce the lands usually return to the original owners as long as there are no children. The lands are also said to return in at least some cases if one of the spouses dies early without children and a replacement is not available from the same lineage. Evidently when there are children the man does not take his land back, and perhaps does not want to since his children are of his wife's lineage and the land can be used for their support.

Nowhere in the islands of Truk and Ponape District does a person have any automatic customary right to inherit lands of his or her spouse on the latter's death. Any transfer of land to a spouse if made at all is usually made well in advance of the probable death of either of the couple. A person, male or female, living on his spouse's land at the time of the latter's death often returns to live with his own relatives. If the marriage has produced children however the bereaved spouse may remain with the children as long as he or she does not remarry someone not of the deceased's family. Children who have been living on the land of a deceased parent usually have some rights in this land, even if the surviving parent does not. If the children are minor the surviving parent may remain to take care of the children on their land. If the parent is aged and the children are adult, the surviving parent may remain for the children to take care of him or her.

The gifts of land to young men and women on marriage on Mokil discussed above suggest the marriage gifts in Truk. There is a difference here however. On Mokil it is the family of the bride which sets aside land for the bride and the family of the groom which sets aside land for him. There is no full transfer of land between families, although if the bride goes to live with her husband's family as is customary on the island the man's family has the use of her land as long as the marriage persists; and conversely, in the rarer case where the couple goes to live with the bride's family, use rights to the husband's personal land are exercised by the woman's family.

On Ponape neither side customarily gives the other land on marriage but as noted above during the Japanese regime parents would sometimes arrange by pseudo-adoption to have a son-in-law inherit official title to their land so that it would in effect be used for the benefit of their daughter. This was done especially when the girl's parents had no sons of their own and wanted to entice their son-in-law to stay with them.

On Kusaie it is said that formerly families of a couple exchanged land to validate the marriage. It is unclear whether this practice is still followed.

The inheritance of other types of corporeal property is generally less complicated than the inheritance of real estate because in contrast to land full title to movable goods, tools, cash, and the like is usually in the hands of a single person. Throughout the area a person's children and brothers or sisters appear to be considered to be the primary natural heirs in that order of small personally owned objects. In general, property suited for use by men goes to sons and brothers; property used by women, to daughters and sisters.

Information on the inheritance of lore and skills is available mainly from Truk Lagoon and Ponape. Certain types of lore, such as the kinds of medicine involving animal spirits, clan history, and in Truk the lore of the war magician (itang) are said to have formerly been considered the property of a given matrilineal lineage. This would imply transmission from a man to his younger brother or sister's son rather than to his own son. Even before foreign contact however it is reported for Truk that the sons of persons possessing such lore were often taught it.

There is a suggestion in some statements by Trukese that the transmission of some lore to the sons of men of a lineage was permissible but that there was some sort of control on the sons transmitting the lore to sons of sons. These controls if they did exist are now no longer operative and persons possessing such lore now teach it to whichever close younger relative they please.

A child is not automatically taught in either Truk or Ponape all the lore or skills his parent or aunt or uncle knows. The adult selects the child he considers most capable, interested, and helpful for teaching. Order of birth appears to make no difference but sex does to some extent. It is felt more proper for men to know clan history and war magic than women, for instance, while it is more proper for women to know certain kinds of medicine connected with diseases of women and infants.

Other types of lore and skills (many kinds of magic and medicine, canoe and house building) appear to have never been limited to matrilineal inheritance in any way on either Truk or Ponape and were probably passed on regardless of line of relationship to any close younger relative in the past as they are today.

Lore and skills must be transmitted orally while the possessor is still alive, of course. However on both Truk and Ponape the people have traditionally believed that the spirits of dead relatives can impart such knowledge in dreams to living people. The spirit teacher dreamed of is often a man's father.

On Ponape but not elsewhere as far as is known, an apprentice to a practitioner of Ponapean magic or medicine of the more secret kinds is not supposed to be able to apply his knowledge until the death of his teacher.

The title system is found mainly on Ponape and in modified form on the three low island communities in the Ponape area (Mokil, Pingelap, and Ngatik). On Ponape the conferring of titles is ultimately at the discretion of the two senior chiefs but there is also a sentiment of ownership of titles by matrilineal lineages, so that if one man of a lineage received a title his lineage mates feel that on the first title holder's death another of their lineage should receive the same title or one of equivalent prestige. This sentiment is connected with political system and the Ponapean title system is discussed further there. On the three low islands there is a sentiment of ownership of titles by patrilineal extended families, so that if a man receives a title his eldest son feels he should receive it on his father's death.

CHAPTER VII

ECONOMY

This chapter considers the exchange of labor, services, and property. Exchange is considered within the family, between different families of a community, between different communities in the two districts, and between the districts and the outside world. The more or less permanent transfer of rights to property within a family at some definite stage of the life cycle or at death of a senior member is considered separately in Chapter VI, Property, although it has an economic aspect. The transfer of property to pay for damages and settle grievances is considered under Chapter VIII, Political Organization.

The island economy may be divided everywhere into two or in some places three systems which are not too tightly integrated with each other: subsistence, cash, and prestige economy. The subsistence economy characteristically uses local materials to produce the basic necessities of life: food, shelter, clothing, and water transportation. It involves mostly relatively small groups of relatives (extended families) and occasionally groups of neighbors for such things as hauling out a large tree trunk for a canoe or thatching a roof. Most of the important daily needs can be provided and still are by the cooperation of people in such groups.

A native prestige economy is at present most highly developed on Ponape, where it is connected with the political system and the honorary titles. In brief it involves the production of prize tropical yams, kava plants, and pigs in return for prestige and advancement in the system of honorary titles. It also involves local materials and relatively small groups of relatives in the production of the livestock and cultivated plants but the distribution of titles is made at feasts which often involves the entire political "district" or petty state (Ponapean term wehi).

A form of cash economy is present on all islands. Copra and a few miscellaneous products are sold for export and a number of islanders receive cash wages for work for the government, especially in the two district administrative centers. With this cash imported trade goods are purchased from the local stores and traders accompanying the government field trip ships. Items purchased in great quantity are rice, flour, sugar, cigarettes, canned fish and meat, cloth, and clothes. The foods, which have made up the major part of the value of all imports are a necessary supplement to the diet of those full-time government workers who have no access to nearby agricultural land of their own or of relatives. For the mass of the population and for those government workers who live on their own land imported food is a convenience because of its ease of preparation and a source of prestige but not usually a necessity. The ease of preparation is probably often a short-run view since it would appear to take more energy to husk, open, cut out, dry, and transport to the trader enough copra to buy a pound of rice than to pick and prepare an equivalent amount of bananas, breadfruit, or other local food.

The three systems of economy do intermesh to some extent. Since the traditional techniques of making cloth have been almost lost except in the Puluwat area it cannot be said that a pure subsistence economy including local production of clothing is possible for the people on most of the islands in the two districts. Knives and other tools, nails, lamps, and fuel for lamps are some of the common everyday items in addition to clothing which the islanders also obtain from the traders, and for which satisfactory local substitutes are not available.

Just as some items purchased with cash have become necessities in daily living, so are some of the things locally produced for immediate use also now sold for cash occasionally, such as local foods. It is considered somewhat shameful to have to ask anyone else for local vegetable food but fresh and salted fish are purchased for cash without shame at least in Truk Lagoon and on Ponape proper and the demand has usually exceeded the supply. There has been almost as good a market for local pork and beef.

On Ponape cash has also been integrated in the prestige economy, to a certain extent. Individuals sometimes buy pigs and even kava plants to present to chiefs at feasts. Yams are usually not bought to present at feasts but men often buy yams of a superior variety which they do not possess in order to get planting stock. Again some of the chiefs sell for cash some of the yams which their people give them.

ECONOMIC BALANCE WITHIN THE FAMILY

As in other cultures of the world there tends to be a division of labor by sex in the islands of Truk and Ponape District in which the heavy labor away from home is performed by men and light labor around the home is performed by women. Men exclusively climb breadfruit trees, while women plait pandanus sleeping mats for instance. Men fish in deep water while women usually collect shellfish and fish in the shallow water in the reef. Men prepare the framework of a building, women prepare most of the thatch. Men make more trips to other islands or communities and formerly fought in wars (more recently the men were in effect conscript labor for the Japanese military) while women stay home and watch the children.

However much of the labor required in the course of daily life is well within the physical capacity of both men and women. For some of these tasks the islands vary as to whether these tasks are assigned to men or to women. Cooking food in stone "ovens" (see Chapter IV, Technology) in Truk Lagoon and on Ponape and Kusaie is considered purely a man's task. In the Mortlocks however both men and women customarily use stone ovens. Cultivating swamp taro in the Mortlocks is considered a fine thing for men to do, although women are also allowed to cultivate taro on the poorer pieces of ground. In the Puluwat area however taro cultivation is restricted to women. In Truk, Kusaie, and probably Ponape men only pound breadfruit and other starch foods. In the Mortlocks, women pound more food than men.

In addition to the division of labor by sex there is also a division of labor by age. In all societies individuals are an economic liability for the first few years of life and for the last years as well if they live long enough. In a relatively easy environment there can be considerable variation in the age when a person starts working enough to become an economic asset and again lets down on work enough to become a liability again.

In general children are set to work at an earlier age in most traditionally nonliterate societies than in our own, since there is less need for an elaborate education. However Micronesian societies in general and those of the Eastern Carolines in particular are a partial exception to this generalization. There seems to be a general sentiment that young people are too occupied with enjoying life and love to work reliably and intensely, and the parents do not demand too much of their children unless the former begin to have actual physical difficulty in getting their daily necessities.

154

This leniency toward youth appears to be most marked in Truk Lagoon and lasts until about the age of thirty. In the Mortlocks it appears that there is greater indulgence of young women than young men. Of all the cultures in the two districts the greatest pressure on young people to do their share of meeting daily needs is probably found in Ponape or perhaps Mokil, but even on these islands there is considerable indulgence of youthful amusements at the expense of "serious" work.

Correlated with this is a tendency to give responsible positions in the political systems or elsewhere only to older men. The lack of respect given to young men with a good foreign education sometimes distresses outsiders. This is more a disrespect or distrust of youth than of foreign ways however and has its beneficial aspects as well: the foreign ideas will probably fit better into islander society if they are worked over by a mature native mind first instead of being applied in a great hurry by some boy just out of school.

The more marked hereditary differences in rank on Ponape seem to somewhat counteract the sentiment of indulgence of youth. Individuals, especially males, of high hereditary rank may have high positions thrust on them while still young and are expected to fill these. The opportunity to rise in the title system by good work at feasts also helps counteract the sentiment of indulgence of youth on Ponape. The successful man must start fairly young to perform miscellaneous tasks and errands for the chiefs in order to get ahead in the title system.

Within the household and family there is throughout the Eastern Carolines a rough balance of labor contributed by husband and wife and even young and old over a lifetime, but there is nothing suggesting the calculated exchanges of food and native money found in Palau between a man and his wife's family. Between old and young there is more an element of calculation as the children approach middle age. If the child fails to support his parents they may limit his inheritance of real estate or withhold from him certain knowledge and skills. Due to acculturation,, however, native lore and skills are less valued by young people than they used to be, and this inducement has lost its force in varying degree (in order of greatest to least loss of force a rough estimate might be: Kusaie, Mokil, Ngatik, Nukuoro, Kapingamarangi, Mortlocks, Losap, Halls, Pingelap, Truk, Ponape, Namonuito, and the Puluwat area).

ECONOMIC BALANCE WITHIN THE COMMUNITY

Exchange of services and products within a community involves both

specialists and nonspecialists. The simplest sort of exchange is typified by
that generally practiced in thatching a house or felling and moving a large
tree. This exchange has been described most carefully for Mokil. In
thatching a canoe house each family group on the island which owns a canoe
house itself is assigned a quota of thatch shingles to prepare. (Thatch is
used on Mokil mainly for canoe houses and corrugated iron for dwelling
houses.) This system enables use of the pandanus supply throughout the
island and also concentrates labor, making the house ready to use in much
shorter time than would be possible if only the people of the family group
worked at it. A single family group would also probably lack enough dry
pandanus leaves on their trees to thatch an entire building even if they
wished to do the work themselves.

On Ponape proper, Mokil, Kusaie, and Truk, young men are reported to form work groups of several to maybe twenty men each for
various sorts of work including bushing land, building houses, digging taro
pits (this on the low islands), and so forth. These groups are known as
"companies" or on Kusaie by the Japanese term kumi. On Ponape the
Japanese term seinendan(g) is also sometimes used to refer to similar
groups. (The seinendan organized by the Japanese was a community-wide
youth organization whose purposes were public works and athletics rather
than private gain.) The group agrees to work for an equal number of days
for each member in turn. Such groups are said to be especially popular
on Kusaie, but are probably found in some form on most of the islands in
the two districts. On Kusaie the kumi appear to be permanent organizations
to which nearly all men belong. Elsewhere they seem to include groups
of friends or neighbors who get together for a while and then break up again
after everyone has had his turn at using the group's labor. It is said that
the Japanese encouraged the formation of these work groups but there are
also indications that they were known aboriginally on Kusaie and Ponape
at least. Spoehr reported that on Majuro such work groups were known in
Japanese times but were not found when he was there in 1947. This suggests
that the Japanese government may have somehow encouraged formation of
work groups all over the Trust Territory but that different island communities
reacted with different degrees of enthusiasm to the suggestion. These work
groups enable concentration of workers where heavy labor is required but
for other tasks they serve no purpose except maintaining social contacts.

On all the islands there is some exchange between households of
food which happens to be in unequal supply. This occurs especially between
households of relatives as far as starch food is concerned. On Ponape and

probably elsewhere neighboring households sometimes cooperate by some going fishing and others preparing starch food. This transfers to family groups a pattern found within the family where different members often fish and prepare starch food on the same day. Fish, pork, and some beef are also sold for cash on all the high islands and possibly on some of the low islands as well.

The physical resources of the high islands, especially Ponape, would permit some expansion of livestock production as production figures from the Japanese period suggest in the following table.

TABLE ?

LIVESTOCK PRODUCTION IN THE PONAPE,
TRUK, AND SAIPAN DISTRICTS, 1937

Commodity	Ponape	Truk	Saipan
Hen's eggs	378,876	178,388	1,890,529
Poultry meat, lbs.	6,731	2,252	64,432
Other meat, lbs.			
(mostly pork and beef)	94,624	39,379	513,572
Milk, gallons	1,627	1,769	12,672

Saipan District had the greatest livestock production of all the districts in the territory in Japanese times and is included for comparison. These figures probably omit some non-commercial production.

At this time a livestock census revealed 613 cattle and 6,810 pigs for Ponape District while the figures for Truk District were 79 cattle and 2,593 pigs. The pigs were mostly on the high islands and the cattle entirely so.

This production of meat, milk, and eggs is actually not so large per capita for either Ponape or Truk but to achieve again even this much might help reduce the need for imported canned fish and meat a little. It must be realized however that much of the care of livestock was in the hands of Japanese. The direction of experienced foreigners appears to be essential to the initial stage of reviving livestock and poultry on a commercial scale, and the potentialities of livestock are probably less than deep sea fishing for bonito.

157

On Truk, Ponape, and Kusaie there are some men who make a good part of their living as fishermen. On Ponape and Kusaie these are mostly immigrants. On Kusaie the most active fishermen have been Mokilese, on Ponape men from Kapingamarangi, Mokil, and Yap. These specialist fishermen are a post contact development and even they are not full-time specialists as a rule. They fish for sale when the season and weather are appropriate for their fishing technique and live like everyone else at other times.

On Ponape and Kusaie hunting wild animals and birds is something of a specialty. Wild pigs are hunted on Kusaie while deer introduced by the Germans are hunted on Ponape. After acquiring .22 caliber rifles in the American period some Ponapeans made a specialty of shooting the native pigeons for sale both to American personnel and other islanders. There are a few communities in Ponape which are far enough inland so that they cannot rely on fishing as a regular source of protein. These have traditionally depended more on hunting.

Before foreign contact there were probably no full-time specialists of any sort. Certainly there seem to have been none in any of the low islands or in Truk Lagoon, although it is possible that on the two islands of Ponape and Kusaie the people at the top of the political system lived purely on tribute of the masses.

The principal part-time specialists found before contact and still found on most or all of the islands today are the traditional chiefs, house and canoe builders, and practitioners of traditional medicine. On the low islands of Truk District and especially in the Puluwat area there are still some individuals who are master navigators. In Truk Lagoon and on Ponape proper there are still people who are recognized as specialists in the semi-secret traditional history and myths.

Formerly there were also certain specialists connected with the original religion, such as priests, diviners, and spirit mediums. As far as is known there are no practicing priests of the original religions at present since nearly the entire population on all islands professes Christianity. Forms of divination are still frequently practiced on Truk but probably the more secret kinds which require the employment of a special diviner are used much less than formerly. Spirit mediums, who go into a trance in which it is believed that a spirit or god is "riding" them, are still found very rarely on Ponape and possibly also on Pingelap, Namonuito, and in

the Puluwat area. In Truk Lagoon they reappeared during the tension of
World War II but have since subsided and apparently no longer practice.
In Truk Lagoon a further craft which is still practiced as a part-time
specialty is the manufacture of large, red painted wooden feast bowls.

The modern economic position of the traditional chiefs varies
considerably from island to island. Before contact the chiefs on Ponape
and Kusaie were in the most favored economic position and got much,
perhaps all, of their daily food and other necessities in tribute of various
kinds from their people. On other islands the chiefly families probably
had to work like everyone else to make a living although everywhere they
received food offerings on fixed occasions.

At present the position of the traditional chiefs appears to be most
favorable on Ponape, followed not very closely by the Puluwat area and
Truk Lagoon. The traditional chiefs on Ponape have maintained their
importance as the leaders of the feast and title system. They receive many
voluntary contributions of food and kava plants (used for making a local
beverage) from people who enjoy attending feasts and have hopes of receiving one of the numerous titles.

Also according to the German land code each Ponapean landowner
was bound to give the chief a kava plant and a tropical yam once a year.
This was evidently intended to compensate or appease the chiefs in part
for relinquishing claims to ownership of all land in their petty states. Most
landowners still follow this practice and many consider that it is something
to which the chiefs have a moral right, although resentment of the demands
of the chiefs seems to have been a traditionally strong semiconcealed
sentiment among the people of Ponape.

Not all of the food which a Ponapean chief receives in a feast is
kept by him. Usually the largest part is divided among the people attending
the feast. Especially large portions are given to visitors from outside the
community, so that the orginal donors of the food often do not receive much
themselves immediately. However at other feasts the donors have the opportunity to become visitors.

The share of food a man receives at a feast is partly in proportion
to the rank of his title but in the long run the rank of his title is also partly
in proportion to the amount of food he has contributed to feasts. The feast
and title system is something like a voluntary old age pension system in

which the more one contributes in youth the more he receives in middle and old age.

Nowhere in Ponape District, nor apparently elsewhere in American Micronesia, do the chiefs obtain a share of copra sales on the basis of their rights in land as they do in the Marshalls. The chiefs on Ponape receive a certain amount of labor from young men who wish to gain their favor but this is not too great. Chiefs no longer requisition labor at will.

On Kusaie, the low islands of Ponape District and the islands south of Truk the traditional chiefs or their descendants still command considerable respect and often occupy important positions in the modern local governments or churches, but the economic benefits accruing to them directly by virtue of their traditional high rank are minor.

Master house builders in the island tradition are of varying importance. On all islands except the two Polynesian atolls of Kapingamarangi and Nukuoro and in the Puluwat and Namonuito areas native style houses are a decided minority, or even nonexistent, but a predominantly native-style construction is still frequently used for canoe houses, cook houses, and feast or meeting houses on all islands. All men have a general understanding of house construction, but for important buildings a master house builder is called in to supervise the measurements of the timbers. If he is not a close relative of the group putting up the building he is paid in cash (probably formerly native valuables) and provided with food while his services are required and given a special share of the food at feasts to celebrate the completion of the buildings.

Carpenters trained by the Japanese or by other islanders who originally got their knowledge from Western sailors and traders in the last century are often but not always specially versed in native style construction as well. Their compensation is similar to the traditional master house builder.

The islands vary in respect in the degree to which the average man is expected to be familiar with foreign carpentry. On the three low islands of the greater Ponape area, Mokil, Pingelap, and Ngatik, the average adult considers himself capable enough to build a house with the aid of his close relatives. In Truk Lagoon on the other hand people often hire the services of a carpenter to get a house built. Information on other islands is meager.

160

Native style canoes of one or more kinds are used on all islands. Here again all men have a general understanding of how to make a canoe but only master canoe builders know the correct proportions and must be called in to give the hull its basic shape. Some men have a master canoe builder build the entire canoe while other men do much of the work themselves, only calling in a canoe builder for the more difficult work. Compensation is similar to that for the master house builders. Where a fairly large sum of money is agreed on as compensation for houses or canoes it is most commonly paid in installments as the work progresses and as the client obtains money. However, there is no fixed number of installments or time for payment.

Makers of carved wooden bowls on Truk work mostly on specific orders for compensation agreed in advance. Cash is now an important part of the payment and the purchase of a large bowl is a major outlay for a Trukese family.

On Mokil, Pingelap, and Ponape locally built whaleboats are also common. The men of most families of Mokil and Pingelap can build these. Ponapeans have usually bought theirs for cash from a Mokilese or other low islander, however.

Throughout the Trust Territory the practice of traditional medicine goes on side by side with government and mission sponsored Western medicine. Of all the islands in Truk and Ponape Districts native medicine is probably practiced least in Kusaie. On other islands it is still practiced widely, although some of the traditional beliefs about supernatural causes of illness seem to be imperfectly known to the younger people. Often there are two stages in medical practice, diagnosis and curing. Both diviners and formerly spirit mediums may serve as diagnosticians. The diagnostician is often not the same person as the curer and both individuals receive compensation if not relatives.

The greatest pay is given to the curer. In Truk District this sometimes used to include plots of land or single trees for serious illness.

Land and trees are no longer used as payment for treatment. This may be because the products of such land and trees become taboo to all except the curer and his family, which probably appeared to be a non-Christian practice to the missionaries. Large amounts of cash and trade goods are still frequently given to practitioners of native medicine in Truk

District, Ponape, and probably in most of the other islands in Ponape District.

In Truk the patient's family makes two payments to the curer: an initial one to obtain the good will of the curer and persuade him to use his most powerful medicine and a final one after the patient is well again. The second payment is normally the largest. The amount of payment is determined solely by the desires of the patient's family. If too low a payment is made however it is understood that the curer may withhold some of his abilities when needed in the future. There is evidently also an unexpressed fear that the curer may reverse his medicine, since some kinds of Trukese sorcery involve only a slight alteration of the medicine and a person knowing the medicine almost automatically knows the associated sorcery. On Ponape also more than one payment may be made to the curer although it is unclear whether a payment is made in advance of treatment.

Puluwat informants have denied that sorcery is known on their island. It is not reported whether payments for traditional medicine are consequently lower there.

A number of specialists have arisen as a result of partial acculturation to Western ways. The foreign governments themselves have employed varying numbers of islanders as laborers, mechanics, clerks, craftsmen, medical aides, teachers, police, and local officials. Many of these employees working in the vicinity of the administrative centers have been more or less full time, although most have been unable to support their immediate families on their wages and have had to rely in part on food brought in by other close relatives. Official employees working away from the administrative centers have in general worked only part time regardless of official hours for pay purposes, since in general they have not had enough training to initiate work in the absence of close supervision.

Official employees working on a part time basis near their own homes seem to be in the most favorable position, since they can get food from their lands and make a certain amount of copra. Thus the money they get from their job can be used for luxuries. A disadvantage is that they are in the midst of demanding relatives who expect to share the good fortune and have nothing to give in return that the employees cannot get for themselves.

An important distinction is that between government employees paid by the territorial government through the district administration and the local ("municipal", that is, community or tribal) employees whose pay is derived directly from taxes on their neighbors. Territorial employees have in general received higher pay in proportion to the amount of responsibility required than have the community employees and the pay of the local employees in some communities has been more irregular than that of territorial employees because of difficulties in collecting taxes locally and managing funds. Even so, in most communities most of the local taxes have gone to pay the salaries of the magistrate (a sort of headman, not a judge), secretary, and treasurer.

Stores, bakeries, and restaurants are found in most communities except the Namonuito and Puluwat areas. The operators of these businesses are mostly part time except for a few individuals around the district administrative center. On the low islands businesses have not usually carried enough stock to remain in operation for more than a short while after the visit of the field trip ship which brings the trade goods.

Such records as these businesses keep often indicate that they are continually depleting their original capital investment and then the "owner" must acquire more "capital" from his relatives to maintain his operations. Actually these records are misleading. The stores serve two functions: first, supplying the demands of a rather small public for the most common kinds of trade goods, and second, serving as a purchasing agency for a group of related families. The "capital investments" of cash by the relatives of the owner can be considered functionally in the light of payment for the goods these relatives receive as gifts from the store from time to time. Of course the individuals concerned do not like to consider this openly as a special case of sale of goods or services and the "owner" does not record it as such, since relatives are supposed to help each other without calculation of gain and loss. However, where small businesses continue to operate for a long time (and not all succeed), it can be assumed that the business owner and his relatives have reached a tacit working agreement.

The small retail stores do not always sell for cash. Often in Ponape District and probably Truk District too they accept ripe coconuts in stated numbers from which they then make copra. Then when they go to the wholesaler to get further supplies they can also take a load of copra and get cash for their purchases. The storekeepers do not commonly accept the finished copra as payment for trade goods. This may be because the storekeeper can make more profit from accepting nuts than the copra. If a customer has finished copra he knows just how much he can get for it and in the three high island groups can get cash for it within a day.

In the three high island groups the copra trade has produced boat and truck operators and mechanics who are part time specialists and whose most important function is to carry copra to market. To date trucks have been used for bringing copra to market mostly on Kusaie. On Ponape a large volume of copra has recently been brought to market in open whale-boats and canoes powered by outboard motors. In Truk where the lagoon is larger and rougher somewhat larger boats powered by inboard motors have been used more. Pay for transport of copra is usually in cash following sale of the copra. Sometimes the owner goes along to sell his copra and at other times he entrusts it to the boat operator.

On the low islands there are no special persons who spend any con-siderable part of their time transporting the copra of others to a central point. There are economic problems involved in loading copra on the field trip ship however. The ship is almost always in a hurry and strong pressure is put on the communities to use all available labor to get the copra loaded quickly. This means that some men who have little copra themselves must help carry the copra of those who have more. If ties between relatives are strong and if the amount of copra per capita is small as in the Western Islands of Truk District this is no problem. But where there is a strong individualist and competitive sentiment and where much copra per capita is made as on Ngatik and Mokil, people expect to be re-warded for helping a neighbor load his copra. At the same time people with a lot of copra who would be able to load it all themselves if the ship stayed long enough resent having to pay others to help carry their copra. So far this situation does not seem to have been solved satisfactorily for all concerned.

The copra trade has also brought into existence a group of workers on islander plantations. These men make copra on the land of richer land owners in return for a share of the proceeds. The share is usually 50 per cent but it varies depending on how much bushing is needed along with the harvest of the nuts, whether food is provided by the landowner, who takes the copra in for sale, and so on. The greatest number of copra laborers in the two districts is on the Nanpei lands in Kiti, Ponape. Some of these laborers or their parents and grandparents immigrated from other islands back in the German period and have lived as tenants ever since. They are given usufruct rights to agricultural land for growing their own food. With

164

most other landowners laborers are not permanent residents but simply come in periodically as needed and then return to their own land. Probably this type of work is found rarely or not at all on most of the low islands where the amount of land per capita is smaller.

Another activity involving islander specialists is the church. Some of the islander members of the clergy approach or reach the stage of full time specialists and are supported by cash received from their church and food and housing provided by their congregation. In Ponape District especially there have been flourishing lay organizations of both Catholic and Protestant churches whose leaders devote considerable time and energy to their work. They do not receive pay for this, merely the respect of others.

In modern Micronesia certain key full-time positions are occupied partly or exclusively by Americans or other foreigners. These include top positions in the district and territorial governments, in religion, and in business. Foreigners in government, religious organizations, and shipping are supported by outside funds. Foreigners in trade are supported by the profits of their organizations. Most foreigners in Truk and Ponape Districts as in the other districts except the Marshalls are concentrated around the two district administrative centers. There are however a few on Kusaie permanently, and foreign missionaries and government officials make extended stays on the various low islands from time to time.

ECONOMIC BALANCE BETWEEN COMMUNITIES

Before foreign contact most of the various islands of Micronesia were connected with each other by sailing canoe for trade and visits. In Ponape and Truk Districts the people of the low islands in general were competent sailors and provided transportation for native trade goods while the people of the three island groups simply remained at home and waited for the low islanders to visit them. The two Polynesian atolls of Kapingamarangi and Nukuoro were an exception. The people there had also lost the art of navigation and were isolated from the world except for occasional Micronesian castaways.

The range of navigation of the people from the islands between Truk and Yap, including Namonuito and the Puluwat area, was considerable. People from these islands were part of the Yap Empire and sailed not only to Yap but to Guam and the other Marianas. During much of the nineteenth century in fact men from the low islands of the Central Carolines provided the transportation for the Spanish government between the different islands of the Marianas. It was a result of this activity in trade and transport that a colony of Central Carolinians became established on Saipan where their descendants are found to this day. A Puluwat canoe visited Ponape in German times and Puluwat canoes have continued to visit Truk up to American times.

However foreign ships have been plying the waters of the Carolines in considerable numbers for over a hundred years. The number of ships was greater earlier than more recently when it has been restricted by the Japanese and American governments for military security. Since the foreign ships were safer and had a much greater capacity than local seagoing canoes the art of navigation has declined considerably everywhere, especially in Ponape District.

In former times the low islands produced certain items of handicraft in exchange for certain high island products which were not available in quantity or at all on the low islands. Details of the trade are clearer for Truk District since the trade persisted there longer and may have been more flourishing to begin with. The low islands produced pandanus sleeping mats, sennit twine, shell beads, woven cloth of hibiscus or banana fiber. From the high islands they obtained extra supplies of food (especially preserved breadfruit and giant swamp taro), turmeric for cosmetic purposes, tobacco, and sometimes basalt rocks for use in cooking.

The low islands still produce some surplus sennit twine and pandanus mats for trade to the high islands. High islanders can and do make these products but it is easier to buy them or barter them with the low islanders. Shell beads are no longer made and native-style cloth is no longer desired by the people of the high islands. even though some has been made in the American period by women in the Puluwat area. Turmeric was produced by some Trukese for the Puluwat trade up into the American period but now apparently production has ceased. Locally grown tobacco has lost importance now that trade cigarettes are usually available.

Considerable amounts of food are still sent to the low islands from the high, although the exporters are now more often low island immigrants who have acquired land on the high islands than the high islanders themselves. The low islanders also send considerable amounts of food to their relatives who have settled at the administrative centers on Ponape and Truk, especially to those employed by the government who find it hard to cultivate all the food they need.

In Ponape District the low islanders in the Greater Ponape area now sometimes export salt fish and coconut molasses to Ponape. The men of Mokil make sailing canoes and whaleboats for sale on Ponape, although only on order. When the field trip ship has refused to carry the finished boats to Ponape for lack of space the builders have sailed these into Ponape or even rowed them in a calm, a distance of about ninety miles of open sea. The Mokilese have not recently used these vessels to sail back to their own island from Ponape against the prevailing winds and current however.

In Truk District there is a certain amount of trade between different communities in Truk Lagoon or between nearby low islands. Lukunor in the Mortlocks produces more taro than any other nearby island and the people of Lukunor occasionally take presents of taro to other islands in the Mortlocks which reciprocate with fish. This trade is combined with recreation inasmuch as the Lukunor people hold a canoe race to the other islands along with the taro presentations.

In general, however, the greatest inter-island trade is between high and low islands. Trade between islands of the same geographic type is limited. Because of the importance of the basic subsistence economy it is mostly islands with different natural resources which have something to offer to each other.

ECONOMIC RELATIONS WITH THE OUTSIDE WORLD

The people of Truk and Ponape Districts buy the imported foods, cloth, tobacco, tools, and other trade goods with money obtained mostly from the sale of copra for export and from wages for working for the government. Copra sales have in both districts supplied a greater amount of the cash to finance imports than have government wages. The Marianas and Palau Districts have been in contrast to this and the chief source of cash in these two districts has been government wages, directly or indirectly. Due to the ravages of coconut beetles and Japanese plans for colonization the coconut plantations in Palau and Saipan are in poor condition.

In spite of a price stabilization program initiated by the United States Naval Administration the price of copra has still been allowed to vary considerably with the world market. Production of copra has tended to go up and down with the price of copra, especially on Ponape Island where people have enough coconuts so that they do not need all of their copra money for

167

necessities. Since bushing is usually carried out at the same time as the collection of nuts the plantations also tend to be neglected at times of low price. As long as copra is salable at all, a minimum production needed to buy a few clothes and tools is probably assured. Because of the variable price of copra and low purchasing power of the dollar when transportation costs are added to the cost of merchandise, it is unlikely that there will be any great spontaneous expansion of copra production per capita.

Exports of trochus shell (used in the Orient in making buttons) and handicraft have also provided additional income. Trochus is not native to the Eastern Carolines and was introduced in Truk, Ponape, and Kapingamarangi by the Japanese. The other islands have none. In handicraft the islands are variable. Kapingamarangi and Nukuoro in Ponape District and Losap and Nama in Truk District have produced the best quality pandanus floor and place mats. Other items of good craftsmanship are made by the people of the low islands of both districts. The high islands have produced less and poorer handicraft. A good market for Micronesian handicraft remains to be developed. Exports of handicraft have tended to decrease as the government sponsored United States Commercial Company and Island Trading Company have run into trouble disposing of their local purchases. Handicraft cannot be expected to compare with copra as a source of income for the two districts as long as the price of copra holds, but handicraft sales have been important for some of the more crowded low islands and could be again if a market could be found.

Steps have been taken to provide a market for fresh produce, meat, and fish with employees of the territorial government at the district administrative centers and with military personnel in the Marshalls. The military market is presumably the largest potentially, and should remain fairly stable as world conditions stay unsettled, but transportation is a problem, and must be provided by the military.

In Japanese times a number of products were a source of cash in both districts which are now being exported or sold to foreigners. Some of these required Japanese or Okinawan labor to produce such as the dried bonito sticks (Japanese katsuo-bushi).

Other products such as dried trepang (sea cucumber of béche-de mer), mangrove charcoal, wild hibiscus fiber, coconut husk fiber, palm leaf fiber, and ivory nuts could be prepared or collected by the islanders themselves with little or no training.

TABLE 4

FISH PRODUCTION IN TRUK, PONAPE, AND PALAU DISTRICTS, 1937

District	Metric tons of fish, total	Bonito only
Truk	12,950.9	12,433.6
Ponape	4,187.0	4,064.0
Palau	14,021.2	13,744.7

Palau was the leading district for fisheries in the territory in the Japanese period.

Fiber products assumed an increasing importance just before World War II. In 1940 fiber exports had a greater cash value than copra on Ponape, and most of this went to the islanders. Changing market conditions and the greater cost of American shipping have so far prevented revival of these products.

CHAPTER VIII

POLITICAL ORGANIZATION

POLITICAL UNITS

Present political organization in Truk and Ponape Districts is a mixture of native and foreign. Foreign political concepts have been accepted most where foreign governmental and mission influence has been greatest (Kusaie, Mortlocks, Truk Lagoon, Ponape in order of decreasing political change). The least political change has occurred in the Puluwat area but even here significant changes have occurred. The amount of territory integrated in the most inclusive independent unit varied considerably over the two districts. The largest well-organized political unit was the island of Kusaie, united under a single "king". In general the islands of Ponape District had more highly developed political institutions than those of Truk District and the low islands immediately to the west of Truk District. Truk stands out in Micronesia as the area with the simplest native political organization, as more complicated native governments were found in the Palaus, Marianas, Marshalls, and Gilberts.

Namonuito and the islands of the Puluwat area, and possibly the Halls, were loosely joined into the Yap empire, which meant mainly that they had trade relations with Yap via the intervening low islands and forwarded some tribute annually to appease Yap magicians who otherwise, it was thought, would cause famine, disease, and storms. Puluwat itself controlled a subdivision of this empire consisting of the other low islands north and west of Truk now in Truk District. (Information on the Halls is not clear however.)

The political ties uniting these low islands were loose and even the larger inhabited islands themselves were not very tightly organized. On Puluwat there were three territorial subdivisions. Two of these were independent of each other in the sense that they each had chiefs of equal rank.

The third subdivision was tributary to one of the other two. It was only following foreign contact that one of the chiefs, having a better anchorage for traders, gradually acquired a sort of authority over the whole island.

A similar division of each inhabited island into independent subdivisions is reported for the Mortlocks. On the other hand the subdivisions of a single low island community did usually keep peace with each other and act in concert against people from other communities. In speaking of "other communities" it must be understood that this does not mean other atolls. In Satawan Atoll there are four communities and in Lukunor two. The Mortlock communities were further aligned in two opposed alliances, but these again were loosely organized as were the communities, and there was apparently not even a nominal head or senior community in either alliance.

Losap Atoll, between the Mortlocks and Truk, was more tightly organized. The two communities of Losap proper and Pis and the nearby low island of Nama are said to have been under a single chief.

In Truk Lagoon it is difficult to disentangle legend from fact and from the innovations of the German and Japanese governments. Each of the larger islands had a dozen or more small sections or subdivisions, each with its own chief. In some cases at least a number of these sections were grouped into a few larger districts on an island. Small nearby inhabited islands were sometimes attached to one of the districts of a larger island, for example, Parem was attached to the north district of Fefan; Falo was attached to the Tunnuk District of Moen. Trukese tradition tells of times when each of the larger islands was under a single chief. Further investigation is needed to determine whether any of the large islands were under a single chief at the beginning of foreign contact. It is safe to say at any rate that wars did occur between districts of a single large island and that at least some of the islands were not united politically when the German government assumed control at the beginning of this century.

Ponape represented an intermediate stage before contact between Kusaie and Truk. The island had no overall government at time of contact but it did have five rather well-organized districts or petty states which persist to the present. Traditions on both Ponape and Kusaie tell of a time when Ponape was politically united under a dynasty whose seat was at the ruins of Nan Matol. It is said that these rulers were deposed with the aid of Kusaiean invaders.

The five petty states on Ponape are ranked for purposes of etiquette only in terms of the order in which they split off from the control of this Kusaiean invader. This rank has no political significance at present. The order of the states is Matolenim, U, Kiti, Net, Jokaj. Net and Jokaj changed places when the population of Jokaj was exiled by the Germans for their rebellion.

The three low island communities in the Greater Ponape area (Mokil, Pingelap, and Ngatik) were pale reflections of the Ponapean petty states in their political organization. Each was a single independent political unit with subdivisions. The two Polynesian communities of Kapingamarangi and Nukuoro were also independent political units.

Foreign contact in Truk District tended to produce greater political integration of the communities. The German administration appointed a chief to each community in the district, whether it had had one or not. In Truk Lagoon the "flag" chiefs were created with jurisdiction over one large island and any nearby smaller islands. These areas apparently followed native traditions of previous political units. It remains a question how much the Germans forced people into these positions just to produce administrative simplicity and how much certain ambitious Trukese chiefs enlisted German support to extend their jurisdiction to accord with traditional ideas of the area these chiefs ought to control. The old alliances in the Mortlocks and the Yap and Puluwat empires tended to decrease in importance under foreign rule, although Puluwat people did not entirely stop sending tribute to Yap until World War II.

In Ponape District foreign rule utilized the existing political units. While new official positions were created in the five districts of Ponape Island, no need appears to have been felt to combine previously independent political units. The municipalities recognized at the beginning of the American period are all continuations of formerly independent tribes or petty states.

In the Spanish regime Truk was theoretically administered from Ponape, but in fact mostly left alone. The constitution of Truk and Ponape Districts dates from German times and has been continued by the Japanese and American governments. It should be kept in mind that any political unity of the two districts is to date something imposed by foreign regimes for administrative convenience. There is no traditional political unity of either district. Although there is some feeling of cultural unity in Truk

District based on a certain degree of similarity of language and custom, in Ponape District there is little feeling of relationship between Ponape and Kusaie, or between the two Polynesian atolls and the rest of the district.

Ponape Island has become something of a melting pot because of the importation of plantation laborers and colonists from other islands. This mixture of different peoples will probably help to produce a feeling of unity within Ponape District as a mixed population develops on Ponape with ties on the other islands. As yet however the immigrant communities have largely kept to themselves for residence and marriage, although mixing some with the true Ponapeans and each other socially and in church and community work.

POLITICAL OFFICES AND ORGANS

The political positions found in the various islands were not every-where the same. In Truk District each community or independent subdivision of a community ("section") had a single chief. The chieftainship was inherited matrilineally by the eldest male of the chiefly matrilineal lineage. It normally passed from elder to younger brother, and then to sister's sons, although apparently there was sometimes an opportunity for choice by the lineage between two members close in age of varying ability. As with property, if the lineage died out then a son of the chief came in line for the position and the chieftainship passed over to the son's lineage.

The functions of the chief included maintaining peace within his jurisdiction and prescribing public activities such as feasts and dances. Theoretically the chief held a power of eminent domain over all land under his jurisdiction and could redistribute it at will. Actually he seems to have confiscated land only in the case of severe offenses and at the risk of rebellion. A chief received first fruits from all holding land in his section and also received special portions of food at public feasts given in his name.

In Truk Lagoon some section chiefs were also district chiefs, in that several nearby sections recognized the chief of one section as superior to their local chiefs, and paid first fruits to both.

A second type of official was the itang or "war leader". These men were military strategists, repositories of historical lore and myth, orators, ambassadors, magicians, and so forth. They appear to have been found only in Truk District with this particular combination of duties and

173

abilities, but they were somewhat similar to the Nanikens of Ponape and the "talking chiefs" found in Samoa and parts of Polynesia. Itangs are specifically reported for both Truk Lagoon and the Mortlocks. Evidently they were not found in the Puluwat area or in the other low islands between Puluwat and Yap.

A hereditary chief might be an itang and itang lore was considered to be primarily the property of the chiefly clan and lineage. However sons of men of chiefly lineage and possibly other men could also become itangs while they could not normally become chiefs. Anyone intending to become an itang had to undergo an apprenticeship and pass through two lower degrees before he was formally pronounced to be an itang. The degree of itang is no longer conferred formally as some of the associated practices are felt to be contrary to Christianity. However, much of the itang lore is still retained.

On Ponape Island the political system has been considerably more complex than in Truk District. In each of the five petty states or districts there were and still are two lines of chiefs, the Nanmarki and Naniken lines, each of which contained twelve title holders in ranked order. There are in addition an undetermined number of other honorary titles at the disposal of the senior chiefs, enough so that nearly every adult man has a state ("district") title. These titles are not all ranked in strict order but they do differ in prestige.

Each of the five petty states is composed of one to several dozen sections, and each section of any size has its own two lines of titles. Many men therefore possess both section and state titles.

Before conversion of the islanders to Christianity there was a third line of titles in each of the petty states. This was the line of priests. The priestly titles have now lost their original function but they have been preserved and interlarded with the Naniken line, which formerly had fewer titles.

The two main lines of titles retain some political function. The senior chief in the Nanmarki line (the Nanmarki himself) is considered senior to the Naniken and is the nominal head of the petty state according to custom. Formerly he was not allowed to mix with the people and at feasts sat concealed in a special little room. The Nanmarki was still supposed to have the final word on all matters of policy but it was the Naniken

174

who transmitted this to the public and probably had greater actual power.

At present the taboos on the person of the Nanmarki have greatly weakened and while he is still treated with considerable respect it is not unusual for him to speak in public and his presence is not avoided. The existence of two high chiefs has given considerable flexibility to the political system under acculturation. Where the Nanmarki has failed to adapt to changing conditions the Naniken has been able to take the lead and vice versa. Where one chief has tended to exploit the people the other has tended to protect them. Such a system might seem to make for confusion but to counteract the division of authority are several devices, discussed below, connected with the system of promotion to the titles which tend to bind the two chiefs and lines together.

The manner of selection of the chiefs on Ponape is less simple than in Truk District and involves both inherited rank and demonstrated ability. To begin with, in each petty state there is a chiefly matrilineal clan (see Chapter V, Family Relationships) with a number of sub-clans of varying rank. It is considered desirable that the Nanmarki be chosen from a high-ranking sub-clan of this clan and this has usually but not always been done. Eligibility to hold the titles of the Naniken line is also increased by membership in specific clans, but in some of the petty states there are two or three clans which claim this privilege.

Another rule involves the lines of twelve titles leading up to the Nanmarki and Naniken. Whenever one of these titles in either line, including the top ones, is vacated by death or loss of title it is considered proper that the others in the line below the vacated title each advance one rank, preserving their same relative order.

In theory an advance may be held up if the title-holder has not been industrious at feasts and in work for the public welfare or if he lacks high hereditary status. Likewise a title holder may "leap" over several others if he is considered to have accomplished much in the public interest or to have high hereditary rank. These irregularities of promotion are normal in the lower ranks but also occur in the very top ranks. When they occur in the top ranks the losers are liable to feel great resentment and may even resign their titles. (The usual response to this is to hold the resigned title in reserve until the previous holder's anger abates and accepts it again.)

All title decisions are supposed to be made by the Nanmarki in consultation with the Naniken and are publicly announced by the Naniken. The two top titles are an exception since the Nanmarki appoints the Naniken directly and vice versa on the death of the other. This custom helps make for a pair who can work with each other. Both are supposed to have discussed this choice with the previous holders of the title and to give due consideration to native custom, but there is traditionally no appeal from the decision of the surviving top chief except rebellion. The threat of rebellion at the time of the installation of a new senior chief, especially a new Nanmarki, was formerly considered quite real by the Ponapeans. Accordingly the exact moment of the death of the old Nanmarki was formerly concealed until the new Nanmarki was chosen and crowned. This secrecy was intended to prevent rivals from interrupting the coronation ceremony.

This secrecy is no longer observed today but the identity of the receiver of a title is still kept secret until the actual moment of conferral. This does not prevent the chief from indirectly sounding out in advance the public reaction to conferring a title on a given person.

Another bond between the two lines is the feeling that it is desirable for the Naniken to be the son of a Nanmarki, either the present one or a previous one, or someone in the Nanmarki line. There is a lesser sentiment that the Nanmarki should also be the son of a Naniken.

These requirements were formerly worked in with the other requirements about membership in the right matrilineal clan by intermarriage of certain first cousins. A man in line for either the position of Naniken or Nanmarki was encouraged to marry his father's sister's daughter. Thus a Nanmarki might appoint his own son to be Naniken. The son would necessarily be of a different clan from the Nanmarki because a man cannot marry a woman of his own clan and all children inherit clan membership from their mother. But the Nanmarki's sister and her daughter would both be of the Nanmarki's clan. If the son-Naniken married the father-Nanmarki's sister's daughter the Naniken's son would be of the Nanmarki clan and eligible to become Nanmarki himself. If this second Nanmarki in turn married his own father's sister's daughter, the second Nanmarki's son would be of the same clan as the Nanmarki's father and would be eligible to become Naniken.

This custom of marriage made it possible for the titles of Nanmarki and Naniken each to remain with a single matrilineal clan, inherited from uncle to maternal nephew (sister's son), while at the same time the men of the two clans holding the titles could be in father-son relationships. In

176

effect both male and female lines of inheritance were taken into account. This type of marriage is no longer strictly practiced but intermarriage between the Nanmarki and Naniken clans is still considered favorably and a man's eligibility for promotion in one line is said by some to be increased if his father holds or once held a title in the other line.

A further consideration in the assignment of titles is the sentiment that the titles within a single line should be spread around among several families and sub-clans. This is in part contradictory to the sentiment that the highest ranking sub-clan should have the highest titles. In effect the combination of the two means that a group of full brothers should not monopolize a bloc of titles in a row, but that people of other families should receive titles ahead of the younger brothers. This rule makes for solidarity of the different branches of the matrilineal clan associated with a given line of titles.

The criteria for conferring titles in the two lines of chieftainship are obviously conflicting and the conflict produces confusion and tension, in spite of the devices noted above for reducing conflict. But the very conflict of criteria means that there is more latitude for choice of a new chief on his individual merits than in the Trukese system.

As noted above each of the sections or territorial subdivisions of the petty states on Ponape has its own two lines of chiefs. The line in the sections corresponding to the Nanmarki line tends to be kept by the men of a single matrilineal clan. This is not necessarily the same clan as that of the Nanmarki line of the state. However the titles of the opposite line, corresponding to the Naniken line, are usually distributed among men of different clans in the sections. The Naniken line on the section level is less important than on the state level.

When the senior chief of a section in the Nanmarki line dies, it is the state Nanmarki, not any other section chief, who installs the new senior section chief. In theory the Nanmarki has had the right to assign the top chieftainship of a section to anyone he pleases. In fact public opinion would not normally permit him to assign it to anyone except the matrilineal heir of the previous senior section chief, and the appointment by the Nanmarki is a formality. However if there is some cause for objection to the normal heir or if there is a dispute as to who is the proper heir the Nanmarki's personal decision is important.

177

Women also hold titles on Ponape, but their responsibilities politically are minor. Each male title has a corresponding female title for the man's wife. There are also a few titles which are given to women of high hereditary rank in their own right. Sometimes the husband of a woman of high rank is given a high title by virtue of his marriage. This may involve any title in the Nanmarki and Naniken lines except the two top ones and probably most other titles. In the event of divorce the man would lose the title. This is as close as women come to holding men's titles on Ponape.

The meaning of many of the Ponapean titles is unclear, which suggests the antiquity of the system. Some of the titles suggest that the holders may have originally been assigned to supervise different types of food production: "Master of the Banana Plantation", "Master of the Forest", "Master of the Sea". Others suggest that the holders had religious functions connected with various shrines. Some of the titles include names of places which are found in the islands of Nan Matol where the famous ruins are located. Perhaps the original holders of some of these titles were officials at the court of the legendary rulers of all Ponape. At any rate nothing is left of the original special functions of these titles and their main importance at present is as symbols of prestige and as qualifications for receiving special shares of food at feasts.

Detailed reports of the pre-contact political system of Kusaie are not available. What is available is somewhat suggestive of Ponape, although on Kusaie the whole island was a single undivided petty state.

As on Ponape the chiefs were chosen partly for hereditary rank and partly for achievements and ability. Counting the senior chief or king there are said to have been eighteen state chiefs or nobles. As on Ponape these were arranged in rank order and in case of a vacancy at the top each chief was supposed to advance a rank. However only one line of chiefs is reported for Kusaie, in contrast to two for Ponape (three, counting the pre-foreign priests). All the Kusaiean state chiefs or nobles were required to live near the king.

The second ranking chief, known as the <u>Kanka</u>, was of special importance. His position suggests the Nanikens of Ponape and the itang's of Truk, but detailed information to assess the degree of similarity is lacking. An important difference from the Ponapean Nanikens is that the Kanka could and often did succeed to the position of king.

The king was elected to his position by the chiefs from among them-selves. Once chosen he appears to have been considered to have had absolute power, but in fact the chiefs could and did lead revolts and depose a king who abused his power excessively. Once elected the king had the power to fill vacancies among the chieftainships from his own partisans in the various noble families so that the longer he remained in office the more secure his position tended to grow.

As on Ponape, the state was divided into a number of administrative sections (about fifty) each with its own section chief or headman. The sections and section chiefs were divided by the king among the higher ranking nobles or state chiefs, who acted as the king's representatives. The king also retained two or three sections under direct personal control. The chief of a section was appointed by the state chief to whom his section was assigned, but it may be surmised that the position was also in part hereditary.

The political system on Kusaie has changed considerably under contact. Christianity and depopulation have both played a part in the changes. The common people accepted Christianity before the kings and many of the chiefs. In 1874 the common people participated in the deposition of a king and election of his successor. Since that time the kings have been more responsible to popular opinion which has tended to follow the leadership of local church leaders.

With the severe depopulation in the later part of the nineteenth century most of the former dwelling sites and sections were abandoned and the complex system of titles fell into disuse. At present the population is back to what it was at the time of first contact according to some estimates, but the settlement pattern has changed and most of the people live in the village centers of the four modern districts of the island: Lele, Malem, Tafunsak, and Utwe. Under the American regime the people have continued to respect the aged king, who has also been the senior ordained minister of the Kusaiean church, but control of both village and island affairs has been officially in the hands of elected officials.

The three low island communities in the greater Ponape area—Mokil, Pingelap, and Ngatik—have rather similar political systems to each other. This similarity is partly due to the fact that the inhabitants were converted to Christianity with the aid of Ponapean missionaries and local people who went to mission school on Ponape. Along with Christianity these people also brought Ponapean ideas about how titles should be bestowed.

179

All of these islands had had some sort of title system before mission contact and the original title systems appear to have involved two lines of titles, sacred and secular, but the old titles were abandoned in favor of the new. This process of adjustment to Ponapean standards is still going on. One of the officials of Ngatik asked recently for an authoritative list of the titles in Matolenim District, which is considered to be the arbiter of such matters, so that Ngatik could make the necessary adjustment in their titles!

One difference from Ponape that all three of these islands share is that eligibility for titles is inherited from father to son. Another is that there is no regular promotion in the titles from rank to rank. These two differences mean that the Nanmarki has traditionally been succeeded by his son, not as on Ponape by the number two man in the Nanmarki line.

The low island communities are much more closely knit than the petty states on Ponape. The traditional chiefs are respected but the gulf between them and the people is much narrower than on Ponape. Special etiquette and respect forms of language used to the chiefs are almost entirely lacking. At feasts the chiefs receive a slightly larger share of food but this has little economic significance. Of the three islands the influence of the chiefs has probably declined most on Ngatik due to the greater social disorganization imposed on the island during early acculturation.

Little is reported to date on the native political organization of Kapingamarangi and Nukuoro. There was both a hereditary chief and an elected priest. On Nukuoro, but not Kapingamarangi, the office of the secular chief was formerly often held by women and was restricted to members of one of the five descent groups described in the chapter on family and social organization. A chief is said to have had the option of choosing his successor from his own close relatives of the proper descent group. On Kapingamarangi the secular chief's office was passed from father to eldest son. On both islands the office of priest appears to have been elective. Dr. Kenneth Emory notes that the secular chief on Nukuoro had greater power than on Kapingamarangi.

PROBLEMS IN THE INTRODUCTION OF WESTERN POLITICAL INSTITUTIONS AND LAW

This section does not purport to summarize the laws of the Trust Territory establishing various sorts of governmental positions and organs. The main purpose of this section is to discuss some points of conflict between foreign and native political institutions which have been noted by anthropologists and other students of island life. This discussion is based especially on conditions in Truk and Ponape Districts but much of it applies to some or all of the other districts in the Trust Territory.

One of the most outstanding conflicts is that between the restricted political loyalties of the islanders and the more inclusive institutions imposed by foreign regimes. Especially important among these more inclusive institutions are the district administrations and all-territorial government. Persons not thoroughly acquainted with the languages and cultures of the islanders often fail to realize the degree of difference between many of the islands and the feeling of separateness which accompanies these differences. Even where there is considerable cultural similarity, as among the five petty states of Ponape or among the islands of Truk Lagoon or of the Mortlock group, the people of these formerly independent communities do not all consider that their cultural similarity inevitably implies that they should be politically united.

It should be remembered that in many of these communities there are still men alive who as youths witnessed wars with their neighboring communities. Effective independence of the various communities in most of both Ponape and Truk Districts lasted up to the beginning of this century. This was later than in some other parts of American-administered Micronesia although foreign contact on a large scale started before, in the first half of the nineteenth century. The foreign government post was established on Ponape by the Spanish in 1887 but the Spanish never effectively controlled the entire island and complete pacification cannot be said to have been achieved until the close of the Jokaj Rebellion in 1910 under the German regime. It was after this that the Ponapeans appear to have fully realized the extent of foreign military power.

On Ponape and perhaps elsewhere even after pacification there have been occasional mysterious deaths which have been attributed by the general public to political feuds within the island, especially between people of different petty states. These incidents serve to illustrate the degree to which law and order are maintained by fear of outside force.

It would be false to give the impression that the islanders spend all their time thinking about what they would do to the people of the next community if there were no foreign administration. However it does seem plausible that fighting between some communities would break out

181

eventually in the hypothetical event that all American and other non-Micronesian officials, missionaries, and teachers suddenly pulled out. And without dragging up hypothetical cases the lack of confidence which the people of any one community feel in a man of another community is great enough to make most responsible leaders hesitant about accepting official positions outside of their own community, and to put a considerable burden on those who do.

A further important conflict between islander concepts and Western political institutions occurs with the attempt to introduce independent specialized branches of government including our basic distinction of legislative, executive, and judicial. In none of the original native governments of Truk and Ponape Districts was there any very clear distinction between these three functions.

All were exercised, insofar as they were exercised at all, by the same chiefs or "kings".

Before foreign contact the legislative and judicial functions of local governments were not very great. People lived by custom rather than written law, and the customs needed no extensive revision as long as the basic economy and conditions of life remained roughly the same generation after generation. Moreover, as noted below, the notion of crime (against the community) was not clearly distinguished from that of tort (damage to an individual or family group). Settlement of torts was most commonly either by negotiation or by fighting between the families of the parties and the chiefs often did not intervene in any judicial capacity.

The previous foreign regimes have not given much example of the independence of these three functions of government. The Spanish and German governments both had such small staffs that the same individuals necessarily combined these functions. Moreover neither of these regimes had the primary objective of encouraging political development. The Spanish wanted the islanders to become civilized Christians, while the Germans wanted them to become productive peasants.

The Japanese eventually had a larger official staff than the two previous regimes, even larger than our own, but much of the effort of this staff was devoted to assisting and administering Japanese, Okinawan, and Korean immigrants, who with the military came to outnumber the islanders on Ponape proper and in Truk Lagoon. As far as the islanders themselves

182

were concerned their affairs were largely in the hands of the local police-masters (on Ponape, Kusaie, and in Truk Lagoon) or on the other islands, in the hands of local chiefs whose power was recognized by the Japanese. The policemasters had judicial powers sufficient to take care of most criminal cases arising. Whether judicial powers were formally assigned to the local chiefs in areas away from the administrative centers is unclear but at any rate there was little need to try crimes on the low islands because of the low crime rate. On Kusaie the people conspired to keep local affairs secret from the authorities. A public confession and promise to reform made in church was enough to satisfy the public and the injured parties in most crimes. Serious crimes by islanders in the Japanese regime were tried by professional Japanese judges.

Under none of the previous regimes were legislative bodies organized. Local officials had the power to make minor regulations while major laws were promulgated with the approval of the territorial or colonial office. In any case the same officials were both the source of the laws and the executives of the laws as far as the islanders were concerned.

The policy of the territorial government under the American regime, both in the naval and civilian eras, has favored the formation of representative advisory bodies for districts or parts thereof to assist in formulating legislation. These bodies have been considered as first steps toward the formation of representative bodies with true legislative powers.

The first such bodies formed in both Ponape and Truk Districts were groups of those community ("municipal") officials around the district administrative centers that is, those on Ponape Island and Truk Lagoon. Both these bodies had the advantage of representing single cultural areas with common problems. They also had the advantage that the members were responsible for administering any proposals in their own communities, and this arrangement made for reasonable proposals.

There was the disadvantage (from the legislative point of view) that American officials tended to consider the administrative functions of these "chiefs' meetings" as primary, and placed primary emphasis on promulgation of orders and laws received from the territorial government and on checking the community records and finances. The criticism was also made that the native executive officials were not well suited to finding out the people's will.

Accordingly an advisory "congress" was eventually organized in Ponape District containing two houses, one elected and the other composed of certain of the traditional chiefs of Ponape Island whose positions are partly hereditary and partly appointed (see section on political offices and organs). As first organized it was primarily representative of Ponape Island but the immigrant outisland colonies on Ponape also received special representation. It is too early to make a definite evaluation of the success of this project but some of the difficulties which have already arisen may be listed.

Perhaps the trouble least anticipated and least appreciated by many of the Americans who helped plan the congress is that the elected representatives have been considered by the islanders as additional executive officials in the chain of command from the district administrator through the petty state ("municipal") officials. The electoral districts, which were drawn up purely on the basis of equal numbers of people, were assumed by the Ponapeans to be new administrative divisions of the petty states, and the "congressmen" took over the duties of seeing that their constituents did their share of community road work and made reports required by the government, and so forth. In doing this they partly duplicated the efforts of the section chiefs on the one hand and the officials of the five petty states on the other. Whereas formerly an order or notice from the petty state officials to an individual citizen went directly to the appropriate section chief and then to the individual, with the introduction of congressmen the islanders assumed it to be appropriate for such communications to be routed through an extra individual, the congressman, before reaching the section chief and the ultimate addressee.

This additional administrative level was not necessitated by the size of the political units and merely constituted an extra source of slow down and distortion of communication. But the greatest disadvantage of this twist given to the institution of the congress is that the intended separation of legislative and executive is no nearer than it was before except on paper. Instead of consciously using native executive officials as representatives, as was done initially in the "chiefs' meeting" system, the American administration was doing the same thing on a grander scale unknowingly with the "congress" and confusing local government in the bargain.

This confusion was also aided in Ponapean minds by the fact that the congress was not initially granted any actual legislative power and that action on most of its recommendations had to wait months for decision by the High Commissioner's office, which was at times negative. Many islanders

184

felt that this advisory function was of so little importance that there must be some other function of the members (i.e., executive) to justify the troubles of election and the fuss which American officials had made about the congress.

Considerable efforts have been made by the Ponape District Administration to educate the islanders and the members of the congress as to its proper function. It cannot however be assumed that the educational efforts to date have produced any great permanent results. A periodic field check by the local anthropologist on the local conceptions of the congress and the extra-curricular duties assumed by congressmen would provide reliable information on the degree of progress in understanding the congress.

Another problem arising in the operation of the congress and in the election of officials generally is the effect of formal voting on political unity and cooperation. In spite of the great powers of the traditional chiefs in theory the island governments in many places in Micronesia before foreign contact were probably much more democratic in effect than reports sound. The threat of rebellion compelled the chiefs to take account of popular opinion and before the introduction of firearms the chiefs possessed no arsenals of special weapons by the use of which they could remain in power indefinitely with only a minority of supporters. Moreover the communities and petty states were everywhere small enough so that there were not too many administrative echelons between the lowest commoner and the highest chief. In fact the chiefs probably rarely made decisions without sounding out public opinion rather carefully. To judge from present practice this sounding out took two forms: informal conversations with a sample of representative individuals and public discussion such as at feasts, and dances. At present, the chiefs in introducing a matter for public discussion in traditional circumstances, whatever their personal opinion, do not go farther than outlining the obvious alternatives of action, if that far. If the people present all agree on one course then the chief announces this as a decision. If they fail to agree he usually simply waits and perhaps brings up the matter again some other time. Eventually a sort of unanimity is usually achieved, if only that the minority keeps its peace realizing there is no hope to get its views adopted by the others.

Of course chiefs who abused their powers and forced the will of a minority on the masses for a time did occur occasionally but tradition records what often happened to these: they were killed or chased away in rebellions. Actually the personal power of the chiefs may have reached its greatest peak in the period after foreign contact but before foreign political control. In this period astute chiefs were able to arm their partisans with imported rifles and increase their economic power by alliances with foreign traders. Even after foreign political control some astute chiefs were able to use their positions of favor with the conquering powers to exploit their people in ways which they might not have dared in the pre-contact days. But this situation was tempered by the fact that word of abuses might reach the foreign administrators who could remove the offending chief from office and replace him with a new favorite. So the old sentiment for unanimous informal consent to all important community actions was never entirely lost.

The congress on the other hand does not reach its decisions as delicately and leisurely as the communities formerly did. The members do not feel that they can personally afford to remain away from home for more than a few days and are in a hurry. The congress is called together specifically to come to decisions. If decisions are postponed there is a feeling that nothing has been accomplished by both islanders and American officials.

Moreover the Americans encourage free debate and the use of voting to come to a decision where unanimity cannot be reached. Voting and unrestrained debate tend to leave a more embittered minority than the traditional leisurely process of arriving at a formal unanimity. It is one thing for a minority to cautiously venture objections and finally lapse into silence when it realizes the weakness of its position. It is another thing for the members of the minority to be encouraged to let loose with extreme statements they would normally make only to each other in private and then find themselves publicly shamed and defeated in the ensuing vote.

Of course such disappointments are common enough in American society and are well within human capacity to bear once one is used to them. The point here is simply that the average Micronesian and especially the average Ponapean is not yet used to considering such social shocks as trivial.

The prospect of campaigning for election to a congress is also offensive to the modesty of the average Ponapean and Micronesian at large. To put oneself unequivocally on record as favoring certain decisions not yet made appears presumptuous. Moreover it puts the candidate in the position of being rejected by either the electorate or his colleagues in congress. Without making a blanket disparagement of all members of congress one may wonder how many are elected because the voters have confidence in them and how many simply because there is almost no one else who would consent to run, or simply because they know a little English and therefore presumably will get along well with American officials.

This question cannot be reliably answered without periodic objective study, as may be conducted by the district anthropologist. Obvious difficulties are involved in asking the American administrative officials to judge their own success in encouraging public confidence in the congress. Even assuming a work load which would enable an administrative official to spend say half of his time away from the administrative center talking informally to people and assuming an awareness on the part of the American involved of the danger of saying the program had succeeded simply because he personally had tried to promote it, experience shows that it is unlikely except in the most extreme situations that the islanders would be so impolite as to give their opinions freely on the deficiencies of a program to someone who had publicly shown interest in promoting it.

It is to be hoped that the public confidence in the congress and its members will grow steadily with the passage of years. Whether confidence actually does grow and how fast it does are questions for study by disinterested trained observers. The answer depends on the experience of the congress, the issues which it takes up for discussion, the quality of the decisions which it makes, the support which it receives from the American administration, the degree of responsibility which it is permitted and a number of other factors which cannot be predicted in detail at present.

Examples of confusion of the functions of island officials are not limited to the case of the Ponape Congress. Another notable example occurred in Truk during the early part of the naval administration and was eliminated after attention was called to it by the CIMA team of anthropologists on Romonum. Here the confusion was between staff and line functions.

A system of government of several echelons of islander officials had been set up which included an "atoll chief" for all of Truk Lagoon who was supposed to be assisted by a staff of two advisers, one advising on affairs pertaining to the western half, the other advising on affairs pertaining to the eastern islands. These advisers were immediately assumed by the Trukese to be an additional echelon intervening between the district administration and the individual citizens. This made a total of five echelons of native officials intervening between American officials and the people in Truk Lagoon: atoll, sub-atoll, "flag", community, and section (or "village";

see previous sections on political units and offices and organs). A greater efficiency was later attained by reducing this to two or three intervening echelons, varying somewhat from island to island.

In general the islanders will naturally assume that any new office created has executive powers unless its functions are very clearly defined in the beginning and redefined over and over again from time to time after establishment. This does not mean that people are inherently incapable of grasping new forms of government, but it does mean that the whole experience of the island cultures to date has taught a different lesson from the one the American administration has been trying to teach about the functions of political leaders. While there is some political specialization in the traditional systems of the islanders the most outstanding difference is between chiefs with high symbolic value (for example, the Ponapean Nanmarki) and their representatives or executive officers (such as the Ponapean Naniken). In the eyes of the islanders the two kinds of chiefs do not greatly differ in the type of authority which they exercise over people; the difference is mostly that the highest chief is due more respect and cannot be approached as freely, and that many of his powers are delegated tacitly or expressly to other chiefs.

A further important conflict in the introduction of Western political institutions can be described in terms of Westernization (progress, social advancement) and dependence on foreigners versus isolation, conservatism, and relative self-government. In general the greater the changes that the administration wishes to introduce in island political institutions the more these institutions must be run or carefully supervised by educated outsiders, at least initially. The amount of training needed to get islanders to take over jobs is often underestimated. In the United States nearly everyone has gone to grammar school and knows how to read and write efficiently, and has had courses in American history which give him some understanding of our political institutions. In the Trust Territory nearly everyone lacks such an educational background.

Of course there is an increasing number of students who have graduated from the district intermediate schools and the central school at Truk but these students because of their youth lack sufficient maturity and do not command enough respect in their home communities to immediately fulfill positions of responsibility. Moreover their formal higher education has necessarily been received in boarding schools away from the homes of most and has consequently isolated the students considerably from their home communities, both physically and psychologically. Even those who learn their school lessons well are liable to lack sufficient understanding and appreciation of the ways of life of their community to fulfill positions of responsibility. And without implying criticism of the educational program, the general level of education achieved in the island schools to date is so low because of the lack of enough well-educated teachers that even graduates of the central school on Truk are far from being ideally trained to cope with many of the problems of the government of their communities in relation to the territory as a whole and the world at large.

On the other hand as far as the maintenance of a minimum standard of living and the customary activities of the communities are concerned, considerably less attention by American officials is needed than has been given so far. In fact, in general the less active intervention the less disturbance, both for good and for bad, will occur in the traditional patterns of living in the various communities, although the need for occasional correction of gross injustices and arbitration of disputes threatening an outbreak of violence would remain, and accordingly some means of acquiring reliable information about current political developments among the island communities would still be of great value.

It would be out of place in this handbook to presume to recommend either of the two alternative policies presented or any balance in between them. The concern here is to present possible alternatives which could be achieved while maintaining law and order. The main point here is that the tempting logical alternative of rapid introduction of new political institutions with little outside supervision is not practical. The result will be disorder and disillusionment.

The optimum rate of political change under various degrees of American supervision also cannot be predicted here. Much depends on the personalities of American officials and islanders involved, on changes in the price of copra and other events affecting the public mood, and on other factors whose effects can only be assessed at the time in question by on-the-spot investigators. However it would be hard to over-emphasize the general caution that any and all political innovations will for a generation or more require much American supervision if they are to be taken seriously by the islanders and not receive unexpected twists which may often defeat the original purpose.

It is to be hoped that as the educational level of the population continues to rise with time the dilemma presented above will not be so sharp, and that the islanders themselves will be able to initiate desirable political changes with little supervision. Experience with the administration of other dependent peoples, however, illustrates a danger here. Once a people becomes dependent on outside supervision both the people and the supervisors are often reluctant to change the pattern developed.

In the Trust Territory a marked difference can be seen between the peoples around the administrative centers and those on islands farther out. The Trukese and Ponapeans got into the habit of bringing problems to the German and Japanese officials for settlement, and have continued this habit to the present with American officials. The people on the outer islands however have had to continue to rely more on themselves, as they had to before there were any foreign officials.

When the American-staffed district courts began to hear suits involving disputes between islanders as to land rights there were many more land cases from the areas around the district administrative centers than elsewhere. This was to be sure partly because customary land tenure had become more confused around the administrative centers and there was consequently a greater rate of occurence of disputes about land. Also, the people around the administrative centers had greater opportunity to present their cases. Even so, the outislanders did not immediately take as much advantage of the opportunities given them as did the Trukese and Ponapeans, and this can be attributed to a greater habitual dependence on foreigners, or greater interest in using them, on the part of the people of the communities near the administrative centers.

Another group of serious problems arises in the application of written law to the island peoples. The islanders' respect for written law is less than ours. In the past life was governed largely by unwritten custom. If new rules were needed or if a custom became unduly burdensome the necessary action could be taken by personal decree of the chief, usually after sounding out public opinion, but new rules of a lasting sort were rarely necessary. The islanders accordingly find it hard to appreciate the degree to which written law is immune to alteration by any high foreign official. In fact not all foreign officials have scrupulously discouraged these notions of their personal power in the belief that the islanders will have more respect for them if the officials appear to have as much authority as possible. Moreover considerable personal authority seems to have been delegated to the district administrators and other foreign officials in the field under the previous foreign regimes.

Even officials not concerned about maintaining an appearance of great personal authority are sometimes constrained by local circumstances to suspend, in effect, impractical legislation. This supports the islanders' "common sense" notion of the personal nature of written law. For instance, in an effort to control the plant pest Lantana, the American administration promulgated a territorial law prescribing penalties for anyone failing to eradicate the plant from his land. However no reasonable attempt could be made to enforce the law on Ponape Island due to the fact that the plant was too long and firmly established on both public and private land. Even assuming that every man could be forced to clear his own land it would be rapidly reinfested by seed carried by birds from the public land. In such a case as this it is pointless for all practical purposes to argue that the American official has not suspended the law but has rather simply chosen to be derelict in enforcing it.

The volume of written law produced under the American administration to date is beyond the comprehension of most island leaders, not to mention the average citizen. It is not only that they are unable to be personally familiar with the details of the law, which would be expecting too much for a lawyer, but that they do not have enough of a general grasp of the system of laws to find provisions which they need to find. Obviously it is hard to have respect for written law whose contents one is unable to learn. (The Japanese administration eventually accumulated many more regulations for the then mandated territory than the Americans have so far. But they made no attempt to promulgate the law except occasionally for selected excerpts through interpreters. The interpreting was probably a source of error which was compounded with the misunderstanding of the audience.)

It is not impossible for an American official reading the original English to obtain a working knowledge of the volume of regulations promulgated by our administration to date. The difficulty for the islanders is greatly magnified by problems of translation and literacy even where respectable translations of the regulations into Trukese or Ponapean have been made. (Translations of some into Kusaiean have also been made but we do not know what attempts if any have been made to assess objectively the accuracy of these.) For a fuller discussion of these problems see Chapter X, Languages. Here let it suffice to state that while a majority of people on nearly all the islands are literate after a fashion in their own language, few can read easily or efficiently even a letter from a friend describing common everyday events. When one adds to the basic difficulty in reading the strain put on islander vocabulary and concepts by trying to translate American legal terminology it is little wonder that a general lack of understanding regulations of any length and complexity is to be assumed, unless a short, non-technical paraphrase and explanation of the regulation has been prepared.

Not only the wording and reading difficulties render written regulations hard to understand for the islanders. The purpose of some laws is unclear to them even when the literal sense is clear. For instance, many islanders have failed to understand why American-staffed courts refuse to honor forced confessions when these are true. They see no objection to the use of third degree methods with known criminals where the police"know" that a man is guilty, although they are aware that abuses can occur. They feel that a criminal has an obligation to confess his crime and deserves a beating if he will not. By ordering the police never to beat suspects or use other third degree methods many feel that we are coddling criminals.

This misunderstanding might have been greatly reduced by initially including a statement of the purpose of the provision along with the translations into the local languages: The object is to prevent conviction of innocent people and any assistance to criminals is an unavoidable accompaniment. A failure to understand the purpose of a regulation not only produces misunderstanding of the motives of the administration; it makes the regulation itself harder to remember and may lead the islander to feel that the translation is mistaken or that the regulation itself has limited application.

The fixed nature of written law unless repealed by proper procedure is hard for the islanders to appreciate. The confusion of law with personal decree has already been noted above. The tendency of some islanders to think of law in terms of "written custom" is also confusing. While some customs are analogous to law in that violation is considered wrong and leads to punishment or retaliation, other customs are not at all like law and are merely rules of conduct which people observe because they personally prefer to do as everyone else does. An example of the legal type of custom would be the prohibition on murder; an example of the non-legal type would be styles of dress (beyond the basic requirements of modesty).

But while with written law something is either covered by law or not, with custom there is a continuous shading from customs whose violation involves penalties to those whose violation does not. Moreover a custom at one time may be held to be very important and later be gradually abandoned. The point at which one says "this custom is no longer of legal significance" is somewhat arbitrary.

For instance, it appears that on Ponape before foreign contact any man who tried to marry a woman of his own matrilineal clan (see Chapter V, Family Relationships) was severly punished. The vast majority of Ponapeans still observe this prohibition and consider that violation is morally wrong. However, at least one marriage of two Ponapeans of the same clan has occurred recently without any penalty being imposed on the parties. This custom is evidently on the way to becoming a matter of personal preference. If contact with the outside world continues, the custom may vanish entirely within a few generations as it has already on Kusaie and Mokil.

If an islander applies the same attitude towards written law as to custom he will tend to ignore laws which he feels the general (islander) public hold to be of little importance. Thus a law against theft will be highly regarded while a law against burning over agricultural land or harvesting turtle eggs will be generally ignored — and with some safety too as long as law enforcement is in the hands of a like-minded islander police force.

Another carry over from customary attitudes toward offenses which conflicts with written law is the traditional islander tendency to regard most offenses as torts, that is, wrongs against an individual or group which may be settled by compensation, rather than as crimes, or wrongs against the community. In the section on political offices and organs, the traditional absence of specialized judges in the island governments was noted. This absence of judges is partly because in island custom the community tended to let the families of the offender and offended settle most disputes between themselves.

Formerly, for instance, if a man of one family injured a man of another family in a fight the offender's family was often ready to pay compensation to avoid retaliation. Or again if the injured man's family retaliated in kind the offender's family would often let the matter rest to avoid expanding the conflict. This put people with few relatives in an unfortunate position but they were usually able to attach themselves to some more powerful family if they wished.

Under this system the ability to get compensation for a wrong suffered without calling in the chief of the community or distant relatives was a measure of respect enjoyed by one's family in the community. It was a matter of honor, so to speak, to settle injuries without the assistance of others. This sentiment still persists so that where a criminal has made amends to the injured party and received forgiveness it is often very difficult to get any witness for a criminal prosecution. Offenders do not seem to find this type of treatment of their offense too discouraging and are prone to repeat their offense, for example, petty theft or assault with knives.

However, there is little information as to whether imprisoning the offenders would reduce the frequency of offenses as long as they are made responsible for their offense privately. Logically arguments can be advanced in favor of both sides of the proposition. Probably type of crime and individual factors would make trial and imprisonment more effective in some cases and private settlement in others. But it is not known just when one treatment is effective and when another. It can only be said that court and police experience in the United States is not the best guide for law enforcement among the islanders, even if better than none. An anthropological field study comparing a number of offenders who have been convicted legally with those who have settled their offenses privately (and are thus under pressure from their family) could provide considerable information with implications for the formulation of law enforcement policy, the optimum size of the police force, and the like.

This tendency to forgive and forget outside the law has been particularly noted on Ponape and Kusaie. On Kusaie forgiveness is usually now dependent on a public church confession but it seems likely that an old sentiment of readiness for private settlement has combined with a practice introduced by the missionaries.

Certain common offenses are regarded with mixed feelings by the islanders, mainly fighting short of murder and adultery. The Ponapeans and Trukese and probably other islanders, have a certain admiration for a man who commits these offenses although they also have recognized traditionally that apology or compensation is due to the persons injured. There is perhaps a special readiness to keep these "admired" crimes out of court.

Other common offenses are more despised, even though they may not be regarded as resulting in as serious damage. These include theft, no matter how minor (distinguished however from some appropriation of property of relatives or members of the same household), and the widespread Oceanic custom of "night crawling", that is attempting to have

194

sexual relations with a girl in her sleep. The latter offense, usually com-
mitted by inexperienced youths, has been traditionally despised because it
is considered distasteful for a girl to have relations in her sleep with someone who lacks the self-confidence to make a direct request.

The Western notion of equal rights for all before the law runs into
some conflict with islander notions of rank, although there is nothing like
the elaborate class and caste system of Yap in Truk or Ponape Districts.
The most extreme difference in status between chiefs and commoners in
the area today is found on Ponape. Probably in pre-foreign times similar
differences were found also on Kusaie but these largely disappeared with depopulation and Christianization. Status on Ponape and Kusaie appears
always to have been partly earned and never hereditary. This has prevented
the development of a rigid separation of the classes. Nevertheless the
traditional chiefs are still able to "get away" with a little more than the
average man if they are so inclined. In point of fact most of them are
reasonably responsive to the obligations of their positions and alleged abuses
by chiefs appear to be much greater in gossip (especially on Ponape) than
in reality.

A second point of conflict with the notion of equality occurs with
reference to women's rights. Ensuring women's rights was not a point with
which previous foreign governments were much concerned. The Japanese
by example showed less willingness to consider women as the equals of men
than the islanders themselves had shown.

In the absence of more specific information it is impossible to discuss the differing position of women on the various islands. It is safe to say
that women were nowhere in the area treated as lightly as they are in some
patriarchal societies elsewhere in the world. In Truk District and on
Ponape family relationships in the female line are still especially valued
and this was formerly true of Kusaie and perhaps the low islands of the
Greater Ponape area. Gladwin's psychological data collected under the
CIMA program indicate that Romonum (Trukese) women on the whole feel
more secure than the men.

Nevertheless it is the men who at least nominally control family,
political, and economic affairs and are shown special marks of respect.
For instance, a man walks ahead of his wife on the road; Ponapean women
often use the special polite vocabulary to their husbands but not the other
way around. It is probably significant that as far as is known to us the

Ponapeans do not yet have a female member in their congress, while the corresponding bodies in the Palaus and the Marshalls have had female members. The position of women on Ponape Island may prove to be a little less favorable than elsewhere in Truk and Ponape Districts.

The final point of conflict concerning the notion of equality to be mentioned here arises not out of native custom but out of the cultural differences between the islanders and their foreign administrators. Because of these differences and because of the strategic military value of the islands of Micronesia to our country it is inevitable for a time at least that Americans should occupy the key power positions in the government, and should attempt to ensure for themselves enough public respect to exercise their power effectively. It is also inevitable that those American personnel whose jobs are mostly paper work or base maintenance are largely isolated from social contact with the islanders and tend to constitute a self-centered foreign colony which draws to it even those personnel who have more contact with the islanders in their work. These facts in turn tend to produce in the minds of both governing and governed the belief that American citizens have special rights for lenient treatment before the law.

While islanders feel that Americans and other foreigners are in a superior position because of greater education and military power, this does not mean that many islanders concede that their own relative social and political inferiority is based on any inevitable or innate racial inferiority. The islanders are openly critical of anything they consider to be unjust use of power by foreign officials. While they consider it to be poor manners to criticise a man to his face except most obliquely, they are prepared to go over his head and present the criticism to the man's superior if needed. Even in the Japanese regime, which appears to have been less responsive to petitions from the islanders than the American, the recall of a Japanese district administrator on Ponape was forced by the complaints of a Ponapean leader.

A belief in special rights of foreigners started before the American regime of course. The belief in special rights of Americans is a product of attitudes developed toward the Spanish, German, and Japanese officials, traders, and missionaries as well as of the current situation. In fact islanders often express to American friends their admiration of the greater liberality of most Americans they know in dealing with the islanders socially and officially.

196

In spite of these compliments the existence of a conflict here cannot be denied. The alleviation of this conflict presents special problems which it would be out of place to discuss here with concrete material. Suffice it to note that legally the conflict is practically non-existent and it can be alleviated or aggravated primarily by the cumulative behavior of American official personnel over the years, not by further legal reform nor by mass education of the islanders.

CHAPTER IX

ARTS AND GAMES

SCULPTURE AND PAINTING

Throughout Truk and Ponape Districts there was originally little development of sculpture and painting. The low development of the plastic arts is general in Micronesia. The greatest development was probably manifested in the painted bas-reliefs on the beams of Palauan club houses. Nothing of comparable variety and complexity can be cited from the two districts considered here.

What sculpture there was was mainly wood carving. Carved objects of esthetic interest generally had some additional value besides their appearance: the large bowls carved on Truk and elsewhere were used as food containers at feasts; the hour-glass shaped drums of Ponape, Kusaie, and possibly the Mortlocks were used with dances or as signalling devices. The stool type coconut graters of Kapingamarangi and Nukuoro have also appealed to the esthetic interest of Westerners but are eminently practical in their proper function.

Objects made primarily for appearance's sake are carved masks painted black and white from the Mortlocks, a little sculpture of the human figure from Nukuoro and Trukese canoe prow heads. The Mortlock masks are made in miniature now as a tourist item. Formerly, a native carver reports, they were made much larger than life size. They represented gods or spirits and were highly stylized and with somewhat angular lines.

A little stonework was done in making food pounders from coral rock but there are no reports of stone statues anywhere in the area (except one unimpressive specimen from Kusaie of unknown age). There are no clay figurines or pots and no pottery has ever been reported from the area. The reason for the absence is unclear since pottery was known for Yap and the Marianas and trade relations were maintained with these areas. There is no suitable clay on the low islands but there appears to be some on the high islands, although this is not certain.

Little is known about the Nukuoro sculpture. It is extremely simplified, yet balanced. Apparently the human forms are no longer being produced. Trukese canoe prow heads contain profile views of two frigate birds facing each other and are painted red, black, and white. Without being told a Westerner would not know what the design was.

Almost no representative painting or drawing is reported for any island in the two districts. Crude figures are sometimes drawn on bark by Trukese in medicine and sorcery but this is not usual. Children sometimes draw in the sand or dirt in Truk and probably elsewhere but this is not a common pastime. The lack of drawing and painting is to be ascribed to historical accident rather than inherent lack of ability. School children are interested in drawing and capable of it when given materials.

Decorative painting is more common but not unusually well developed. The greatest use of colored designs on everyday tools and household objects appears to have been on Kusaie, but this has largely disappeared with acculturation. On all the islands canoes are painted decoratively, although the paint on the hull is not purely decorative as it is believed by some of the islanders to lessen the resistance of the canoe to the water as well as to preserve the wood. On Truk decorative painting (red with black trim) is applied to the wooden feast bowls. On Ponape, and possibly Nukuoro, stylized canoe paddles used in dancing were painted with small triangles of alternating colors and ornamented with fiber tufts. Dance paddles are still made and used occasionally on Ponape. On Nukuoro they appear to be obsolete.

PERSONAL ORNAMENT

A number of forms of personal ornament were originally practiced by the islanders of Truk and Ponape Districts. Most of these have fallen into disuse since foreign contact.

One of the most common forms of personal ornament throughout the two districts in ancient times and today (to judge from old stories) is the flower garland. This is short and worn on the head rather than around the neck like the Hawaiian lei. Considerable effort often goes into making these yet most of them fade in the same day that they are made. Shell head garlands are sometimes made and are more permanent.

Necklaces of shell beads, shell breast pendants, wooden combs, wrist, ankle, and arm bracelets of turtle shell are other forms of ornament which used to be made and are now obsolete.

The Trukese used to make a hole in their earlobes and distend this with plugs of leaves until it was several inches in diameter. On the strand of flesh they would hang numerous small rings carved out of coconut shell. These are no longer used but old men and women with the distended ear-lobes can still be seen.

Woven belts in Ponape and Kusaie, and in Truk District woven wrap-arounds for women and loincloths for men contained decorative designs. The Kusaiean belts, now no longer made, are noted for their quality. The Trukese woven wraparounds and loincloths were a coarser weave and the fabric appears stiffer as well. The art of weaving was practiced until re-cently in the Puluwat area of Truk District but is dying out even there in the face of the superior softness and low cost of imported cloth.

Yellow-orange body paint composed of turmeric and coconut oil was used throughout Truk District and on Ponape. Sometimes the powdered turmeric was used by itself. This was also believed to have medicinal qualities. This use of turmeric was abandoned only in the American era in the Puluwat area. Ponapean men sometimes simply rub themselves with coconut oil on the occasion of the dances.

Perfume was and still is used by both sexes throughout the area. Native perfume has a coconut oil base. The scent commonly came from flowers but on Ponape and possibly elsewhere a certain kind of dead fish was also formerly used! Hair oil, scented pomade, commercial perfumes, are all considered acceptable substitutes. Certain flowers are included in head garlands primarily or partly for their scent.

FOLKTALE

There is a great variety of folktales still to be found in Truk and Ponape Districts. A simple division of tales into those told for amusement and those which are purportedly true is universal throughout the Micronesian islands of the area (that is, all except Kapingamarangi and Nukuoro which are Polynesian), although the assignment of tales to one or the other category often seems arbitrary to Western listeners. Prominent among the tales told for amusement are tales of encounters with supernatural beings and monsters, often cannibalistic, romantic love stories, and animal stories, the latter especially for children. The subjects of the allegedly true stories are often similar to those of the tales told for amusement but also include legends of the origin of clans and the first peopling of the islands, legends of wars and the development of political units, myths about the activities of the native gods, the origin of magic and medicine, and about the formation of local landmarks.

The tales told for amusement are considered to be "lies" of little value and the principal reluctance to tell them is based on a desire not to waste the hearer's time. There is also a belief among the Trukese that telling many tales will cause the group listening to break up, and a belief among the Ponapeans that telling tales in the daytime will hasten nightfall and thus interfere with work. The Ponapean belief at least is not a very gross exaggeration. Neither of these beliefs are taken seriously enough to interfere much with the collection of tales.

Many of the tales considered to be true are treated as valuable private knowledge. The general outlines of these tales are often widely known but the full versions are often known only to a few experts. In the past these experts would not reveal their knowledge to someone outside of the family without receiving considerable payment for the instruction. At present some but not all experts are willing to divulge their knowledge to the public at large. Even those willing may desire payment.

For Ponape many of these valued tales were received by the German anthropologist Paul Hambruch in 1910. Hambruch's collection of tales is very good and by far the best published from the area but more complete and probably more accurate versions of many of his tales could still be collected from living Ponapeans. Other smaller published collections of tales are listed in the bibliography.

Folktales of native origin appear to be most highly developed in Truk Lagoon, and next on Ponape Island. On Kusaie folktales of native origin have mostly been forgotten although apparently at one time there was a large body of tales. Foreign folktales have also largely displaced native tales in the Mortlocks.

Each of the various culture areas in the two districts gives its own twist to tales found widely in the Pacific Ocean area. For instance in a common Polynesian and Melanesian tale a man goes to chop a tree down to make a canoe; each morning he finds the tree standing again in full foliage; finally he makes the appropriate offering to some nature spirit and is able to complete his work. This tale is also known in Ponape but here the cause of the inability to fell the tree once and for all is that the canoe-maker has failed to apologize for his poor work to an insignificant looking passerby who was really a supernatural being. The emphasis on the need for speaking modestly is characteristically Ponapean.

Stories resembling part of the Oedipus myth of Greece are found in the Pacific area: a man orders his wife to kill any boy baby born, fearing that the son will be dangerous to him; the wife bears a boy baby which is secretly kept alive and later returns to supplant his father. In a Trukese version the hero is not the man's own son but rather his sister's son. The man's sister's son is his matrilineal successor. It would appear that much of the suppressed tension which normally exists between father and son in societies where the son is the father's heir is transferred to the maternal uncle-nephew relationship when a man's sister's son is in line to succeed to important rights of the man, as in Truk.

The proportion of "amusement" tales to the total body of tales appears to be especially high in Truk Lagoon. The proportion of allegedly true tales appears to be higher on Ponape. Among these Ponapeans are especially fond of tales of oppressive chiefs who meet retribution for their misdeeds, also of tales which explain the origin of their more elaborate political system. Trukese tales are often quite lengthy and contain many incidents, some of which are rather loosely connected. Ponapean tales tend to be shorter and more tightly organized.

As in our own culture a distinction is made between tales which it is suitable for children to hear and those which it is not. The line between the two is not the same as in our culture however and the original versions of Trukese and Ponapean children's tales sometimes contain references to bodily functions which would not be permitted in tales for American children.

Both children's and adults folktales contain much violence, as do folktales in most cultures the world over. Ponapean tales are perhaps more violent than Trukese. In one popular Ponapean tale a king sets fire to the house of his mother-in-law (who happens to be a monstrous lizard); his wife jumps into the flames to die with her mother, and the king jumps to join his wife. In another, one chief sends a man and his son to get some bananas from another chief; the second chief secretly wraps up the corpse of a pregnant woman instead; when the boy reaches into the basket for a banana as they are paddling home he grabs the breast of the corpse instead; the corpse arises to devour him but the father throws it into the water; in revenge for this trick the first chief sends a school of sting rays which lure the second chief out of his house at night and then whip him to pieces with their tails.

Not all stories are as gruesome as these but at least these should serve to illustrate the point that there is no possibility of protecting islander children from notions of violence by carefully screening English reading material or movies. They will get the violence in the home anyway; although the specific techniques of violence will often be different.

INSTRUMENTAL MUSIC

Instrumental music was poorly developed in Truk and Ponape Districts, but the islanders were and still are very fond of singing. The same may be said of Micronesia in general.

The few native musical instruments are now obsolete or nearly so and are replaced by the guitar, harmonica, and ukulele. Formerly the nose flute was a popular instrument in Truk Lagoon and the Mortlocks and is also reported for Ponape. In Truk at least it was used mainly by young men serenading their girl friends and calling them forth to rendezvous. As such it was a target for missionary prohibition, although perhaps a more important factor in its disappearance was the great popularity of Western music and introduced instruments. There is hardly anyone left, if anyone at all, who knows how to play the nose flute. On Kusaie the nose flute is said to have been absent but panpipes were present (several hollow reed whistles of varying length tied together).

Hourglass shaped wooden drums with fishskin heads are reported for Ponape, Mokil, Nukuoro, and the Mortlocks. On Kusaie drums were imported from the Marshalls for a Marshallese dance but not used otherwise. All the old drums have apparently been purchased by foreign collectors and new ones are no longer made. Drums were formerly important as signalling devices on Ponape, and were also used with dances. Drums were not found in Truk proper as far as is known, nor west of Truk in Micronesia.

Large sea shells are blown as trumpets for signalling throughout the South Seas. These can hardly be called musical instruments as they possess only one note and do not appear to be combined with singing or other musical instruments.

Small dance sticks are used to mark rhythm on Ponape in women's dances. The sticks are either hit against each other or against a board laid on the women's laps. Large staffs or dance sticks are used as percussive instruments in some men's dances in the Mortlocks and on Pingelap. The movements made with these sticks are as important as the noise made with them.

On Ponape the stone slabs used for pounding the kava root (for beverage) are specially selected for their bell-like tone. While kava is being pounded the pounders take turns pounding rhythms on the edge of the stone slab. When a batch of kava is finished the pounders all unite in a special rhythm. The Kusaiean "clinkstones", now no longer used, appear to have been similar.

A few islanders today know how to play other Western instruments besides the common guitar, harmonica, and ukulele. Since Japanese times Western-style bands have been organized sporadically on Ponape. Missionaries have introduced a few reed organs but these are not widely available. The main obstacle to wider use of a greater variety of Western instruments is financial as a large number of the islanders are musically inclined.

SONGS AND CHANTS

The islanders originally had a rich body of traditional songs but most of the native-style songs are now remembered only by old people or not at all.

Native songs had a range of only a few notes, sometimes only two, and complexity was introduced by rhythm and syncopations in the shift from one note to the other. It is surprising how subtle and difficult a two note song can be to a Westerner used to less complex rhythms and more regular tone shifts.

The range of notes in surviving native songs tends to be greater in Truk than in Ponape. This may be connected with the greater use there of the nose flute which operated partly by harmonics, like the bugle.

A form of harmony was used in some dance songs on Ponape and perhaps elsewhere. This sounded strange to Western ears as it involved the use of seconds, that is, the parts kept one full tone apart (or an octave intervened giving much the same effect).

Rhythm in most songs was highly complex although an underlying one-two beat was usually present. It was the basic duple rhythm which the percussion instruments and dance movements mostly marked.

The content of traditional island songs falls into several categories: love songs, work songs, dance songs, feast songs, children's game songs, and lullabies may be mentioned.

Old love songs are no longer in use as far as is known although they are remembered by some old Trukese and Ponapeans. Modern love songs with Western style music both original and borrowed, preserve many of the phrases of the old songs but are generally much shorter. There is no compulsion felt to use only antique wording in modern love songs. Any phrase or word a little out of the ordinary will do and Japanese and English words are also freely introduced to help express the unique sentiments of the composers.

Work songs are reported for Kusaie and Truk and were probably general. They were used especially in dragging out and raising large timbers, launching large canoes, and the like. Like Western sea chanteys these work songs had a solo part interrupted by shouts in which all the workers joined in and pulled or pushed. The solo part appears to have been regarded as the private possession of the soloist or his family.

A wide variety of dance songs formerly existed in Truk and Ponape Districts. Dances and songs used to be spread from island to island by sailing canoe voyagers. Consequently popular dance songs are still spreading throughout the area but not as fast as formerly since dancing has been severely discouraged by some missionaries. Young Trukese in 1950 knew mostly dance songs learned from Nauruans imported by the Japanese in World War II. Puluwat informants say that many of the dance songs current in the Puluwat area until the beginning of the American era originated on other islands with which they had trade connections and the Puluwat people did not understand many of the words.

Other traditional dance songs were peculiar to one island and commemorated important myths and semihistorical events. The language of these songs is highly metaphorical and allusive and the listener must know the story to which the song refers to understand it. Songs of this type are best preserved on Ponape.

Feast songs on Ponape and Truk were allied to both dance and work songs and celebrated the amount of food a family or section was providing for a feast or the difficulty of providing the food. Some were sung as the large yams (on Ponape) or on Truk bowls of pounded breadfruit were being carried into the feast house.

The words of many of the feast, dance, and work songs in Truk District, on Ponape and evidently on Kusaie as well have a poetic meter which is independent of the rhythm of the tunes. Most of the lines contain five or seven syllables and words sometimes are altered and extra vowels added to fit the poetic meter.

There are on Truk especially and also on Ponape a large number of poems or chants which do not have associated melodies. Like some of the dance songs, these commemorate legendary events in the island history. Unlike the dance songs these poems are considered to be privately owned knowledge and are recited publicly only on special occasions and then often in fragments.

The Mortlock men's stick dance "songs" also lack any associated times, and have a poetic meter.

Traditional lullabies and songs of children's games are of simple tunes and rhythms. However, the words are archaic and hard to understand.

Hymn singing is very popular now among the people of all the communities in Truk and Ponape Districts. Many popular Western hymns have been translated into the island languages and some new hymns have been specially composed by islanders. Singing in four part harmony is common and even arrangements in eight parts are sometimes performed. The singing of the Mortlock Islanders is especially fine by Western standards.

Hymns are sung at feast, political meetings, and other non-religious occasions as well as in church. On informal occasions some popular Japanese and American songs are also sung. Both hymns and foreign secular

206

songs are sometimes sung to the accompaniment of guitar, harmonica, or ukulele, although these instruments are not usually used with hymns on formal occasions.

DANCING

Formerly a wide variety of dances was found in the two districts as elsewhere in Micronesia but on most islands these have been repressed by missionaries and are no longer practiced. The missionaries opposed dancing on the grounds that it stimulated extra-marital affairs. This criticism has some justice for some of the dances, especially in Truk District, where dances were often held just to give young people a chance to show themselves off to the other sex and where dance songs sometimes celebrated adulterous love affairs. Even these dances did not involve mixing of the sexes in the fashion of Western ballroom dancing although lines of men and women sometimes danced opposite each other.

In Truk District new dances were sometimes believed to be ordained by the gods or ancestral spirits for their pleasure. The gods would announce their desires and give detailed instructions for performance of the dance in dreams or via spirit mediums. This presented another incompatibility between dancing and Christianity. Not all missionaries have regarded all native dancing as incompatible with Christianity. The Mortlock stick dances were considered to be a sort of military or athletic training for men and boys and have persisted to the present. In these men take large staffs and leap about, striking the sticks sharply together in fixed patterns. When performed at top speed it is a considerable gymnastic exercise. A similar dance is also performed by Pingelap men. Similar dances are known in Western Micronesia.

On Ponape some of the missionaries, especially American Catholic, have been tolerant of traditional group dances which celebrate legendary events in the island's history. Ponapean group dances are remarkable for their seemingly loose and relaxed but actually very precisely controlled movements.

On Ponape several different dances are sometimes performed to the same song. Men have standing dances with and without decorated stylized dance paddles which they flash and turn. Women have sitting dances with and without small dance sticks which they strike against each other or against a board resting on their laps.

207

Ponapean traditional dances now performed are mainly stationary and emphasize hand and head movements. In the standing dances the dancers also stamp their feet with percussive effect but do not move from one place to another.

The dances performed in the Puluwat area until recently survived largely because of the rarity of missionaries there. In the men's dances the men leap about vigorously, clap the hollow of their elbow and other parts of their body with percussive effect, and emit loud shouts from time to time. The unrestrained nature of these dances was in great contrast to the Ponapean dances.

The dances of the two Polynesian atolls of Kapingamarangi and Nukuoro are apparently no longer performed for religious reasons although probably still remembered by the older people. A circle dance is reported for Kapingamarangi and the use of dance paddles for Nukuoro but details are lacking.

A "marching dance", which is a product of acculturation, is known on most of the islands of any size in Truk and Ponape Districts. A similar dance is known as far west as Palau. The men dress up in white trousers and shirts and march onto a field or stage where they perform close order drill with Japanese or American commands to the accompaniment of a harmonica.

Some Western ballroom dancing of a sort is known from movies and from American military men. There is a strong belief among the island leaders that ballroom dancing is immoral for Micronesians and ballroom dancing is a controversial subject when it is proposed or performed. By traditional Carolinian standards of behavior, ballroom dancing is immoral as is any public display of affection between the sexes. (However, this ban on public display of affection between the sexes should not be taken to imply a feeling of embarrassment or restriction extending to private hetero-sexual relations.)

SPORTS

A few traditional island sports are practiced, including foot races, canoe races, toy canoe sailing (on Truk), dart throwing (on Ponape), and wrestling. Probably all of these are practiced less frequently than in former times, partly because introduced sports have replaced them and

partly because organized amusements have tended to lapse with acculturation. Of introduced sports the most popular in the communities around the
district administrative centers is baseball which was introduced by the Japanese. Other introduced sports include Japanese wrestling (sumo), many
Western track events, and a kickball game from the Marshalls.

Of traditional sports the most elaborate is canoe racing. Both sailing and paddling canoe races were held until Japanese times on a number
of the islands. Special racing canoes were constructed for these. As far
as is known no racing canoes have been constructed during the American
period but ordinary canoes have been raced occasionally on important holi-
days on Ponape, Mokil, Lukunor, and no doubt other islands.

The sailing of toy canoes is a pastime of Trukese men, although
only men of certain communities in Truk Lagoon have practiced it since
World War II. Most of the sailing does not take the form of races. En-
thusiasts seem to be comparable to Americans whose hobby is flying model
airplanes. Formerly the sailing of toy canoes sometimes had ritual connections with the breadfruit crop. Apparently it was also done for amusement in olden times and is done solely for amusement now.

Foot races appear to have been considered a child's game in pre-
foreign times. On Ponape foot races Western style are now important in
the annual track meet.

Dart throwing is fairly popular on Ponape both among children and
adults. Cane darts are bounced off a small mound of hard-packed earth.
The object is to see who can make his dart go farthest. This game is also
known farther east in the Pacific in parts of Polynesia.

A game of kickball introduced from the Marshalls via Kusaie is
popular among the older boys of school age. An imported ball is usually
used. The players form a circle, clap hands rhythmically and try to keep
the ball from touching the ground.

Native wrestling was formerly taught to island youths as a part of
their military training. As such it was practiced mostly among relatives or
very close friends. For competitive wrestling in track events the Japanese
sumo has been very popular on Ponape. The object here is merely to make
the opponent step out of the ring. This is more peaceful than island wrestling. Yet on at least one occasion it has given rise to a small riot among
sympathetic spectators.

Baseball, the most popular introduced sport, is especially popular on the high islands which have room enough for a field. Low islanders also enjoy the game but some have been reluctant to use community funds to buy the necessary plots of land which would form a good ball field. Hardball is played almost exclusively.

CHAPTER X

LANGUAGES

All languages in the Truk and Ponape Districts belong to branches of the Malayo-Polynesian family. Malayo-Polynesian languages are spoken in most of the islands of the Pacific as far north as Hawaii. They are also found in Madagascar off the coast of Africa. The main areas in the Pacific where unrelated languages are spoken are New Guinea, except for the northern and eastern coasts, Australia, Japan, and the islands of the North Pacific.

In the past scholars have divided the Malayo-Polynesian languages into several great branches on a geographic basis: Indonesian, Melanesian, Polynesian, and Micronesian. Indonesian includes roughly those languages spoken by the inhabitants of Malaya, Indonesia, and the Philippines; Melanesian, roughly those languages spoken in the arc of islands from New Britain and north and east New Guinea down south to New Caledonia; Polynesian is spoken mostly in a triangle formed by Hawaii in the north, New Zealand in the south and Easter Island (2,000 miles west of South America) in the east; and Micronesian languages are spoken mostly by the inhabitants of the U.S. administered Trust Territory and the British administered Gilbert Islands.

Recently, however, this classification has been undergoing revision by linguists. The unity of the Micronesian group within the Malayo-Polynesian family is no longer admitted. The Western Micronesian languages (Yapese, Palauan, and Chamorro) are said to be more closely related to some Filipino languages than to languages spoken farther east in Micronesia. It is clear at any rate that the languages of Truk and Ponape form a single related group which might be termed Nuclear Micronesian. The languages of the low islands between Truk and Yap and those southwest of Palau all fall in this group also. Marshallese, Kusaiean, and Gilbertese may also be more divergent members of this group but a judgment on the relations of these languages by comparative linguists on the basis of a full modern description of them is not yet available. The languages of the two low islands of Kapingamarangi and Nukuoro are Polynesian and thus more closely related to Hawaiian, Tahitian, Samoan, and so forth, than to any of the other languages in Micronesia.

In the Truk District the Truk Lagoon dialects are widely understood by adult men on the outer islands. In Ponape District Ponapean dialects are widely understood on the low islands, even including the two Polynesian atolls, by adult men and in some cases women and fairly small children as well. On the high island of Kusaie, Ponapean is less widely understood and is not as useful for talking with the local people. The spread of Trukese and Ponapean as second languages has been encouraged since foreign rule began by the fact that the two high island groups have been centers of trade, government, education, and mission activity. This is true even though Protestant activity in the Truk District began first in the Mortlocks and then spread to Truk proper, the Truk stations becoming more prominent later. Before foreign rule as well, the two languages were evidently spread by sailing canoe voyages between the high and low islands for trade and social visiting. Some of the out-island dialects of Trukese have been further spread by migration. People from the islands to the north of Truk migrated to Saipan in the Spanish period and Mortlockese were settled on Ponape by the Germans after the Jokaj rebellion.

The influence of European and Oriental languages on Carolinian languages has not yet been very great, in spite of statements sometimes heard to the contrary. There are commonly used words of American, Japanese, German, or Spanish origin for some introduced plants, animals, trade goods, and for a few foreign political and religious concepts. English words come from two periods: from the whalers and missionaries of the nineteenth century and from the contemporary American occupation of the islands. These foreign words are nearly all additions to the native vocabulary rather than replacements. And sometimes a native term was used for a foreign object instead of a foreign one. Trukese, Ponapean, and Kusaiean all refer to guns by native words for bow-and-arrow, and today many islanders do not know that their ancestors had bows. The degree of foreign influence on the other languages of Micronesia with the exception of Chamorro seems to be about the same as on those of Truk and Ponape Districts. Chamorro, the language of the Marianas, took over many words from Spanish and from Filipino languages during the long Spanish regime on Guam.

The sounds of the languages of Truk and Ponape Districts are somewhat different from English but not too hard to pronounce as sounds of languages of the world go. Some sound distinctions which we make in English such as b and p, k and hard g, make no difference in the meaning of Nuclear Micronesian languages. What is psychologically the same sound in the local languages may sound sometimes like one and sometimes like another sound to a European. On the other hand some distinctions which we do not notice in English make a difference in the meaning of words in the Micronesian languages. The most important of these differences is the difference between long and short sounds, both vowels and consonants. In Ponapean, for instance, where a long vowel is indicated by an h following the vowel, pahpa means "father" or "papa" while papah means "to serve". Other differences in vowel quality and in pronunciation of consonants are probably best learned by imitation in the field.

It is advisable for a foreigner making a serious attempt to learn one of the languages to rely as much as possible on listening to islanders speak and to rely very little on written or printed material. While a majority of Trukese and Ponapeans are literate in their own languages, as of this date there are too few really fluent enough in reading and writing their own language to enable much local written literature to have grown up. There are many translations from European languages into the native languages prepared by the government and missions but some of these contain atrocious errors. Few of even the most skillful could claim to illustrate typical native style and constructions because the translators are generally (and properly) motivated by accuracy first and literary quality second.

The spelling in documents printed to date in island languages varies in quality considerably, but because of dialectic variations from village to village on the large islands it is safe to say that no printed document is likely to reflect with accuracy all the meaningful sounds ("phonemes" in linguistic terminology) that any particular speaker would use. Different spelling systems for both Truk and Ponape were originally devised by missionaries of different nationalities: American, Spanish, and German. None of these was entirely adequate in its initial form. The originators tended to try to distinguish sound differences meaningful in their European languages (as k and g) while at the same time failing to distinguish some differences important in the native languages which were lacking in their own languages (as some of the vowel sounds or p and pw, m and mw in some positions).

Native users of these spelling systems inevitably failed to understand

213

the unnecessary distinctions and tended to equate letters such as k̲ and g̲, t̲ and d̲, p̲ and b̲ and some of the vowels as free alternants. They also have tended to merge the spelling systems of different foreign origins. This has increased even more the ambiguities and latitude in native spelling. The inadequate spelling systems evidently explain why most islanders find reading and writing in their own languages so laborious and uncertain. Many individuals have several ways of spelling their own names for instance.

Postwar linguistic studies in Truk and Ponape have provided the scientific knowledge on which a practical standard spelling system for both languages could be worked out. The standard spelling system now in use on Ponape comes reasonably close to being as simple and accurate as possible. The spelling used in Elbert's Trukese Dictionary with the addition of a way of showing long vowels (such as writing the vowel twice) would be an equally effective system for Trukese but as of this date Truk appears to be behind Ponape in the adoption of a psychologically representative spelling. The particular symbols used are not so important as simply ensuring that there is one and only one symbol for each meaningful sound in the language, and that refinements of sound which make no difference in the meaning of words are ignored.

Another disadvantage of relying on written material for learning the language is that in normal speech the end of one word often fuses or elides with the beginning of another and the sounds of one or both change at the point of fusion. These changes are especially noticeable in Trukese but are also found in Ponapean and other languages. Such changes have rarely been indicated in native writing but one cannot hope to ever be able to listen in on a meeting or an ordinary conversation without becoming familiar with these changes through a good deal of listening to the islanders talk at normal speed. It is a good idea to insist that the islander from whom one is learning the local language should always speak at normal speed. He should simplify things by cutting down vocabulary and sentence length but not by an exaggeratedly clear and slow pronunciation.

The grammar of Nuclear Micronesian languages is fairly simple. Nouns have no special form for plural number. Number is indicated by numerals, demonstratives (such as "this", "that", "those") or associated pronouns, which do have number. There are no case endings as in Latin or German but many of the common nouns have special endings to indicate possession (for example, Ponapean saling̲: ear; salingei̲: my ear). There are several slightly different ways which different words have of forming these endings which need to be memorized.

In addition to the possessive endings, all nouns have a special ending in some vowel plus n (-en and -in are very frequent) which is usually best translated as "of" (for example, Ponapean saling: ear; kidi: dog; salingen kidi: ear of dog, dog's ear). This ending is not the same as the genitive case in English and other European languages. In the example above ("dog's ear") the genitive ending in English ('s) is attached to "dog". In the island languages the special ending is attached to "ear". The foreigners who devised Ponapean and Trukese writing often wrote this ending as a separate word, like "of" in English. This is misleading since in slow speech or when an islander stops to reconsider the next word the pause occurs after the -en, not before. Moreover in Trukese, Ponapean, and related languages when either the possessive or "of" endings are added to a noun, the original vowel of the noun often changes or is shortened as well. This is something like the changes in vowels of verbs in English to indicate tense (such as, sing, sang, sung). A common change is a to e (for example, Ponapean mahs: eye; mes-ei: my eye; mes-en: eye of; the vowel here is shortened as well as changed).

One unusual feature of these languages for English speakers is the different numerical classifiers usually used in giving numbers of different kinds of things. There is a general series (Ponapean ehu, riau, siluh, etc. ; Trukese eeu, ruwu, ünülngat, etc. ; English one, two, three, etc.) which can be used for anything in an emergency and be understood, but in normal correct speech long objects are counted with one special series, flat objects with another, live animals with another, and so on. Ponapean also has special series for counting some kinds of feast food. There are probably several dozen of these series in each language but only about five of them are of great importance.

Many nouns do not have special possessive endings. With these a separate possessive word is used as in English ("my", "his", "our", etc.). As with numerals there are series of possessive classifiers which are used with different classes of things; a general series, another with food, another with children and tools, and so forth. The two kinds of classifiers group things under different principles: the possessive classifiers group on the basis of use while the numerical classifiers group on the basis of shape or nature. In Ponapean there is also a special set of possessive classifiers used to refer to things belonging to high chiefs.

The pronoun systems of the languages make finer distinctions than modern English. There is a distinct singular form for all persons including second (like old English "thou"). On the other hand there is no distinction of gender in the third person: one word is used for "he", "she", and "it". In the first person plural (we, us) there is an important distinction between exclusive (they and I) and inclusive (you and I). Ponapean proper has three forms of the second person singular which could be called familiar, polite, and honorific. The honorific is used in speaking to the highest chiefs and a special vocabulary goes with it. The polite form is commonly used between adults who come from different places or toward older people. The familiar form is used toward children or with intimate friends. These distinctions of intimacy are not found in the out-island dialects of Ponapean nor in any of the Trukese dialects but similar distinctions are reported for Kusaiean.

Ponapean, Kusaiean, and the Polynesian dialects also have special forms of pronouns to refer to two people only ("we two", "you two", "they two") in addition to plural and singular forms. Kusaiean also has forms for three people. Trukese, like English, has only singular and plural.

Verbs have special endings to indicate direction of motion such as "up", "down", "out", "in". There is no distinct past tense in island languages; the general form of the verb is used for both past and present. The Ponapean verb ending -er is sometimes incorrectly said to mean past tense. Actually it is more like what we call a perfect tense: instead of corresponding to "he did" it corresponds to "he has done" or "he had done (already")".

Other endings on verbs are pronoun object endings (corresponding to English "me", "us", "him", "her", etc.). These are fused closely to the verb instead of being independent words as in English. In fact, where they are combined with the directional endings, the pronoun object endings come first.

In both Trukese and Ponapean negatives and an immediate, general, and subsequent future tense (and a few other things) are indicated by particles between the subject and the verb. A doubling of the first syllable of a verb indicates a progressive aspect: as in English "he is doing" "he was doing". Passive forms of verbs ("it is done") are uncommon in either language but are found for some Ponapean verbs. In general Nuclear Micronesian interpreters have trouble with passive constructions and they should be avoided in English speeches and documents for translation.

Word order in the island languages is much as in English. The main exceptions are with adjective-like words, which sometimes come after the noun instead of before as in English. The order of some kinds of clauses is a little more restricted than in English. In Trukese and Ponapean clauses starting with "because", "since", or "for", nearly always follow the main clause (for example, "John went fishing since the fish were running", not "Because the fish were running, John went fishing."). Quotations, direct or indirect, nearly always follow the main clause. (For example, "John said, 'I want to go fishing'" not " 'I want to go fishing,' said John."). "If" clauses are nearly always put before the main clause. Adherence to this order in preparing things in English for translation will facilitate translation.

It is sometimes said that primitive languages have a small number of words. While it is true that a language restricted to any small community will lack many technical terms because of the lack of specialists there is little reason to believe that the average islander has a speaking knowledge of fewer words than the average American. Elbert's Trukese Dictionary, which does not claim to be complete, has about five thousand major entries and a number of additional compounds. The student, then, will not lack a problem in memorizing words.

At the same time the areas of meaning covered by words in the island languages do not closely correspond to those in English. To give an obvious example a legal term such as "bail" may have to be translated in an island language by a phrase meaning "money which takes the place of the person under accusation". But we on the other hand will have to learn separate island words for "very young coconut", "drinking coconut", and "ripe coconut", or "hermit crab", "mangrove crab", "coconut crab", and so on, since the island languages have no single general word for "coconut" or "crab".

This difference in coverage of meaning areas extends even to parts of speech. The island languages have many nouns and verbs but few adjectives and adverbs and do not use adjectives and adverbs much. The relative rareness of adjectives and adverbs is connected with the preciseness of many of the nouns and verbs. If the nouns and verbs are precise enough ("ripe-coconut", "mangrove-crab") they do not need to be qualified.

In English adjectives are sometimes employed redundantly for stylistic vividness ("the blue sea", "the green forest"; what other color would they be under normal lighting?). The island languages use this

217

device much less frequently. Persons preparing speeches or textbooks in English for translation would do well to keep this fact in mind.

CHAPTER XI

MEDICINE

This chapter discusses the traditional beliefs and practices of the islanders concerning disease and how this affects acceptance of Western medicine.

CAUSE OF DISEASE

Traditionally the islanders have believed that most disease comes from a number of supernatural sources. These include sorcery, supernatural punishment, and more or less unprovoked attacks by spirits. Information on these beliefs is best for Ponape Island and Truk Lagoon although similar beliefs are probably held throughout the area with minor variations.

In some parts of the world actual sorcery is not practiced as far as outside observers can tell. The belief in sorcery is kept alive solely by unjust suspicions whenever someone falls victim to disease or an unusual accident. In the Eastern Carolines suspicions of sorcery are also undoubtedly often unfounded. Nevertheless it appears that sorcery was formerly practiced fairly frequently and that the traditional techniques are still fairly widely known and sometimes practiced.

Sorcery is thought to be able to inflict harm on property as well as persons. On Ponape, for instance it is believed that sorcery can cause land to be infertile or interfere with the sound construction of a building. On Truk it is believed that sorcery can make canoe hulls crack and make the waves wash away the shores of a victim's property.

Some common means of sorcery are by the use of charmed objects which are hidden around the victim's house and by reciting magical curses. On Ponape a common form is alleged to be sending fire from a charmed burning coconut frond. Individuals claim they have seen the fire traveling from the sorcerer's place to the victim's house. Ponapeans believe that an especially potent form of sorcery can be conducted using a drop of blood of a victim which may be obtained either by a knife fight or when the victim has some accident which breaks the skin. Other things connected with a victim such as hair, clothing, chewed sugar cane, and excreta are thought to be used by sorcerers on occasion. However none of the people in the Truk and Ponape Districts appear to manifest the obsessive care in hiding these objects from potential sorcerers that is found in some primitive societies.

On Truk sorcerers throw charmed pebbles on the roof of their victim's house. Also on Truk if a sorcerer and his victim eat certain kinds of food together (chicken or certain fish) the sorcerer himself may then afterwards consume a special medicine and this is thought to make the other man sick. Spells or curses are also used with food on Ponape and Truk.

The possibility that actual poisonous substance may sometimes be introduced into the victim's food should not be ignored. This practice has not been specifically reported from the Eastern Carolines but it is said to occur elsewhere in the Pacific Ocean area. This might well be classified as sorcery by the islanders but not by Western standards.

There are several common occasions thought to provoke sorcery. Any rich or prominent man is thought to be especially liable to sorcery by envious rivals. On Ponape sorcery is allegedly used against rivals in the competition for the honorary titles given by the chiefs. In former times sorcery was used in war; now it is said to be used at important ball games and athletic events. Both sorcery and love magic may be employed on the rival and the loved one respectively in love triangles. A property owner may use sorcery or employ a sorcerer to afflict a thief. Especially on Truk, parties in land disputes, who are often related, are alleged to use sorcery against each other at times.

Another supernatural source of disease is punishment by spirits or gods, including now the Christian God, for disrespect, prohibited acts and violations of taboos. This cause appears to be more commonly invoked on Ponape than Truk. On Ponape it is believed by many that supernatural punishment will fall on persons who are disrespectful to the traditional chiefs, or who keep to themselves turtles and other food which is supposed to be shared with the chiefs according to custom. The chiefs themselves do not have to know about the act of disrespect. Their clan or ancestral spirits will take care of this automatically without being invoked according to traditional belief. Authority within the family has also been partly maintained by a belief that the spirits of deceased ancestors can detect and punish violations.

In addition to purposeful punishment by spirits it is believed that there are a number of malevolent spirits which are more or less waiting for an opportunity to cause sickness to people regardless of how good they may be. In Truk the sea and shore is a popular haunt of such spirits. In Ponape the extensive mangrove swamps and mountain forests are alleged to be haunts of such spirits.

Especially on Ponape certain places are said to cause various diseases if one approaches them without the proper magical precautions which are valued secrets of a few specialists, if remembered at all now. Most of these places are ruins of pre-Christian tombs and sacred places. Probably it was originally believed that these places were guarded by spirits or gods but, if so, the belief is less explicit now.

On Ponape, totem fish, birds, animals were associated with many of the matrilineal clans (see Chapter V, Family Relationships). It was believed to be wrong and dangerous for a member of a clan or a child of a man of the clan to eat the clan totem animal. It was also disrespectful for anyone to eat the totem animal of someone else's clan in his presence. Almost everyone respects the taboo on eating or harming the totem animals of some powerful clans, such as the fresh-water eel, which is the totem of the Lasialap clan, the senior clan of the petty state of U. These food taboos are still observed by many Ponapeans. Others who have tried violating them as during the food shortage of the war, have experienced stomach sickness and skin trouble, evidently psychogenic.

On Truk there are also some suggestions of clan totem animals but such animals are not of much importance as a cause of disease. However it is believed that fish or other animals are connected with certain types of medicine. The specialists knowing such medicine, members of his lineage, his children, and patients who once undergo treatment with such medicine are all believed to be in a special relation to the fish or animal and cannot eat it (except in some cases the specialist himself).

The islanders also recognize the existence of some common, mild or chronic diseases, especially those introduced by foreigners, which are not attributed to any supernatural agency. Probably the early stages of yaws, which used to affect almost every child before controlled by American penicillin, are an example of an indigenous disease not attributed to any supernatural cause. Traditionally the islanders appear to have had no explanation for these diseases. Now most of them give more or less credence to Western explanations involving germs and other parasites.

It is confusing to attempt to classify the symptoms produced by the various causes listed above. Some of the causes are supposed to have specific results. Thus one kind of sorcery produces eye infection and blindness, another kind produces vomiting of blood, another crippling, and so forth. If members of a certain Ponapean clan eat their totem fish, which has a speckled skin, it is believed that in addition to other symptoms their own skin will become similarly speckled. Certain forms of temporary psychosis are considered to be the result of possession by a demon.

But a wide variety of symptoms is allegedly produced by some other kinds of sorcery and by the action of spirits. And at the same time a single constellation of symptoms is often attributed to different causes in different individuals. This is not at all unreasonable if one accepts the premise that spirits are involved: why should a spirit always punish or express aggression in the same way?

Actually diagnosis involves both forms of divination and observance of symptoms. Unless the symptoms fit some stereotype very closely, divination or simply an attempt to recall recent offenses are usually more important in determining the cause of the disease. The medicine therefore is at times more adapted to divination or to the patient's feelings of guilt than to the physical symptoms.

FORMS OF TREATMENT

The most common forms of treatment involve the use of herbs and other natural products of land and sea. Herbs may be made into packets with which the curer strokes the patient. Following this the herbs are usually boiled in water, the liquid from a drinking coconut or expressed coconut cream. The infusion is then drunk by the patient. Liquid squeezed from the packets may be applied to external sores or in sore eyes. Herb poultices are also sometimes used for sores.

The Truk herbal infusions may be poured on heated rocks to produce steam. The patient is held over this and the whole covered with a blanket or tarpaulin. The steaming may be of value in colds but the rationale of the treatment so far as there is one appears to be to scare away the spirit by the objectionable (to the spirit) scent of the steaming infusion.

Where herbs or other small objects are used the medicine is supposed to be carefully disposed of after treatment. In Truk this usually means sinking it in a deep part of the lagoon. In Ponape, it may also be burned in a fire, put in flowing fresh water, or buried depending on the type of medicine.

Massage is commonly used, especially in Truk District. Masseurs use coconut oil which usually contains herbs which themselves are supposed to be of medicinal value. It is unclear how much value is attributed by the islanders to the physical effects of the massage and how much to the medicinal oil. At any rate skilled island masseurs appear to help patients in pain to relax effectively.

Little traditional surgery is reported. Some masseurs also practice bone setting. A little blood letting is reported for bruises but blood letting is not apparently believed to have general curative powers. The most comlicated surgery practiced was probably the removal of testicles. It is reported that on Puluwat and Ponape men would remove testicles affected with elephantiasis. The operation may have been known more widely. On Ponape it was customary until German times for young men to remove one testicle before marriage as a sign of bravery. This custom is now extinct but some of the older men now alive underwent it.

The traditional equivalents of preventive medicine are also found in the area. Packets of herbs are prepared to hang in one's house, or wear around one's neck. Other charmed objects may be buried under one's door. Spells are said over small bracelets or strings which are then worn on the wrist.

With sorcery it is believed that the cure of the victim may mean the death of the sorcerer. Certain magical practices are believed to return the sorcery to its originator and numerous deaths are attributed to this practice. Some people express the opinion that it is un-Christian to send back sorcery and that anyway God will punish the sorcerer eventually. The Trukese appear to believe that knowledge of sorcery is dangerous to its possessor and is especially dangerous if used, even if not sent back. For this reason old people who know they will die in a few years anyway are thought

223

to be more interested in sorcery.

COMPARISON OF WESTERN AND ISLAND MEDICINE

To a certain extent Western and island medicine are complementary. Western medicine is especially suited for severe infections and other acute disorders, while traditional medicine is especially suited for complaints of psychological origin and minor infectious diseases where the principal pre-scription of a Western doctor would be rest. To be sure, island medicine is not always in itself restful but the very fact that it is being performed relieves anxiety and is a concrete sign that the patient's family is supporting him (by arranging for the visit of the curer and his compensation). This reassurance is perhaps mainly what many patients are seeking. Some individuals are occasionally afflicted with psychotic episodes which are often relieved following traditional treatment designed to drive away spirits. One wonders whether economically practical forms of psychotherapy could do as much for these people.

However, Western and island medicine do not entirely complement one another. On the one hand traditional medicine is fairly often used to attempt cure of conditions for which Western techniques seem clearly super-ior such as tuberculosis, gonorrhea, and tetanus. On the other hand it is likely that some of the techniques of traditional medicine are physically therapeutic and duplicate or overlap Western medicine. Just which these are cannot be told in detail without a fuller study. Some of the local med-icines for control of diarrhea and astringents for control of bleeding may be of value, for instance. Collection by the local anthropologists of informa-tion on herbs used by islanders in medicine with evaluation by the district medical officers of case histories involving traditional medical treatment might eventually enable the American administration to selectively encour-age certain kinds of traditional treatment. Increased use of effective local remedies and the abandonment of ineffective ones would enable the govern-mental medical facilities to be used to a greater advantage. A few local remedies might even prove to be of general value outside the Trust Territory as have quinine, digitalis, and other folk remedies elsewhere.

The flourishing use of traditional medicine along with Western medicine by a majority of the people of the two districts may be attributed in part to feelings of modesty. The islanders, especially the women, are reluctant to let themselves be examined naked by others, especially by island men. Since foreign doctors are located only at the district

224

administrative centers and even there cannot see all patients (nor should they if one of their objects is to train islanders to take their place), this means that the more modest women often do not come in for treatment until it is too late. While there is a certain amount of general modesty women are especially afraid that islander medical personnel will gossip and criticize the conformation of their genitals afterwards, a fear which has some basis in custom and past incidents. By custom girls in Truk District and Ponape enlarge the labia minora by pulling on them to make themselves more attractive to men. Medical practitioners have unusual opportunities to compare the success of different women in this practice and have been known to discuss their findings in blasé tones.

Training practitioners in discretion should eventually produce less reluctance on the part of patients to submit themselves to examination. Both the training and significant reduction of reluctance after the practitioners have learned to be discrete will take time, since the islanders are fond of gossip and will not readily trust the discretion of other islanders outside of their circle of relatives and intimate friends.

Islanders comparing Western and island medicine often tell of people given up for hopeless by the American doctors who were cured by traditional medicine. It seems unlikely that many of these cases are correctly reported. Occasionally perhaps the doctor sent the patient away saying that he could find nothing wrong to treat, especially in cases of psychological origin. Doctors also have made a practice of letting hopeless patients return to their home to die if they desired. It is not inconceivable that there may have been an occasional rare spontaneous recovery in one of these cases but unexpected spontaneous recoveries can hardly have been frequent enough to account for the faith in the superiority of traditional medicine. The faith in traditional medicine is rather based on the greater psychological security which it offers to the patient and his family, by virtue of its familiar surroundings and strengthening of social ties.

The American official and doctor know that Western medicine on the whole can be scientifically shown to be more efficient than island medicine. A continuing program of popular presentation of the scientific facts about health and disease will certainly have effect in the long run in changing the islanders' beliefs. The work of the missionaries in encouraging the people to abandon magical attempts to control supernaturals and simply pray to God will also continue to be of help by providing an alternative way to take care of the emotional needs for reassurance. Both of these tasks are slow-working and long range.

The crucial point to note here is that the acceptance by the islanders of rational arguments for the greater efficiency of Western medicine is severely impeded by the inevitably greater satisfaction of psychological needs provided by island medicine. Most islanders now accept Western medicine as good in certain cases but not everywhere appropriate. Violent criticism of local medicine or attempts to suppress it by force are likely simply to make the islanders distrust the American administration in general and Western medicine in particular.

The extent of the significance of traditional medicine may be appreciated better if the Westerner realizes that in these societies before Christianity many aspects of medicine and religion were intimately bound together. The divorce is still not complete. Traditional medicine still helps provide comfort in other matters besides physical pain and weakness, matters which would most commonly be assigned to the sphere of religion or other activities in Western societies. Forcibly interfering with traditional medicine could accordingly arouse a semi-religious resistance which could have political as well as medical complications.

Elsewhere in Micronesia the revivalist modekngei cult of Palau, a sort of back-to-the-old days island sect, demonstrates more clearly the original religious significance of island medicine. The history of Japanese attempts to control this cult demonstrates the difficulty of forcible suppression. Indeed Japanese attempts to make the Palauans enlightened by decree undoubtedly supplied much of the motivation for the modekngei movement. There were signs of similar movements among the high islanders of Truk and Ponape Districts during World War II when island life was severely dislocated. These movements seem to have subsided following the end of the war, but the probability of more energetic repetitions in the event of certain kinds of administrative pressure is attested to by numerous examples from the history of the administration of dependent peoples in the Pacific and elsewhere.

Even if the people could suddenly be convinced to use only Western medicine, and went to the hospital or dispensary every time they now use local medicine, it would put a severe strain on the existing medical facilities. Some of the added medical expenses might be met by increasing the medical fees in view of the large sums now sometimes given to island curers in appreciation of their services. But much traditional medicine is simply a matter of one relative or close friend treating another and there is no payment at all here. The reader should recall that there are no full time specialists making their living primarily from traditional medicine (see Chapter VII, Economy). Also there is a rough reciprocity in fees for traditional medicine: a family group often both gives and receives money, food, and goods for these services, and can afford to pay large amounts for one formula of medicine if it has good prospects of receiving corresponding amounts for its own services on another occasion. This sort of reciprocity does not exist with Western medicine: if the doctor over-charges his patient one time, the patient has no chance to reverse roles and over-charge the doctor later.

The balance of public confidence in the two systems of medicine, Western and island, varies from island to island. Roughly, it appears that the least confidence in Western medicine is felt in Truk District and the most on Kusaie with the other islands of Ponape District intermediate.

The Trukese seem to have had a greater interest in medicine from the beginning. In fact, Trukese curers and medical diviners enjoy a high prestige on Ponape. But even in Truk District the people at present utilize the hospital and dispensaries in great numbers. There is every reason to believe that the use of these facilities will in the long run continue to increase.

CHAPTER XII

RELIGION AND EDUCATION

RELIGION

This section discusses briefly some of the aspects of islander religion of general interest, including sects active in the area, the communities in which their adherents are numerous, and something of the activities of the sects.

Nearly all the inhabitants of Truk and Ponape Districts have been baptized as Christians and accept Christianity. Pagan religious ceremonies continued in the Puluwat area up until the beginning of the American era but have since been abandoned following conversion of most of the population. In per cent of adherents to Christianity Truk and Ponape Districts are comparable to the Marshalls and Marianas Districts and are more Christian than the Yap and Palau Districts where sizable proportions of adherents of pagan religions are still found.

Christians in Truk and Ponape Districts are divided into two sects, Protestant and (Roman) Catholic. As yet there has been no multiplication of Protestant sects, and Protestant missionary activity has been a continuation of the activity of the American Board of Commissioners for Foreign Missions of Boston which began activity in the area about a century ago. German and Japanese missionaries replaced Americans throughout most of the area in the German and Japanese periods. The American Board itself is Congregational but it also supports missionaries of other like-minded sects.

The Kusaiean Protestant church is officially independent of missionary direction. However, the American Board continues to sponsor a church school at Mwot on Kusaie, and missionaries resident at the school or visiting it are available for consultation with Kusaiean leaders as desired.

No figures for the exact numbers of adherents are available. In general Truk District and the islands of Ngatik and Ponape proper are split between Catholic and Protestant perhaps about equally, although there are concentrations of both sects in certain communities. On Ponape, for instance, Net District, Awak Section of U District, and Wene and Palang sub-districts of Kiti District are predominantly Catholic. Most of Matolenim District and the central part of Kiti District are predominantly Protestant. In Truk District the Halls, Ta, and Oneop in the Mortlocks, Losap, and Nama are predominantly Protestant. On the larger islands of Truk Lagoon both sects are found in sizable numbers but again some communities are predominantly one or the other. For instance, the west side of Fefan Island is almost entirely Catholic while the east side has had a greater concentration of Protestants. Kusaie and the remaining low islands of Ponape District (excluding Ngatik) are predominantly Protestant.

The churches are important educationally since they conduct parochial schools for children in addition to the regular religious activities. The Catholics have established more schools than the Protestants. The remaining Protestant schools are mostly for training older children as religious leaders, although not only religious subjects are taught.

The missionaries also introduced Western medicine into the Eastern Carolines but this aspect of their work has mostly been taken over by the territorial government, which maintains medical dispensaries on each island of any size and maintains hospitals at the two district centers.

SCHOOLS

Public elementary schools are found on practically all inhabited islands in the two districts. The teachers are islanders. The existence of mission schools was noted in the previous section.

After completion of elementary school selected students are eligible to attend the intermediate school at the administrative center of their district. The teachers here are both islanders and Americans. On completion of intermediate school a still further selection is made of students to attend higher school at Truk. This latter school is open to students from other parts of the Trust Territory as well as Truk and Ponape Districts. The teachers here are mostly Americans. Intermediate and higher schools are both boarding schools. So far almost no islanders have gone on to a college education.

General public attitudes toward the schools vary from community to community but are on the whole mildly favorable. Many islanders hold out some hope that schooling will make their children more like Americans and eligible for government employment, and will teach them enough English to be able to use it in trading and talking to American officials.

At the same time many parents find their children useful around the home, such as, as baby sitters while the adults cut copra or gather food. Attendance is accordingly often irregular.

Due to public pressure and even though contrary to official policy, much of the teaching in elementary schools has been devoted to reading and speaking English. This has not been effective as most of the island teachers have not known English too well to begin with so that the teacher's mistakes are compounded by the students.

One of the initial problems in getting island teachers to teach in their own languages in the first grades of the elementary schools has been to prepare suitable material in the island dialects. In the Eastern Carolines alone there are at least twelve dialects which are different enough from each other so that children speaking one would find it considerably harder to learn to read material printed in any of the others (see Chapter X, Languages). If the teachers are given English material to translate, the translations are liable to contain mistakes which destroy the sense and in any case will probably be stilted and devious.

In the Japanese period public elementary schools were established on Ponape and Truk and attendance at these made compulsory. The entire cost of the schools was maintained by the territorial government, in line with the practice in pre-war Japan where schools were run by the Ministry of Education. The American administration has endeavored to place responsibility on the communities for support of their own elementary schools but the change-over has not been smooth. Many islanders have continued to feel that all public schools should be a responsibility of the territorial government.

The islanders themselves lacked formally organized schools before Western contact. Education of young children was in the hands of parents, older brothers and sisters, and other relatives and was mostly informal and individual. The closest thing to a formal school was in the education of the magician-war leaders (itang, see Chapter VIII, Political Organization) of Truk. A group of selected older boys and young men might sometimes meet with an itang to learn the ways of war, local history, and so forth. Only close relatives and paying students were entitled to participate in such groups.

CHAPTER XIII

MIND AND MANNERS

The purpose of this chapter is to present some of the main differences between the various tribes or communities of islanders and ourselves in etiquette, social attitudes, and ways of thought. These remarks, it is hoped, may be of use in facilitating relations of Americans and islanders, especially in the case of new acquaintances.

This chapter does not however constitute a detailed prescription for removing all social friction between islanders and outsiders. Even in a single island community, as anywhere else, there are wide differences in individual personality. Different people will put different interpretations on the same act of the same person. The statements here about attitudes and ways of thought are generalizations about the majority of people. Many persons are exceptions or "deviants". These exceptional persons, moreover, are especially likely to seek out foreigners for the support they often lack in their own community.

This chapter is intended to enable outsiders to adjust somewhat to island ways and manners. A complete adjustment is impractical even as an ideal, since it would demand that the American become himself indistinguishable from an islander. By so doing he would probably accomplish nothing for his job or for the welfare of the community. The very fact that Americans are in the position of administrators, teachers, and missionaries implies that to a certain extent they expect the islanders to do the adjusting. The islanders share this feeling to a degree which is varying but everywhere considerable. They are all quite aware that foreigners have different ways from their own. The islanders consider some of our ways to be superior to their own and the rest they are usually willing to tolerate. Our aim here is to discuss especially some of the differences between the islanders and ourselves which can become needless sources of friction — needless because neither side is usually fully aware of the implications of the differences.

More important than any of the rules or suggestions here is good will

on the part of the outsider. Mechanical observance of local etiquette without good will is of little effect or may be interpreted as a sign of fear. A
reasonable amount of good will will eventually win the confidence and
friendship of most islanders even without initial understanding of etiquette
and popular sentiments.

MANNERS CONNECTED WITH FOOD

An appropriate point to begin a discussion of manners and sentiments
in Micronesia is with those connected with food. While food is relatively
abundant most of the time on most islands in Truk and Ponape Districts and
so should not seem to be a matter of great concern from the point of view
of supply, food nevertheless has important social and ceremonial values.
By gifts of food people acknowledge their respect for their chiefs and the
old people of their family. Welcome to visitors is expressed first of all by
gifts of food. On Ponape the ability to grow large yams is a mark of indus-
triousness and respectability. A similar attitude toward giant swamp taro
is found in the Mortlocks, though not as strong. On all islands, high and
low, the breadfruit is important and the yearly variations in the harvest
have been traditionally considered signs of supernatural favor or displeasure;
ceremonies were conducted to ensure a bountiful crop.

Americans in Truk and Ponape Districts are often embarrassed by
gifts of more food than they can possibly consume. This problem reaches
its extreme on Ponape. Ponapeans feel that to maintain the honor of their
family or community they are obliged to give large gifts of food to every
distinguished visitor, which includes most properly introduced foreigners.
While this obligation is felt as onerous at times, the foreign visitor cannot
simply solve matters by refusing the hospitality point-blank, as this lays
the host open to charges by his neighbors that he was stingy in letting his
guests go away without gifts. Moreover the host may regard an adamant
refusal as a sign that the guest is hostile toward him or does not consider
that island food is good enough for foreigners.

There are ways of accepting gifts of food offered to one which let
the host maintain his self-respect and still reduce somewhat the burden of
hospitality. To begin with the visitor may protest the size of the gift and
need not always accept all the more difficult kinds of food offered, especially in informal situations. By difficult kinds of food are meant chicken,
canned food, whole large fish, and the meat of domestic animals. When
the visitor is served a cooked portion of such food he may restrict himself to
a part of the portion or share it with other members of his party. A host is

flattered if his guest remarks on being unable to eat all the good food provided. Moderation in eating is also respected in itself. In general, helpings may be shared by persons of different status without embarrassment, since there are no elaborate rules about the separate consumption of food by people of different status as in Yap District. It is general practice, however, to offer whole helpings of food first to guests and persons of high rank, and for the hosts and persons of lower rank to eat later and consume the remainder.

In making official visits in island communities it is never thought amiss for foreign visitors to carry canned fish or meat and some bread or rice unless one has been specifically invited in advance to a meal. If on arrival the visitor discovers that the islanders have prepared a meal for him he may leave behind the food he has brought for his own party. Canned fish and meat are especially appreciated.

Another way of repaying hospitality is by carrying around a good supply of cigarettes and sharing these generously. At feasts on Ponape the workers who prepare kava drink are privileged to ask for cigarettes from the chiefs and visitors by singing a special humorous song. It is good form for the visitor to initiate such a gift on his own also. In making the gift some of the cigarettes should first be offered to the senior titled person present and then to the kava pounders. Cigarettes are not everywhere an appropriate gift since the Protestants, especially the older people, often do not smoke. Cigarettes are especially in low repute on Kusaie, although some Kusaieans smoke.

A readiness of the guest to eat different kinds of island food puts less pressure on islander hosts to prepare difficult or rare foods. An American who is interested in eating an occasional meal of fish and preserved breadfruit is easier to entertain than one who will only eat certain foods, such as lobster, chicken, or yams. The act of eating everyday island foods shows the islanders better than words that the visitor does not share in the attitude of superiority and aversion to their food expressed by some other foreigners.

At feasts, especially on Ponape, visitors may receive large gifts of food obviously beyond their capacity to use. While such a gift is usually made in the name of the senior American present it is intended for the entire party of visitors, including, as a rule, members of the boat crew. It is not appropriate to return any of the food to the host but it is appropriate to give some to any of the local men who help transport it for a considerable distance. It is also considered appropriate for the Americans to give surplus food to the District Hospital and Intermediate School.

From time to time the islanders who have entertained may come to the District Administrative Center for official business, medical treatment, church affairs, trade, or visits to their children in school. This is an opportunity for the American to reciprocate with invitations to meals.

Concerning table manners, both Protestants and Catholics often say grace before eating. In any case it is polite not to begin eating immediately that one is served and to wait until one is urged to eat.

Traditionally food is served on leaf platters or plates and eaten with the fingers. Many islanders possess imported plates and eating utensils and use these on special occasions and for foreign visitors.

BEHAVIOR ON FORMAL OCCASIONS

Compared to the average American, most of the people in Truk and Ponape Districts are characterized for formal occasions by quiet speech and non-assertive behavior. This contrast is perhaps strongest with the Ponapeans and Kusaieans and is related to the elaborate etiquette formerly connected on these islands with differences in rank, still partly preserved on Ponape.

The difference in approach is embodied in one's first Eastern Carolinian handshake, a custom borrowed from the West. The vigorous bone-crushing handshake of some Americans is totally absent. Shaking hands as practiced in these islands is usually a brief contact between two almost relaxed hands.

The non-assertive behavior is more a matter of manners than intent. The people of most of these islands would consider it impolite to directly contradict the statement or refuse the request of another, especially of a superior. At the same time they are themselves very careful about making controversial statements in public or difficult requests of strangers. Casual visitors are often initially pleased with the ready assent of the islanders to all sorts of "progressive" ideas. Slightly longer contact often shows that such assent is mostly polite talk designed primarily to put the visitor at his ease. Disillusioned foreigners may charge the islanders with being untruthful. The islanders are liable to regard the same foreigners as rude, unsympathetic, and unacquainted with local conditions.

An extreme example of the sort of approach not productive with the islanders was provided by one American official (not an employee of the

Trust Territory) inspecting Truk who tried to demonstrate the solution of the Micronesian's economic problems by shoving a stalk of bananas into a chief's arms and holding out a five dollar bill in his hand, saying triumphantly, "See? You give me bananas. I give you money. " His further remarks made it clear that the Micronesians could all become prosperous if they would only stop being so lazy and produce more things for sale, such as bananas.

The visitor's particular example was especially inappropriate since at the time bananas were being purchased for sale on Guam under a limited quota system because of inadequate storage, shipping, and marketing facilities. At the time the Trukese were prepared and anxious to sell many times the amount of bananas needed by prospective purchasers. Out of politeness the chief did not tell this to the visitor, who probably went away believing he had given the chief an invaluable reminder of the basic principles of economics. The chief, not a rash man, remarked later that if the visitor had been an islander and talked to him like that he would have fought with him.

If this same visitor had spent his time in asking islanders about their attempts to make money by selling local products he would have acquired a better understanding of the economic potentialities and problems of Truk, certainly an essential first step towards an effective solution. Moreover the islanders themselves would have been more ready to listen seriously to his advice or criticism if he then had had any to offer.

Much of the elaborate formal etiquette used before chiefs on Ponape, Kusaie, and to a lesser extent on other islands is now no longer practiced. Certain observances are still considered good manners, and some are mentioned below.

The head of a person is considered worthy of special respect and is not touched without special reason. Little children are not used to being patted on the head and usually resent it. A barber cutting the hair of a Ponapean chief still utters a word of apology. The entire person of a chief should not be touched lightly. A friendly backslap is unusual and out of order in most circumstances.

In general a person should not raise himself higher than another to whom respect is due. If a chief is sitting it is impolite to stand up in his presence without apologizing, although if he stands one may continue to sit. It is impolite to stand above people to photograph them without their consent, although this is usually freely given. At feasts and meetings foreign visitors are generally offered chairs. If there are not enough chairs to go around the foreigner gets them. On official occasions chairs add to the dignity of the foreign official but on informal occasions they also tend to isolate the occupant. Informal conversation is most easily carried on with all parties on the same level, which usually means without chairs.

In Ponape only the traditional titles are used in polite conversation instead of a man's name. Nearly every man has a title and some of the higher titles have both forms of address (used in speaking to a man) and forms of reference (used to talk about the man to someone else). If anyone but an intimate friend calls a man by his true name it is considered an insult. Foreigners are exempted from this requirement by virtue of their ignorance; nevertheless it is appreciated when they observe it. Elsewhere in Truk and Ponape Districts personal names are used freely, even in abbreviated form, although there is some feeling of embarrassment about saying the name of a dead parent.

Also principally on Ponape there is a marked distinction between polite and intimate speech. The polite speech uses special second person pronouns, possessives, auxiliary verbs, and special words or phrases for common objects and acts such as food, house, eat, come and go. In public speeches polite language is used almost exclusively by the Ponapeans themselves. The polite language is also used between adults who are not on intimate terms and toward older men by younger men. Ponapeans greatly appreciate it if foreigners who learn their language make an attempt to use polite speech. People of the other islands, except possibly Kusaie, are less concerned about this.

GOSSIP

The people of the Eastern Carolines, like the people of many small rural communities in other parts of the world, are much given to gossip, some of which is malicious. Gossip serves some of the same functions as our own daily newspapers, magazines, radio, and motion pictures, being a combination of both entertainment and information. Favorite subjects are romantic and adulterous affairs, alleged thefts, inadequacies in the entertainment of guests and the size of feasts (this especially on Ponape), and political intrigues.

237

No one, not even chiefs or foreign officials and missionaries, is immune from gossip; in fact the more exalted the individual the more he is a subject of gossip.

Cases of the complete fabrication of malicious lies intended to discredit an enemy occur but are not too common. More common is the elaboration of small incidents by fertile imagination. For instance, a man and a woman meet on the road by chance and exchange a few words. A third party spreads the word they are having an adulterous love affair.

Fortunately, the islanders themselves have a critical attitude toward most gossip and do not give complete faith to anything they hear. In spite of this foreigners are well advised to be discreet in their words and acts. For instance a casual answer to a household servant as to whether a certain feast was as big as some other is liable to be broadcast in expanded form to the effect that "Mr. A was angry because the people of X gave him too little food."

Needless to say, foreigners should be careful themselves about giving credence to unfounded rumor, especially where there is a possibility that a rumor could serve some end in political or legal intrigue. Certainly administrative action concerning a man should not be taken simply on the basis of hearsay statements by someone else, however trusted the bearer of the report.

ATTITUDES TOWARD PUBLIC BEHAVIOR OF MEN WITH WOMEN

As far as is known, the people of the Eastern Carolines originally had rather permissive attitudes toward premarital sexual relations and also toward extramarital sexual relations on the part of men with unmarried women. These attitudes have been altered in varying degree by missionary teaching on the different islands but still retain much force everywhere.

At the same time on all the Micronesian islands in the area at least (possibly excluding Kapingamarangi and Nukuoro) the taboos on public contact between the sexes are stronger than in our own society. Women are retiring in public. In walking along the path a wife walks behind her husband.

Most public physical contact between the sexes is considered embarrassing. Kissing in the movies embarrasses the older people (Japanese movies also lacked kissing.) Western style ballroom dancing and even square dancing are also regarded as risqué or improper by most adults. In the Ponapean feast houses men sit on one side and women on the other. This pattern is also followed in churches throughout the area, although families of foreigners are often invited to sit together on the men's side.

ATTITUDES TOWARD ACCULTURATION

Several distinct attitudes toward acculturation may be noted among the peoples of the Eastern Carolines. Officials and other visitors will make a better impression on the islanders if in remarks on the subject of progress they consider the attitude of the local people.

The island most interested in progress and Americanization is probably Kusaie. The Kusaiean interest in adopting foreign ways may be attributed primarily to the example and encouragement of American missionaries over a hundred year period. Also important is the severe depopulation, which did great damage to the native culture. The Kusaieans take considerable pride in what they know of American ways and are decidedly disappointed if visitors extol the wisdom of their traditional ways of living.

A number of low islanders have an interest in foreign ways which approaches that of the Kusaieans. These include the people of the Mortlocks and other islands south of Truk, the Halls, and Mokil. Protestant missionary activity is also probably the main motive force here, although deserting sailors who settled on Mokil were important on that island as well. These low islanders are well aware of the meager resources of their homes and have less lofty hopes than the Kusaieans as to what foreign ways can do for them.

The people of Truk Lagoon are in general less concerned about the problem of foreign versus native customs than the peoples of the above islands. The Trukese tend to take a more practical attitude toward custom: if a foreign custom works they adopt it; if a local custom no longer works they drop it without much sentimentality. In fact, this has meant that less change has taken place thus far in the local culture than on the above islands, since the number of foreign customs with obvious practical advantages to the Eastern Carolines with their present economy is not large.

The attitude of the people of the Puluwat area and Namonuito is perhaps similar to that of the Trukese, but these low islands have had less contact with foreigners and so are in fact less acculturated. Considerable resistance to acculturation was found in the Puluwat area into the Japanese period but now seems to have largely vanished.

The attitude of the people of Ponape is mixed and intense. The Ponapeans are acutely aware that there are such things as "Ponapean customs" and "enlightened customs" and they often discuss articulately just which Ponapean customs should be kept and which replaced. A common sentiment is that "We can't get rid of all Ponapean customs; we want to keep some." The choice of customs to keep varies widely according to the individual. The variation in attitude reflects in part missionary attitudes: for example, devout Protestants do not drink kava, devout Catholics may. Some of the attitudes stem from personnel of the four foreign regimes which have occupied the island in the last seventy years.

While Ponapeans are deferential toward foreigners in positions of power they are discriminating and do not hold all foreigners in great awe. This may be a heritage of the days when each chief had his deserting sailor for his foreign adviser and of the Spanish regime when Ponapeans resisted the government with some military success.

Many of the people of Ngatik have also an ambivalent attitude toward acculturation. This may be attributed in part to the tragic history of the island's early contact with Westerners (see Chapter II, The Past). Compared to Ponape and most of the Eastern Carolines, the Ngatik people have less of their original culture left to cling to because of the slaughter of the males in the nineteenth century, and probably for this reason, and because of Western sailors who settled on the island, are more acculturated than the Ponapeans. Many of the people give the impression of consciously wanting progress and change but secretly being uncertain or resenting it.

The caution that these generalizations about the traits of the peoples of the different islands do not apply to each and every individual particularly deserves repetition and emphasis with respect to attitudes toward Western culture. Attitudes toward Western culture are of fairly recent development. The native cultures, so to speak, have not had time to "make up their mind". In a single community Western culture means one thing for an islander church leader, another for a store keeper, another for a chief, and another for a government worker. The amount known about Western culture varies greatly among individuals according to their experience of it as pupils, workers, and so forth. The various bearers of Western culture

240

themselves have been quite diverse: persons of several nationalities, religious sects and orders, differing economic status, military and civilian.

A further caution to bear in mind is that wherever a foreigner goes he is most likely to be sought out at first by those islanders most interested in Western culture. There are such persons in all communities. Using such persons to make any generalizations about islander attitudes on any subject is liable to be misleading but especially so with regard to attitudes toward foreigners and Western culture.

With all these cautions one must not err in the opposite direction in assessing islander attitudes toward Western culture. While it would be foolish to accept the flattering picture of the islanders as eagerly awaiting the least crumb of wisdom from foreigners, most islanders have considerable respect for Western ways. The type of violent anti-foreign sentiment manifested in some of the French and British possessions recently, and on Ponape during the Spanish and German periods, is little in evidence at present. The people of all the islands are nearly always friendly and courteous toward foreigners who behave reasonably toward them, and the foreign visitor or official entering the area for the first time may anticipate with pleasure his relations with the islanders.

SELECTED ANNOTATED BIBLIOGRAPHY

The purpose of this bibliography is threefold. The first is to ac-knowledge the main written sources consulted in the preparation of this handbook. The second is to list some of the more important and easily ac-cessible scientific works on the Eastern Carolines, regardless of the degree to which they have been used as a source here. The third is to list bibli-ographies where readers interested in special questions may find references to works not listed here.

There are several restrictions on this bibliography. To begin with only works which deal in part or in whole with the Eastern Carolines have been included. However, works on other parts of Micronesia are included in some of the bibliographies listed.

The bibliography is mostly limited to relatively modern works, ex-cept for a few early works of unusual interest. The modern literature gen-erally contains a review of the significant contributions of older literature and often corrects earlier mistakes.

Foreign works on Micronesia have been omitted except for a few major works which were important sources of the material included here. Again, references to these may be found in bibliographies listed.

Works written in technical language which are deemed to be of interest mainly to specialists have been omitted. On the other hand, popu-lar works which rely for effect on sensationalism and ill-founded specula-tion or which report little more than personal travel experiences have also been omitted.

Not all of the references are annotated. We did not consult some of these during the preparation of the text but consider nevertheless that they would be highly useful for any reader desiring to begin a fuller study of a number of the subjects treated here.

American Board of Commissioners for Foreign Missions. Correspondence, Micronesian Mission.

 Consulted only after preparing the manuscript. Valuable historical source. All except recent letters are deposited in the Houghton Library, Harvard University.

Baker, R. H. The Avifauna of Micronesia, its Origin, Evolution, and Distribution. University of Kansas. Publication of the Museum of Natural History, Vol. 3, No. 1. 1951.

Bascom, W. R. Ponapean Prestige Economy. Southwestern Journal of Anthropology, Vol. 4, pp. 211-21. 1948.

 Authoritative discussion of how and why Ponapeans grow yams, etc.

_____. Subsistence Farming on Ponape. New Zealand Geography, Vol. 5, pp. 115-129. 1949.

_____. Ponape: The Cycle of Empire. Scientific Monthly, Vol. 70, pp. 141-50. 1950.

 Comparison of significance of the four foreign régimes since 1887.

_____. Ponape: The Tradition of Retaliation. Far Eastern Quarterly, Vol. 10, pp. 56-62. 1950.

 Discussion of Jokaj Rebellion on Ponape in German period.

_____. (See also U.S. Commercial Co.)

Bentzen, C. Land and Livelihood on Mokil, Part II. Washington, D.C.: Pacific Science Board, 1949 (ditto). CIMA report.

 Complementary to Weckler's work. Overlaps some of Murphy's and gives independent check.

Bollig. P. Laurentius, O.M. Cap. Die Bewohner der Truk-Inseln. Münster i. W., 1927.

 Valuable information on religion.

Bryan, E. H. Jr. Economic Insects of Micronesia. Washington, D.C.: National Research Council, 1949. (processed).

Burns, A., et al. Report of the UN Visiting Mission.....UN Trusteeship Council, Gen. Doc. T/789, 1950.

 On the whole a favorable outside appraisal of U.S. administration in Navy period.

Christian, F.W. The Caroline Islands. London, 1899.

 Contains scattered bits of information on Ponape, much personal experience, not completely reliable.

Clyde, Paul H. Japan's Pacific Mandate. New York, 1935.

 Partly based on a trip of the author's through the present Trust Territory in Japanese times. Moderately sympathetic to Japanese administration.

Coolidge, Harold J. Conservation in Micronesia. Washington, D.C.: Natural Research Council, 1948.

 Contains papers presented at two conferences on

conservation sponsored by the Pacific Science Board.
Includes recommendations as to laws and protected
areas.

Coördinated Investigation of Micronesian Anthropology (CIMA) Interim reports, 35 authors. Washington, D.C.: Pacific Science Board, 1947-48 (processed).
Final reports on Eastern Carolines are listed here under
authors' names. Some interim reports give valuable
information not included in final reports.

Damm, H. et al. See Thilenius.

Dyen, Isidore. Sketch of Trukese Grammar. CIMA Report. Washington,
D.C.: Pacific Science Board, 1948 (typed).
Authoritative description of the sounds and grammar of
Trukese.

Eilers, A. See Thilenius.

Elbert, S.H. Kapingamarangi and Nukuoro Word List, with Notes on Linguistic Position, Pronunciation, and Grammar. U.S. Naval Military
Government, 1946.

_____. Trukese-English and English-Trukese Dictionary....U.S. Naval
Military Government, 1947.
Contains a large vocabulary. Failure to note regularly
double consonants and long vowels detracts somewhat
from value of otherwise excellent work.

_____. Utamatua and Other Legends from Kapingamarangi. Journal of
American Folklore, Vol. 62, pp. 240-46, 1949.

Emory, Kenneth P. Myths and Tales from Kapingamarangi...Journal of
American Folklore, Vol. 62, pp. 230-39, 1949.

_____. A Program for Polynesian Archaeology. American Anthropologist,
Vol. 55, pp. 752-55. 1953.

_____. (Bishop Museum Bulletin on Kapingamarangi based on Dr. Emory's
CIMA and SIM investigations is in preparation at this date. Dr. Emory
has kindly answered a number of questions on Kapingamarangi and
Nukuoro social organization etc. in a personal communication. Presumably this information will be included in his forthcoming work.)

Fischer, Ann. The Role of the Trukese Mother and its Effect on Child Training. Washington, D.C.: Pacific Science Board, 1950 (mimeographed).
Final SIM report.

Fischer, John L. Native Land Tenure in the Truk District. Civil Administration, Truk, 1950 (mimeographed).
Comparison of land tenure in various cultural subdivisions of Truk District.

_____. Contemporary Ponapean Land Tenure. Civil Administration, Ponape, 1951 (mimeographed).
> Discusses interaction of customary land tenure with programs of German, Japanese, and early American regimes on Ponape Island.

Freeman, O.W., ed. Geography of the Pacific. New York, 1951.
> Good coverage of the Carolines and the rest of Micronesia.

Garvin, Paul L. Linguistic Study of Ponape. Washington, D.C.: Pacific Science Board, 1949.
> CIMA Report. Professional description of Ponapean. Minor points on description of sounds have been challenged, but work provided basis for current official spelling of standard Ponapean.

_____, and S.H. Riesenberg. Respect Behavior on Ponape. American Anthropologist, n.s., Vol. 54, pp. 201-20. 1952.
> Describes especially use of respect language on Ponape Island.

Gladwin, Thomas. Civil Administration on Truk: a Rejoinder, Human Organization, Vol. 9, No. 4, pp. 15-24, 1950.
> Defense of naval administration in response to Hall's criticism of same year.

_____ The Role of Man and Woman on Truk. Translation of the New York Academy of Sciences, Set. II, Vol. 15, pp. 305-9. 1953.
> Discusses psychological differences between sexes on Truk and the causes.

_____, and Seymour B. Sarason. Truk: Man in Paradise. Viking Fund Publication in Anthropology, No. 20. New York, 1953.
> Discusses life histories and results of psychological tests and integrates these with cultural and sociological investigations.

Glassman, Sidney F. The Flora of Ponape. Bernice P. Bishop Museum Bulletin No. 209. Honolulu, 1952.
> Thorough professional description and catalog.

Goodenough, Ward H. Premarital Freedom on Truk. American Anthropologist, Vol. 51, pp. 615-20. 1949.
> Based on CIMA work, discusses why Trukese are preoccupied with notion of romantic love in view of their indulgent attitude toward sex.

_____. Property, Kin, and Community on Truk. Yale University Publication in Anthropology, No. 46. New Haven, 1951.

CIMA report. Concentrates on analysis of social organization of Romonum, a small, relatively unaccul-
turated island in the western part of Truk Lagoon.
Most important source of information on Trukese family relations. Bibliography.

_____. Native Astronomy in the Central Carolines. University Museum,
University of Pennsylvania, Philadelphia, 1953.
Astronomy is principally an aid to navigation. This
analyzes previous works and adds some field data.
Bibliography.

Grey, Eve. Legends of Micronesia, Books I and II. High Commissioner,
Trust Territory of the Pacific Islands. Honolulu, 1951.
Legends, myths, and tales selected and adapted for
American school children from rough English texts sup-
plied mostly by islander school teachers and students.

Gulick, Rev. L.H. The Climate and Productions of Ponape or Ascension I.

_____. Lectures on Micronesia. Reprinted from The Polynesian, 1860-61
in Annual Report of the Hawaiian Historical Society for 1943, No. 52,
pp. 6-55. Honolulu, 1944.
Early first hand reports of a perceptive observer, who
played an important role in Ponapean history.

Hall, Edward T. Jr. Military Government on Truk. Human Organization,
Vol. 9, No. 2, pp. 25-30. 1950.
Criticism of naval administration on Truk; see also
Gladwin's article of same year.

Hambruch, Paul, see Thilenius.

Hiroa, Te Rangi (Peter H. Buck) Material Culture of Kapingamarangi.
Bishop Museum Bulletin No. 200. Honolulu, 1950.
Full catalog of objects traditionally made by natives
and methods of manufacture.

Hunt, Edward E., Jr. A view of Somatology and Serology in Micronesia.
American Journal Physical Anthropology, n.s., Vol. 8, pp. 167-84.
1950.
Discusses racial components of native peoples of the
Trust Territory from viewpoint of physical anthropology.
Reviews work of Japanese anthropologist Hasebe.

Imanishi, N. Ecological Study of Ponape Island (Ponape-to seitaigakuteki
kenkyu). Tokyo, 1944.
A cursory examination of this sizable volume suggests

247

that it reports important original research in the fields
of economic geography and native social organization.
As yet untranslated from the Japanese.

Krämer, Augustin, see Thilenius.

LeBar, F.M. Trukese Material Culture. Washington, D.C.: Pacific
Science Board, 1949 (mimeographed).
CIMA Report. Thorough description of traditional ob-
jects and methods of manufacture for the island of
Romonum in Truk Lagoon.

Lewis, James L. Kusaiean Acculturation. Washington, D.C.: Pacific
Science Board, 1949 (typed).
CIMA Report. Reviews history of foreign contact on
Kusaie based on library and field work. The account of
Kusaiean history in this handbook relies heavily on Lewis.

Luomala, K. Micronesian Mythology. Standard Dictionary of Folklore,
Vol. 2, pp. 717-22. New York, 1950.
Recommended for educators, etc., interested in further
exploring this field. Contains bibliography.

Marshall, Colin. Report on Forestry in the Trust Territory....Washington,
D.C.: Pacific Science Board, 1951.
SIM report. Professional forester's report. Includes discussion of land policy and other subjects peripheral but
vital to an effective forestry program.

Murdock, G.P. Anthropology in Micronesia. Transactions of the New York
Academy of Science, Ser. 2, Vol. 2, No. 1, pp. 9-16. 1948.
Reconstruction of development of social organization
in Micronesia based on the author's fieldwork in the
area and on a survey of the literature up to and including the CIMA program.

_____. New Light on the Peoples of Micronesia. Science, n.s., Vol. 108,
pp. 423-25. 1948.
Discusses navy supported research in Trust Territory.
Author directed the CIMA program.

_____, and Ward H. Goodenough. Social Organization of Truk. Southwestern
Journal of Anthropology, Vol. 3, pp. 331-43. 1947.
Concise statement of conclusions of the authors CIMA
fieldwork. A few points superseded by Goodenough,
1951.

Murphy, Raymond E. The Economic Geography of a Micronesian Atoll.
Annals of the Association of American Geographers, Vol. 40, pp. 58-
83. 1950.

This and following two works present results of author's
CIMA investigation on Mokil. Much of the material
overlaps with Weckler and Bentzen's report on the same
island but was collected independently.

_____. Landownership on a Micronesian Atoll. Geographical Review, Vol.
38, pp. 598-614. 1948.

_____. "High" and "Low" Islands in the Eastern Carolines. Geographical
Review, Vol. 39, pp. 425-39. 1949.

Murrill, Rupert I. Anthropological Study of the Ponape Islanders. Washington, D.C.: Pacific Science Board, 1948 (typed).
CIMA Report. Largely technical study of physical anthropology (body measurements, etc.) but discussions
of population growth, dental conditions, and blood pressure are of wider interest.

_____. A Blood Pressure Study of Natives of Ponape Island.... Human Biology,
Vol. 21, pp. 47-57. 1949.

_____. Vital Statistics of Ponape Island. American Journal of Physical An-
thropology, n.s., Vol. 8, pp. 185-93. 1950.
Above two articles are more easily accessible excerpts
from author's CIMA report.

O'Connell, James F. A Residence of Eleven Years in New Holland and the
Caroline Islands. Boston, 1836.
Author was stranded on Ponape 1826-33. Fascinating
adventure plus valuable historical information. Part on
Ponape translated into German by the ethnographer
Hambruch (see Thilenius). English copies rare.

Oliver, Douglas L. The Pacific Islands. Cambridge, Mass., 1951.
Gives a broad historical and geographical perspective
in non-technical language.

_____, ed. Planning Micronesia's Future. Cambridge, Mass., 1951.
Discussion of economic and political policy based on
U.S. Commercial Co. economic survey immediately
after war. Some parts are outdated but much deals with
permanent, basic problems of the area.

Pacific Science Board. Annual Report. Washington, D.C., 1947 to date.
References to scientific publications resulting from work
sponsored by the Board are included. References to
CIMA reports begin in 1949.

_____. Films and Bibliography of Publications and Reports Resulting from
Field Work of Pacific Science Board. Washington, D.C., Oct., 1953
(mimeographed).

Lists both printed and mimeographed material, general and technical publications. Over 100 authors,
many with several items each. Much material on Eastern Carolines and Micronesia as well as other parts of
Pacific.

Pelzer, K.J. Agriculture in the Truk Islands. Foreign Agriculture, Vol.
11, pp. 74-81. 1947.
_____. See also U.S. Commercial Co.

Riesenberg, S.H. Magic and Medicine in Ponape. Southwestern Journal of
Anthropology, Vol. 4, pp. 406-29. 1948.
Discusses procedure in traditional medicine, sorcery
and magic. Includes list of medicines.
_____. Ponapean Political and Social Organization. Washington, D.C.:
Pacific Science Board, 1949 (typed).
Authoritative and detailed description. The most im-
portant written source on its subject. Useful bibliogra-
phy.
_____, and A.H. Gayton. Caroline Island Belt Weaving. Southwestern Jour-
nal of Anthropology, Vol. 8, pp. 342-75. 1952.
Probable origins and technical details.

Sarfert, E. See Thilenius.

Schneider, David. Some Micronesian Matrilinies. Harvard University,
Cambridge, 1954 (ditto).
Includes comparison of Trukese social organization with
other parts of Micronesia. Useful for summary and
interpretations of reports of other authors.

Stillfried, Bernhard. Die sociale Organization in Mikronesien. Acta
Ethnologica et Linguistica, No. 4, Vienna, 1953.
Author has raised some questions which require further
field checking and reviewed much of the CIMA material as well as earlier works.

Thilenius, G., ed. Ergebnisse der Südsee-Expedition 1908-1910, Series
II - Ethnography; B- Micronesia. Hamburg, various dates.
Series IIB is divided into a number of volumes on each
of the main island groups of Micronesia. Some of these
volumes are in turn divided into sub-volumes by different authors. The works on the Eastern Carolines summed
up the previous literature and added important field
data. Reports on areas not covered by the CIMA project
remain the standard works on the island cultures, although they are outdated for description of contemporary
cultures.

Damm, Hans, et al. Vol. 6, Inseln um Truk, subvolume 2. Hamburg, 1935.

Covers Puluwat, Pulusuk (referred to as Hok), and Satawal (the latter is the easternmost island of Yap District). Subvolume 1 by Krämer.

Eilers, A. Inseln um Ponape. Hamburg, 1934.

Brief information on Mokil, Pingelap, Ngatik, Nukuoro, Kapingamarangi.

Hambruch, Paul and A. Eilers. Vol. 7, Ponape, subvolumes 1, 2, 3. Hamburg, 1932, 1936.

The most thorough of all the German reports on the Eastern Carolines. Especially valuable for the historical summary and large number of intelligible Ponapean texts of tales, reports, etc. with good, if not perfect translations into German. Hambruch died before completing publication and Eilers took over his work resulting in some inevitable confusion and errors. Hambruch's history of Ponape through the German period is colorful and at times opinionated. This handbook is the principal source of Ponapean history before the Japanese period. History is subvolume 1; general ethnography is subvolume 2; Matolenim ruins and Ponapean myths and tales are subvolume 3.

Krämer, Augustin. Vol. 5, Truk. Hamburg, 1932.

Perhaps most notable for description of material culture. Many parts of this volume have been superseded by the work of the Yale University CIMA team on Romonum: Murdock, Gladwin, Goodenough, LeBar.

_____. Vol. 6, Inseln um Truk, subvolume 1. Hamburg, 1932.

Covers briefly Lukunor, Namoluk, Losap, Nama, Halls, Namonuito, Pulap. Subvolume 2 by Damm et al.

Sarfert, E. Vol. 4, Kusae. Hamburg, 1919.

Reconstruction of old Kusaiean culture.

Tolerton, B., and J. Rauch. Social Organization, Land Tenure, and Subsistence Economy of Lukunor. Washington, D.C.: Pacific Science Board, 1949 (mimeographed).

CIMA Report based on authors' fieldwork on Lukunor
in Mortlocks.

U.S. Commercial Co. Economic Survey of Micronesia. Honolulu, 1946.
Series of unpublished reports, some mimeographed,
all microfilmed and in Library of Congress, etc. See
especially reports by Bascom, Bryan, Hosaka, Fosberg,
Townes and Oakley, Hall and Pelzer, Piper and Bridge.
Consulted in preparation of this handbook were:
Bascom, W.R. Ponape: A Pacific Economy in Transition (mimeo-
graphed).
Hall, E.T., Jr., and K.J.Pelzer. The Economy of the Truk Is-
lands. Both Bascom's and Hall and Pelzer's works give consider-
able cultural background data for their study of the economy.
Bascom's is the more extensive of the two.

U.S. Department of the Interior. Report on the Administration of the Trust
Territory of the Pacific Islands. Washington, D.C., 1951-53.
Annual report to UN. Official statistics, etc. from
beginning of Interior administration.

_____. Department of the Navy. Agriculture in the Japanese Mandated
Islands. Civil Affairs Guide (OPNAV 13-17), Washington, D.C., 1944.

_____. East Caroline Islands. Civil Affairs Handbook (OPNAV 50E-5),
Washington, D.C., 1944.
The above three works were prepared during the war for
military purposes without firsthand investigation. Somewhat outdated and must be used with caution but contain
valuable information translated from Japanese official
documents and from earlier anthropological literature.

_____. The Fishing Industry of the Japanese Mandated Islands. Civil Af-
fairs Guide (OPNAV 50E-20), Washington, D.C., 1944.

_____. Annual reports to the United Nations on the Administration of the
Trust Territory (OPNAV pp. 22-100), Washington, D.C., 1948-50.
Actual title varies. Official statistics, etc. for period
of Naval administration.

Utinomi, Huzio. Bibliography of Micronesia. Honolulu, 1950.
Translation into English edited and revised by
O.A. Bushnell et al. at University of Hawaii. Includes comprehensive listings of Japanese and Western
works on Micronesia in fields of botany, zoology,
medicine, anthropology, geography, etc. Works
after 1944 not included. About 3500 entries.

Weckler, J. E. Land and Livelihood on Mokil, Part I. Washington, D.C.:
Pacific Science Board, 1949 (ditto).
>History, land tenure, etc. Complementary to
Bentzen's report, which is Part II. Overlaps
Murphy's and provides independent check.

Yale University, Institute of Human Relations. Human Relations Area Files.
New Haven, Conn.
>Existing material on Micronesia was translated where
necessary and catalogued during war. Use of these
files enables the investigator to check quickly any information there may be in the literature on points of
interest. A number of points in this handbook were
checked in the files. The collection of data from
several authors on the same subject in a single place
is especially valuable. The files eliminate the need
for translation from other languages. They include a
large bibliographical section with library references.

Yanaihara, T. Pacific Islands under Japanese Mandate. London, 1940.
>Translation and revision of a work first published in
Japanese. Gives a Japanese viewpoint.

ADDENDUM TO THE BIBLIOGRAPHY, SUMMER 1966

Bascom, W. R. Ponape: A Pacific Economy in Transition. University of
California Anthropological Records, Vol. 22. 1965.
>A publication of Bascom's useful report for the U. S. Commercial
Company (see above, p. 252). A substantial bibliography has been
added.

deYoung, John, ed. Land Tenure Patterns in the Trust Territory of the Pacific
Islands, a Handbook. Guam: Office of the High Commissioner, 1958.
>Includes published versions of Fischer's reports on land tenure in Truk
and Ponape (see above, pp. 245-46).

Emory, Kenneth P. Kapingamarangi, Social and Religious Life of a Polynesian Atoll. Bishop Museum Bulletin No. 228. Honolulu, 1965.
>Thorough coverage of the former religion. Oriented toward describing
the local culture before contact, but also describes modern life.

Fischer, Ann. Reproduction in Truk. Ethnology, Vol. 2, pp. 527-40. 1963.

Fischer, J. L. The Position of Men and Women in Truk and Ponape. Journal
of American Folklore, Vol. 69, pp. 55-62. 1956.
>Compares the image of men and women in myth in the two societies,
and suggests relationships to social organization.

Fischer, J. L. Totemism on Truk and Ponape. American Anthropologist, Vol. 59, pp. 250-65. 1957.

Discusses traditional beliefs about relationships between fish, etc., and humans.

_____. The Japanese Schools for the Natives of Truk, Caroline Islands. Human Organization, Vol. 20, pp. 83-88. 1961.

_____, Ann Fischer, and Frank Mahony. Totemism and Allergy. International Journal of Social Psychiatry, Vol. 5, pp. 33-40. 1959.

Discusses symptoms of violation of traditional food taboos and possible relationships to allergy.

Gladwin, Thomas. Canoe Travel in the Truk Area: Technology and its Psychological Correlates. American Anthropologist, Vol. 60, pp. 893-99. 1958.

_____. Petrus Mailo, Chief of Moen. Pp. 41-62 in Joseph B. Casagrande, ed., In the Company of Man. New York: Harper, 1960.

A sensitive and properly appreciative personal sketch of an outstanding Micronesian leader.

_____. Culture and Logical Process. Pp. 167-77 in Ward Goodenough, ed., Explorations in Cultural Anthropology. New York: McGraw-Hill, 1964.

Hainline, Jane. Culture and Biological Adaptation. American Anthropologist, Vol. 67, pp. 1174-97. 1965.

Includes considerable bibliography on Micronesia. Discusses population size and environment.

LeBar, Frank M. A Household Survey of Economic Goods on Romonum Island, Truk. Pp. 335-49 in Ward Goodenough, ed., Explorations in Cultural Anthropology. New York: McGraw-Hill, 1964.

_____. The Material Culture of Truk. Yale University Publications in Anthropology, Vol. 68. New Haven, 1964.

Describes the traditional artifacts of Truk Lagoon, especially Romonum Island.

Lessa, William A. An Evaluation of Early Descriptions of Carolinian Culture. Ethnohistory, Vol. 9, pp. 313-404. 1962.

Samples of early reports of ethnographic relevance.

Mahony, Frank J. The Innovation of a Savings Institution in Truk. American Anthropologist, Vol. 62, pp. 465-82. 1960.

Swartz, Marc J. Leadership and Status Conflict on Romonum, Truk. Southwestern Journal of Anthropology, Vol. 15, pp. 213-18. 1959.

_____. Situational Determinants of Kinship Terminology. Southwestern Journal of Anthropology, Vol. 16, pp. 393-97. 1960.

Swartz, Marc J. Political Acquiescence in Truk. Pp. 17-39 in Roland W. Force, ed., Induced Political Change in the Pacific: A Symposium, Tenth Pacific Science Congress. Honolulu: Bishop Museum, 1965.

Note: Abbreviations used are mostly standard. CIMA stands for Coordinated Investigation of Micronesian Anthropology. SIM stands for Scientific Investigations in Micronesia (see Introduction).

INDEX

APPENDICES
    Drawings
    Population Statistics

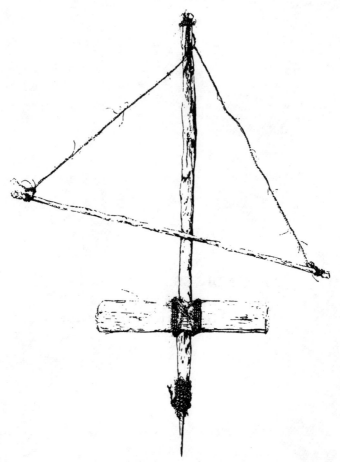

Pump Drill (*nikanen*).

Length of shaft, 28 inches; diameter of shaft, 0.75 inch; length of hand bar, 21 inches; length of drill, 3.5 inches. Point on this demonstration specimen made from a large nail. Yale Peabody Museum, 143646.

Multipronged Fish Spear (*óppong*).
Method of lashing prongs to shaft. Romonum Island. Yale Peabody Museum, 143610.

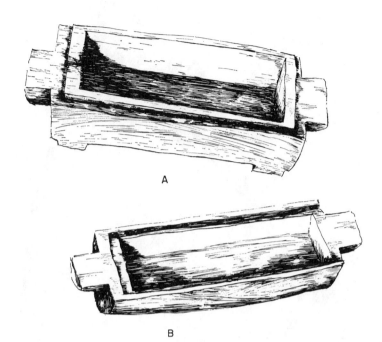

A

B

Wooden Storage Chest (*sop*).
A, Body of chest showing mortising to receive lid. B, Underside of lid. Model specimen made on Romonum Island. Yale Peabody Museum, 143587.

Small Wooden Bowl (*föyjene*).
Somewhat boat-shaped, with flat bottom, inside and out. Flared rim at either end. Length, 15 inches; width, 11 inches; depth, 5 inches. Yale Peabody Museum, 143572.

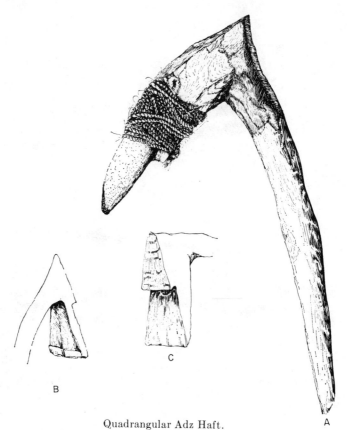

Quadrangular Adz Haft.
A, Side view; B, same, underside; C, same, end view. From model made on Romonum Island.
Yale Peabody Museum, 143666.

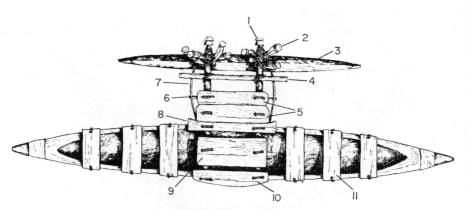

Small Fishing Canoe (*wa fötyn*).
Looking down on hull and outrigger; 1, boom; 2, stanchion; 3, float; 4, crosspiece (*waaiso*);
5, outrigger platform (*cööcöörarau*); 6, longitudinal stringer (*waatippu*); 7, diagonal stringer
(*ceeteam*); 8, crosspiece (*mesenap*); 9, removable board (*maatyng*); 10, weather-side board
(*tinikäsä*); 11, thwart.

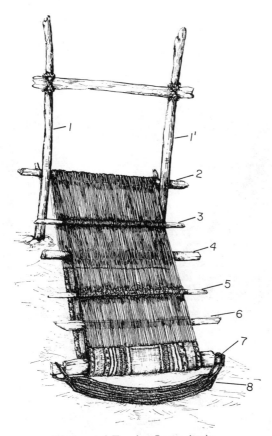

Horizontal Tension Loom (*tyr*).
The cloth and warp beams are about 45 inches long, 2.5 inches wide, and 2 inches thick. Vertical supports 1, 1'; warp beam, 2; lease rod, 3; shed stick, 4; heddle, 5; sword, 6; cloth beam, 7; sling or belt, 8. Yale Peabody Museum, 143699.

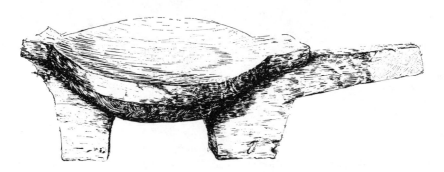

Coconut Grating Stool (*wasan pweiker*).
Overall length, 29.5 inches; overall height, 8 inches; seat length,
21 inches; seat width, 13 inches. Romonum Island. Yale Peabody Museum, 143589.

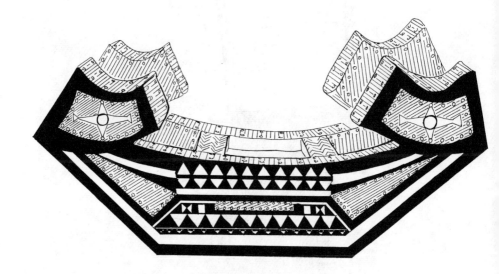

A

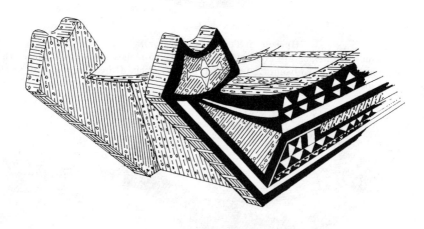

B

Receptacle for Spirit Offerings (*nän*).
A, Side view; B, end view. From a model made on Romonum Island. Yale Peabody Museum, 143657.

POPULATION FOR ISLANDS IN TRUK AND PONAPE DISTRICT, 1964

Truk District, total	24,521
Truk Lagoon, total	16,885
Population of the six largest islands in the lagoon was:	
Tol (four communities)	4,633
Moen	4,115
Dublon (also known as Tolowas)	2,067
Fefan	1,986
Uman	1,725
Udot	823
Southeast Islands (Mortlock Island, etc.), total	5,350
Satawan Atoll (four communities)	1,870
Lukunor Atoll (two communities)	1,145
Nama	932
Losap Atoll (two communities)	775
Namoluk	322
Etal	306
North and West Islands, total	2,286
Hall Islands (four communities)	845
Namonuito Atoll (fice communities)	443
Puluwat	361
Pulap and Tamatam	360
Pulusuk	275
Ponape District, total	18,293
Ponape Island, total (six municipalities)	11,998
Kiti	2,711
Matolenim	2,478
Jokak (Sokehs)	2,378
U	1,690
Net	1,440
Kolonia	1,301
Kusaie	3,245
Pingelap	908
Mokil	658
Kapingamarangi	635
Ngatik	472
Nukuoro	377